ETs and the EXPLORER RACE

Joopah and Zoosh
through Robert Shapiro

Light Technology Publishing

Chapters 14, 15 and
portions of chapter 11
were previously printed in the
Sedona Journal of Emergence!

ISBN 0-929385-79-9

Michael Tyree, Illustrator
Margaret Pinyan, Editor

Published by
Light Technology Publishing
P.O. Box   1526
Sedona, AZ 86339
1-800-450-0985

Printed by
MI**SS**ION
PO**SS**IBLE
COMMERCIAL
PRINTING

P.O. Box 1495
Sedona, AZ 86339

ETs and the EXPLORER RACE

Joopah, Zoosh and others
through Robert Shapiro

For all of you who are ready to embrace
your neighbors even though their appearance
and mannerisms might be unusual.

— Zoosh and Robert

Acknowledgment

I'd like to thank Joopah, whose presence in my life since I was ten years old guided and supported me into my career. I'd also like to thank all my friends, both physical and non-physical, who have guided me, sustained me, supported me, nurtured me and sometimes challenged me to stretch and be more.

Robert Shapiro

Contents

Introduction

The purpose of this book that you are holding in your hands is to guide you toward acceptance of the differences amongst you all, as well as acceptance of the wide variety of life that the universe has in store for you.

It is ironic that the Zeta beings, of whom Joopah is a portion, regard you as their past lives but you have not yet come to terms with their appearance. If we could have you change for a moment your attitude about who's an ET and who isn't, then imagine that all the animals and insects, the butterflies, birds, deer, fish, all these beings on your Earth right now, are from other planets —which, as a matter of fact, they are — and that on their planets they have their own cultures and perhaps appear differently.

Now imagine for a moment that the ETs have arrived in a flying saucer and landed, proverbially, on the White House lawn. But nobody comes out of the ship. Security guards, the press, maybe the President are all there to say, "Well, who's here?" Nothing happens. And the people don't know what to do. They wait for a while as the beings inside the craft are projecting goodwill and telepathic resonance and so on. Nothing happens, and the beings inside the ship realize, "Wait a minute —these people don't understand telepathy. How are we going to communicate with them?" So they have a discussion onboard and they say, "We'll have to invite them aboard, because we surely could not go out there." So they open the door just a little bit, with a "bzzzz," and someone comes up the stairs and peeps in —possibly someone with security, possibly a person from the State Department, maybe a diplomat —and walks inside the ship.

Of course, it's unusual. Its inner corridors and everything tend to be somewhat circular by the nature of the shape of the vehicle. They walk in a little bit farther; it's kind of damp and humid in there —not what you would expect if you were expecting a vehicle crammed with electronics, but the electronics are not apparent. So this diplomat looks around the ship, and suddenly, over against a far wall there is a low hum. A panel slides away, and the diplomat finds himself or herself looking at what is basically a fish tank, with fish swimming around in there. The diplomat thinks, Oh, these ETs are trying to show something in common —that they carry pets just like Earth people have pets. But suddenly, because he's within the insulated environs of the ship, he hears a voice in his head. It says, "What pets? We're the ETs."

I mention this to you because in order for you to appreciate the appearance of ETs — and granted, many of them look very much like you, but they don't all — you need to begin to accept as equals what you call animals. Just because you don't understand their language and their ways of being and their attitudes, this kind of thing is proof that they are from someplace else; they are not from your culture. Begin to consider what you call animals — especially insects like ants; ants are some of the most advanced creatures on your planet. If you can begin to consider them as extraterrestrials who are just visiting here, serving you as you evolve toward being the Explorer Race, then you will truly begin to appreciate that ETs might very well look very different.

Now, the chances of your meeting an ant three stories tall are zero. Granted, they are a little bit larger on their home planet, but by "larger" I mean maybe only two or three inches long. But they have no need for great size, because on their home planet they do not have the wealth of resources you have here. They can't be too big, otherwise there wouldn't be enough to go around.

I want you to understand that the next leap you really have to make is accepting ETs for how they look, because nobody — and many of you reading this know this — likes to be rejected just because of the way they look. So practice with each other, learn how to accept each other and to be curious about each other's differences, and in this way you will be preparing truly to meet your ET friends.

Zoosh
through Robert Shapiro

All right. This is Joopah, hello. I would like to say to all of my Earth companions, welcome to this book which, while not completely my perspective, has some of my perspective in it. I want you to enjoy it as much as you can and let it stimulate your imagination. We know now that you are our past lives, and this is why we cherish you so. Please know that my people are slow in becoming as sophisticated as you are, with all of your contact with unusual races of beings. Even on our planet, the idea of animals is something new, and we don't quite know what to do with the idea of a separate species. You see, we are all truly one, not only with our teachers on our planets, but also with each other.

And we are one with you, too. We know that you are our past lives. We didn't always know that, but we know it now. So understand that we truly do cherish you, and please, please know that you can call us Zetas. We do not need to be called by our color, and we are not all gray. Those from Zeta Reticuli do have that appearance, but I'll let you in on a little secret: Part of the reason we have that appearance is because of a unit we use to protect us from the energies on Earth, which are energies we are not used to. And this unit emits a silver light that goes all around and over our bodies and causes us to look a little bit more gray than we really do look. Some of us are actually sort of a pale white —beige, you might call it —although many of our people are very light gray.

Know that we will look forward to meeting you explorers as you come out to the stars, and we will help you in every way we can. Please enjoy the book.

Joopah
through Robert Shapiro

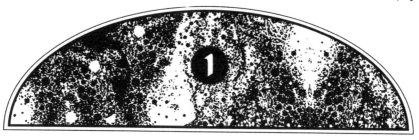

The Great Experiment: Earth Humanity

Zoosh, Joopah and Osiris
Sedona, Arizona, October 13, 1987

oosh speaking. In this day and age your alignment with space (as you understand it) or with beings who are from someplace else (as you like to say) is most constructively involved in your life if you perceive them as actors. If you do perceive them, *allow them to be equals* —not anybody better or greater than yourself, but simply other actors on the stage of life. If you want them to be all-wise and wonderful, powerful and creative, if you want them to be sweet and gentle, if you want them to be anything, they will be what you want and need them to be in any given moment. Recognize that in your interaction with any individual actor in life, such as yourselves (you are all actors in life), you will experience from that actor or individual just exactly what you need. You might experience challenge; you might experience "so what"; you might experience an emotion that equals "Yech! I can live without him or her!" Or you might feel an attraction, almost as though someone reached into your heart and said, "Hey, you, come here."

You might experience many things. But one thing you must be aware of and alert to at all times: You will experience a desire to be saved, guided or led by someone or something that is on the inside track while you are struggling around on the outside track (to use the athletic term). If you're on the outside track all the time, you're running a longer race than the person on the inside track. You don't have to go too far in your society to hear the words, "Well, she's got an in" or "He got in because he knew somebody. It's who you know, that's how you get in."

So I am suggesting that in order to see how you fit in, you must see beings from elsewhere as total equals. Do not confuse yourself with the dilemma and obvious conscious confrontation such as, "Zoosh or Charlie" (pick any name) "seems to know some things that I have momentarily forgotten." As you will notice, when the truth resonates within you — a truth that you can *feel* — then I'm not telling you anything that you don't know. I'm only reminding you of what you already know. If it does not resonate within you, then you can say, "Well, so what! I could have gotten that out of the encyclopedia." It is important for you to have this equal partnership. When you are building a house and putting up a wall that has been formed on the ground, if one side is doing all the pushing, it's hard to raise the wall. *You've got to be equal.*

Technology Not a Measure of Advancement

Allow for the fact that beings here from other planets may well be more technologically advanced, as you perceive it (though it is not possible to be more advanced technologically, since it is merely the development and completion of an idea), but they might never have integrated emotion into their lives. In the case of some of these so-called "advanced" beings, maybe they couldn't get as far in technology as they would have liked because emotions got in the way. Maybe they decided (in the case of the Zeta Reticuli beings, and they know this) that emotions were causing a lot of disturbance, that emotions weren't efficient and that if they could genetically purify the species, then it would be easier to build bigger and better spaceships.

Many beings from Zeta Reticuli are in your skies all the time. They have been here since the beginning of the creation of the human race as you now experience it. You didn't naturally evolve here. You are the result of an experiment, although not from any inbreeding with them; you are not the result of that. They would like to have what you have, but they don't know what it is. It is important for you to recognize that so-called technological advancement is not a measurement of a so-called advanced civilization. That idea has to be dropped.

Technology is like anything else. Maybe you want to explore the idea of growing roses and you grow a rose garden. You say, "I'll start out with A and end with Z. I'll grow every rose I've ever heard of until I've completed that cycle." After you've grown the Z rose, you then go to your neighbors, give out announcements, put ads in the papers and say, "I'm now the most technologically advanced rose-grower in the history of the world." This joke is to point out that there is a tendency in the so-called Western world (of which you are a part, or you wouldn't be here) culturally, politically, historically, to look at some countries that do not have indoor plumbing (for example) as being a little backward.

Maybe some people find that rubbing urine on the body is purifying. You think to yourself philosophically, "Oh, that's all right if they want to do that." If you were confronted with that in your own yard, then you might say, "That's all right if you want to do that in *your* yard." Being philosophical is one thing, but the practical experience in front of you is quite another.

What I am suggesting is that it is vital for you to understand that technological experience means nothing. It is the exploration of roses from A to Z. At some point that Zeta Reticuli example – of a civilization that is technologically and spiritually advanced but emotionally dwarfed – discovered that *emotions are vital* because they are the juice of creativity, not in the sense of technological perfection but because they are the juice, the guts, as it were, of the creative energy. So they are now working to create their species in a way that lasts – because they don't understand love.

Zetas, Watchers of the Experimental Stew

They have been here since the beginning to watch over the experiment here on Earth, the experiment of folding in equal batches of what you now call positivity and negativity, or what I like to call comfort and discomfort. This is the experiment that folds in equal batches and says, "What can we create here? We've got this species of being here that developed on this planet called Yeti or Bigfoot. We see them now and then. Those are the original Earth beings. Sometimes you see them running around a little bit, but not much; they're shy. They live underground, for the most part.

"Folding in this stuff, we've got to have strength. How can we be certain that they'll be strong? Well, they have a pretty hostile environment here, big wild critters running around. So we'll help them to be strong by creating an environment that is safe enough but that they must be able to survive when things get warm. We know they're going to be strong, because the ones that can't run fast enough will be somebody's dinner. So we're going to bring them along slowly.

"We're going to mix in equal batches of Orion beings, Pleiadian beings, beings from Sirius. We're going to make a little stew here. We're going to bring in the mind of Orion. We're going to bring in the joy and childlike sense of discovery and song of Pleiades. We're going to bring in other things. We're going to bring in many things that can be applied.

"We're going to bring in our friends from Zeta Reticuli, the finest technicians known in the universe, to watch over the experience and tell us how the stew is coming. They are here. They like to serve, they say."

But the great God entity says the real reason they're here to report back to the Network how you're coming along is because they need to discover what they left behind to achieve technological perfection. Oh, they have spirituality; they have an understanding of that, but to them it is a separate thing. That is why some beings here on this planet have spirituality that is separated. They might go to church on Sunday, but they practice life as they want during the week, you understand.

Nothing exists here without having existed someplace else. The idea of America being the melting pot? Well, I can assure you that that is an outgrowth of the idea of *Earth* being the melting pot of the genetic experiment to create a powerful race of beings called the human being — *that which wants to know.* That's where Earth is.

Human Curiosity

The human being — that which wants to know. Have you ever met a child who is full of life and isn't curious? *The human being wants to know,* is born with the desire to know, wants to know everything. When? *Now,* not tomorrow. It doesn't understand tomorrow, only integration into the now. Spirituality is now, and it intersects with the material plane right here, now. Now is always now, and the material plane is always as it is, moving through its development.

The human race is in its teenage years, in a sense. What do teenagers want to do? They want to get out of the house and explore. Can't wait to get out and join the Navy. "Maybe I'll go join a theater group and travel around. Want to see what's out there in the world, what's across the river, what's on the other side of the big pond." You want to *know.*

You have been created so that you will want to know. The great adventure in the future is, of course, space exploration, and the tantalizing element is these critters who are flying around in the spaceships. Who are they? Have they got two arms, two heads? How many heads have they got? Two legs? One leg? You want to know.

Curiosity is an emotion that is unknown on Zeta Reticuli. Now, I'm not picking on Zeta Reticuli, just putting them on notice, in a sense. They know this now. They've gradually begun to come around to the idea and knowledge in the last fifty years or so that something is missing from their civilization — the juice that bonds life.

Plants can be created on the ethereal plane out of thin air, so to speak, but *not* plants that need water and live in harmony with all elements, *not* plants that will in time die and gradually become soil in which other plants will grow. In other words, etheric plants are not cyclic life that feeds other life.

You have come from life cycles of other galaxies [star systems]. However, those galaxies are from your dimension. I can assure you that those galaxies have other dimensions just as Earth has its dimension now. You are like the child's toy that is a ball on a rubber string that you can bounce and snap. You are at a certain point in your destiny, which didn't start here and will not end here. It is necessary for you to grasp that you are here *out of your soul's choice,* and your soul manifests itself in the stuff of Earth. There isn't anybody sitting in this room now who isn't created physically out of Earth. Yet nobody here originally developed on Earth, for your souls all owe their origin to other places.

You came here for the Earth experiment to create the Explorer Race ("I want to know") so that you would have a lust for life, so that you would go out into space bringing that lust for life – the desire to get to the top of the mountain – not willing to say "this far and no farther" but to go all the way. You will bring that lust for life back to areas that live interdimensionally (such as Zeta Reticuli) and that need to be reminded energetically why *you* have something *they* need – these great and powerful, knowledgeable beings who can build craft that can fly from their galaxy to yours in a couple of hours (most of the distance is traveled in an instant), who travel in spirit light. How can that be?

Emotions, the Fuel of Creation

In their quest to develop the highest spiritual and physical, technological society with a blending of matter and spirit, the Zeta Reticuli forgot that even though emotion can be tricky stuff that can maybe mess up the works now and then, it is the power, the fuel of creation.

It takes a lot of men to build a machine; it takes a lot of them to get the oil out of the ground for fuel. But did they go into the ground and create that oil? No. They got it out, they refined it, they put it into the machine and it runs the machine, but they didn't make the oil. The "oil" is emotion, heat, pressure – it is many things. It is desire.

It is important for you to recognize that *the key to your power lies in the physical manifestation of your emotions* **while** *you are aware of spirit and* **while** *you have thought included.* It is balanced. No one has ever manifested on this planet without spirit, physical body, mind and emotions. You come here with all four to use them all, so that when you become the Explorer Race and go out and meet those funny people who look and act different and who seem to be so technologically and at times spiritually advanced, you can give *them* something they need. They know this, and that is why they are so interested in your progress.

And there's always this: You manifest here. You have lives on other planets and you understand somewhat (mentally) the idea of all your lives happening at the same time when you take yourself out of the context of time. And you don't necessarily have to have all your lives as an Earth person. Maybe almost everyone here on Earth has a probable future life on Zeta Reticuli – the planet that forgot how to laugh and still does not understand why they should, what's in it for them. Because with laughter goes tears, and tears are oh, so inefficient. It stops everything when you cry. You can't cry comfortably and do your work, not if you get into it all the way and have a good cry. That's inefficient, you see. You can't build taller and better buildings when you're blubbering all over.

The stuff that bonds life together, then, is energy that is charged with a desire to live. Your scientists are familiar with the idea of positive and negative ions and so on. They're just now beginning to discover those tiny little particles that they think don't have any charge, but in reality can adapt to any available charge. They are the catalytic energy that brings together the positive and negative ions to form matter, which eventually becomes you and everything else. So in a sense, the energy of those unknown funny little particles is *the energy of the desire to live.*

"I want to be. I want to be human. I want to be a tree. I want to be a dolphin. How do they live? What do they know? I don't want to just study dolphins, I want to *be* one. I want to be a human being — what are they?"

The Equality of Human-ET Interchange

It could be that many of the Zeta Reticuli beings who are studying you in your probable reality ("But Zoosh, this feels physical to me!" — of course, because you are in it; and their reality also feels very physical to them) are in many senses your future selves reaching back to you for help. They help you and you help them equally, this being a world that is positively and negatively charged, where those charges are brought together with the power and energy of the creative force — emotion. It could be that you help each other.

It could be that those future selves are coming back here to recapture what they left behind so that their race does not have to come to an end — for it is now dying, and they know this. They had been locked into the idea that it is because they had not developed strong enough physical bodies. ("If only our bodies can be stronger. How can we create that?") They, like your scientists, have tried to find the meaning of life by looking with higher and higher magnification. They have concluded that the molecular structure that bonds their physical bodies together has become indifferent to the idea of holding the atomic structure together. There is a loosening of the electron field within their bodies, almost as though the electrons (or the atoms, the cells, the molecules based upon them) no longer have a will or desire to live – they do not have your lust for life, joy of discovery, appreciation for the smell of the flowers and your reaction to it. Not just the *smell* of the flowers – not diagnosing the chemical elements that cause that odor to penetrate your sinus cavities – but your emotional-physical reaction to the smell.

That is why they are here. They know this now. They didn't know this in the beginning. They thought they were performing a service to the Network. ("How can we be of service?") Now they know why they are here.

It is important for you to understand this because there is a tendency, especially in the Western world, to perceive one way of life as being better than another. It is important to perceive the reality of the so-called space brothers and sisters and space "its." (They're not all brothers and sisters, I can assure you; some of them are its.) They are here also for themselves. It just so happens that what's going on on this planet will allow the resolution of future and past ideas you could call mistakes – not because they were "oops!" but because they were dead-end courses of action that could only lead to an ending (such as the exploration of technology without the inclusion of *all* the portions of you – spirit, mind, body, emotions).

What is going on, then, is a *balanced* interchange between you and extraterrestrials. There are many beings here from many different planets and galaxies, because as the Earth experiment evolves it is going to be possible to allow past dead-end experiments to be balanced and moved beyond. Earth is the crux, the *precise place* where the energy is balanced. It is going to be possible for the race, for example, on Zeta Reticuli (who are so many millions of years in the future that they are really in another dimension from you right now), their species, their race consciousness, to not die out. Even though a large portion of their physical, systemic life is almost pseudomechanical, there is still consciousness. It is not going to be necessary for them to die out because they will allow their bodies to become more biological once they understand that the process of life is constant cyclic action – meaning *that which flows through and blesses all that it touches.*

Violence, Anger and the Will to Live

That could be said about life. You could say to me, "But Zoosh, what about violence?" And I would reply that there is a reason for experiencing violence on this planet. Why? Well, if you had a desire to learn a particular course of action on the Pleiades, for example, where there isn't a whole lot of violence (how much? almost none), it would take you many lifetimes to find out, maybe nineteen to twenty. Maybe your spirit guides you and says, "Two lives from now it is going to be absolutely necessary for you to understand the idea of the creative force of energy," and you say to yourself from your soul to your larger spirit, "Well, I don't know whether I'm going to have a complete understanding of that." They reply, "Have I got a place for *you*, a place where energy can be created and uncreated in a moment, where entire civilizations can be created and uncreated like that [snaps fingers]!"

Your civilization was created just as it says in the Bible. Your biblical tome is an allusion (not illusion) to the way things happened. When your species was created on this planet it was through a larger force. Many of the beings who were involved, especially from the galactic region Sirius, are even now similar to yourselves. So the energy involved in that creative power was designed to create within you a desire to *be*, to scream for life, saying, "I want to live!" and not meekly let life parade by you. If a neighbor asks, "What?" say, "I WANT TO LIVE!" not "I want to live" [in a tiny voice].

The desire here is to create life in *all* of its possibilities, in all of its beauty, in all of its ugliness. Because what is ugly to one may be beautiful to another. Maybe some civilizations existing even today consider violence to be beautiful. And now that the world is smaller and you know about them and they know about you, then since you're coming together, maybe you have to throw all of that into a blender, shake it up and reach some kind of understanding so that the drink doesn't poison and kill all of you.

Maybe that's why the communications experience now is changing. People on the other side of the world have said, "Americans are from the devil!" – all Americans, you understand, not this American or that American, but *all* Americans – and you know this is not so. Even though you might allow that some Americans might be bad, you are still willing to allow, in your very magnanimous attitudes, that some Americans, especially yourselves, are okay. Well, it is the same all over. It is time to get beyond a narrow, limited view of life.

There has been a great desire by your source races to explore this planet. Many excuses have been brought forth: "We will bring our way of life to them. We will improve their lives. We will find things there that will be good for us" and so on. But the real reason was to bring you all together, sit you down at one table (so to speak) and see if you could feed each other as well as feed yourselves. You've done a pretty good job. You haven't finished blowing yourselves up, and it doesn't appear that you will this time. You have certainly risen and fallen here before many times and temporarily finished it. But you can't keep a good race down, as you might like to say.

This preamble is just to remind you that in order to fulfill your purpose on this planet it is absolutely necessary that you allow yourself to be emotional as well as mental, that you be spiritual as well as physical, and that you allow all parts of you to be present with you as they are, not as they "should" be. That group of individuals on the other side of the world who thinks that all Americans are bad and should be eliminated obviously doesn't understand how wonderful you are.

Also recognize that it is necessary to allow your emotions when you are angry as well as when you are happy. Otherwise you will not understand the creative power that is behind life here on this planet.

We might hear from a few other beings, someone from Zeta Reticuli, and end up with someone who has some connections here to Earth, talking to you about what you can do for yourselves here on this planet, how you can best align your energy to Earth and how you can be *all* of you without saying, "All Americans are bad; all emotions are bad." Let it stew around in you. I know when you're being emotional, and I'd like you to do *more* of it. It is good. Keep it up.

Joopah speaking. My origin is Zeta Reticuli. My friend and advisor Zoosh has spoken to you of our quest for the knowledge of the energy you humans refer to as emotion. We have studied this for some time and have come to realize that in order to experience emotion, we must increase our physical interactions with the human being as a species. We have therefore over the past five or six hundred years had more open communications with the human being as a race. We have at our convenience established communication with many members of your Earth race and have even reached out to some of your governing bodies. It has been difficult to reach out to the governing bodies because they come and go so quickly and have no lasting effect or guidance. They do not, in a sense, represent any form of Earth philosophical approach to life.

So our attempts to speak to Earth beings through the governments have been put away for now. It is more comfortable for us to speak and communicate directly with an Earth being individually. So I will simply ask, do you have any questions about Zeta Reticuli, why we are here and who we might be to you?

What life span do you have?

We live for several hundreds of your years because our bodies are efficiently created to form a perpetuating energy system in its own right. It is unnecessary for us to eat or even partake of liquid, as our physical bodies are nurtured on what is a more genetically evolved machine (almost). Our systems will thereby function smoothly for two to three hundred years, depending upon the form and function in which we participate in this life. If it is our purpose to lead some group, we will live for perhaps three hundred years. If it is our purpose to follow, we will live for perhaps two hundred years.

Are you saying that your bodies do not have any organs?

As you would understand it, they do not have separate organs. They are made up of a physicalized plasmic form of motion. That is the best way I can describe it to you. If you were to condense light – and you have done so in the form of the primitive laser – and encapsulate that light into a body, it would live indefinitely. So we tap that condensed light energy and exist upon it for as long as our existence is deemed necessary.

Do you have any kind of sexual intercourse at all?

We do not do so for our own perpetuation of the species, nor do we do so for fun as you might do here. We have that experience only when we are involved in breeding experiments in an attempt to achieve a level of physicality to adapt our species to a more physical environment.

Right now it is necessary for us to create a physical shield of energy around us when we have contact with you. This shield creates a severe limit in our communications, for what we wish to understand from you is something that is expressed energetically – emotion. Even though it has physical and mental attributes, it is primarily an energy. Yet because we are affected so severely by any outburst from you of what you call discomfort, we find it necessary to create an energetic field stimulated by a mechanical device around our physical bodies. That shield does not allow us to truly feel your communication but rather to simply hear it, which is not sufficient. In order to have any true contact with physical beings, we must create a hybridization of our physical bodies that can interact with you on a more physical level without the need to create this plasmic shield.

As you beings communicate with one another, your primary means of communication is through what you *feel* from another person rather than what you hear. Then your mind interacts on the level of thought and seems to give you permission to like or not like something. But primarily the physical reaction is stimulated by your emotional-energy interaction on the auric level. We do not allow that interaction with our species because were we to be lanced, so to speak, with some energy of discomfort, it would cause immediate death or isolation from the others of our species. We do not have any system built into our now physical bodies that will protect us from any incompatible energy.

Then how can you thoroughly study our emotions?

Need for Zeta Reticuli Hybrids

We cannot. This is why it is necessary for us to create a form of body into which we can manifest our consciousness. Then we can have a greater understanding of who the human being is. So we have been involved in the experiment of hybridizing your bodies and our bodies for some time with a group of volunteers.

Sometimes the volunteers on your planet do not remember that they volunteered for this, but all who are working with us have given us their conscious or unconscious permission at the soul level. Sometimes people will not remember that permission was given, because they are in their conscious — or separated — state on your world. When you are experiencing your body consciously you are somewhat separated from your all-knowing knowledge, and that knowledge will then not be present to remind you that you have given your permission. So it is necessary for us to create a different form of body so that we can interact with you on a more compatible level.

How many hybrids are now on Earth?

They are not on Earth. They live with us. If the scientist wants to study what is being created, it is rather difficult to study what is being created if that "what" is interacting with beings that are unlike itself. Therefore they live with us so that we can study them and so that they can, by living their lives, demonstrate to us what can be.

Are they born on your ships?

They are born on the ships or on our planet.

Do you know of and/or interact with the angel hierarchy?

We are aware of your understanding of this energetic level to which you ascribe good and evil. Some people consider that some angels are not good and some are good. This is a current separation.

Are you aware of the infinity of the soul?

All souls are infinite.

Are you aware of other dimensions that are in contact with emotion?

We are aware, but mental awareness is not sufficient. We are not experientially aware.

In Earth terms what would your existence, your vibration, be dimensionally — a fifth- or sixth-dimensional level?

Eighth. You do not really understand that frequency is not an outward hierarchy, that frequency simply *is*. And of course there is also pulse. Pulse and frequency are not the same. Pulse is much closer to what you refer to as hierarchy. Frequency is that which exists within a pulse.

Contact with the U.S. Government

Did the United States government come into contact with your race through experiments 44 years ago?

Yes. And before that, in the 1890s, there was contact.

Did the experiments with what you call primitive radar invisibility establish contact between your race and our scientists?

As I said, the original contact was in the 1890s, but as far as what is known to you, there was some contact in the forties.

Have you shared technology with the United States government?

To some extent, as is often the case when even you might go to some other culture and bring along a gift or item that you feel demonstrates something friendly.

Is it propulsion you speak of?

Not so much propulsion as the *method* of traveling. There was some explanation of how ions can move through space and time without loss —no drainage. Atomic theory has been around for a time. There is an idea originally in atomic theory of the wasting away or dying off of energy [entropy] within the atomic cycle. We explained that this was unnecessary.

How do you feel about love?

You are asking me to be something I am not. You are asking, How do you feel? Understand that if I could tell you how I felt, I would not be sitting here talking.

Why not?

Understand clearly that I am here to *learn* how to feel emotionally.

Are you among those beings who take up contactees to examine their bodies, or is that some other race?

We are amongst those.

Are you still doing this?

Yes. We have never taken anyone without their permission, ever. And they rarely remember what we speak about.

Apparently they remember pain and suffering.

We do not fully understand pain and suffering; this is something we are learning. It has been explained to us by those who have greater knowledge than us on a practical level what this pain and suffering is. And we are trying to understand by creating a hybridization of our species so that we will have a cousin species, you might say. Right now there is no species about which we can say, "Ah yes, they are like Uncle Charlie," you understand. We do not have a direct correlation of species to which we can have direct communication that *we* can understand. So there is a communications gap.

Are you in communication with the Altekkians of the Pleiadian system?

What's in a name? We are in communication with all. We are not disconnected from spirit. The idea of love is something that we understand on a universal level. We do not understand very much the idea of hate nor do we understand very much the idea of individualized love. Let me clarify that. We are aware of all beings whose goal is to achieve the highest purpose of all species. We are not much in contact with beings who are simply involved in troublemaking, to use your term.

Zeta Reproduction and Race Consciousness

Are you androgynous beings?

Yes.

Do you reproduce by thought?

No. We have technical means.

Are you speaking of cloning?

Yes, as you would understand it. It is not so much genetic cloning as a form of cloning that is like pressurizing carbon to make a diamond, which becomes this energetic substance of greater mass than the original substance. So it is more a technological and linear thought pattern.

Well, as we have parts of our beingness on other planets and other systems of worlds, you must also.

Indeed.

Then through one or the other wouldn't you be able to experience emotion and . . .

Understand that our consciousness is more of a race consciousness. We do not have what you experience as individual consciousness. What one of us knows, we all know simultaneously because of the nature of our species, whereas in your species even though unconsciously you are aware of all things, on the conscious level one person might know one thing and another not. We do not have that.

So it's kind of redundant to have individualization.

If we were all together on the same planet, yes, but we are throughout the universe performing service as we can.

Do you see this race bringing more of the unconscious material into consciousness in this time period?

Oh, yes. That is part of why we have always been here, to perceive the experiment: Earth Human Being.

The Process of Earth Human Being

Can you tell us more about this process?

Well, of course, the idea is to bring up that which is not known and create an alignment through the use of that which is experienced all the time. Since you experience your mind, your body and your emotions all the time, then with the guiding light of spirit, what will be brought up is all that you have never found a logical placement for or never put in place emotionally or never understood how to deal with physically or never integrated spiritually. When you bring up your unconscious (in spiritual terms, your soul self) and allow it to be your day-to-day self, you necessarily bring up the residual stuff that you have placed under your conscious mind (subconscious) to bridge that gap. We are aware that you are involved in clearing your subconscious mind now so that the clear path of the unconscious or soul self might be consciously tapped during your conscious, day-to-day life.

Very often these days you will have these emotional outbursts. We are round about in the skies, and especially with those we feel a connection to, we will tap in to your physical self. Sometimes we will be present in the form of tones. You might hear us toning in, tuning the crystal frequency within your pulse. And we will then extrapolate as much as we can from the way your physical body reacts in an emotional cycle so we can understand the effect of your emotions on your physical self.

Do the Zetas have the ability to channel as do human beings channeling interdimensional contacts?

It is unnecessary for us to have a separation to do that. We can utilize a form of communication device or simply be involved in a group meditation that we do.

We do things in groups. We can be involved in a group meditation to achieve a quicker pulse within our current bodies and have that pulse gradually merge into our bodies, thus receiving all knowledge in that moment that we need to know. We do not need to know everything everywhere. We will have only that knowledge we need to know in connection with our evolution. So we will utilize that.

We also have the ability to tie in to your soul bodies through the use of a device, a machine to create a greater communication. We create that knowingness in your thought at the subconscious and unconscious level so that you will ofttimes have, when you meet us, a sense of familiarity even though you might be frightened at our appearance. You will sense a vague familiarity because you will, at the unconscious level and sometimes at the subconscious level, remember who we are from the future or from the past in accordance with other lives you have lived or will live. That knowledge can be tapped unconsciously, so we simply reach in and tap that energy of your future or past self and allow that energy to be reflected in us so that you can see us as something other than some monster, some strange-looking person.

We then allow you to experience our race consciousness in that moment, and there will usually be less fear. We notice that less fear is felt toward us when we share our soul selves with you. In that moment when we allow that soul energy to be within you as we probe your unconscious, we also allow our race spirit to be within you so that you can see the familiar in us as well as the dissimilar. This allows a greater sense of communication and peace.

Are we being probed right now?

It is possible, yes. We usually do this through the use of a higher-pulse crystal that is involved in your pineal and sometimes one involved with the hypothalamus. We key into your brain-wave pattern in order to understand how your brain waves receive emotions. We have yet to

achieve a complete understanding of how your emotions speak through your physical body because of our difficulty in communicating physically. But that will come.

There's no lasting positive or negative effects from this?

None at all, because you have given permission on the soul level to be born with the seed crystal within your physical self that will act as a tuning fork to allow us to get in touch with you. That is why sometimes when we are around and need to be directly connected to your emotional self through your physical self, as extrapolated through your brain-wave pattern, you will sometimes hear a tone. The crystal functions as a tuning fork to achieve communication from our pulse to your pulse.

Is a good timing coming up for a worldwide media release that will key in a more pervasive consciousness?

Not yet. That would be interference if we were to create an externalized vision.

I mean from someone here on this planet. There are many people who are working on this right now.

It will be necessary for you all to achieve total and complete harmony individually, to recognize your harmony on a race level. When you are willing to see yourself and everyone on this planet as Earth citizens (not when you have achieved the *total* knowledge and feeling of it) and understand that you have a specific Earth race consciousness, then it will be easier for us to assist in the magic moments that create breakthroughs. Right now it is necessary for us to stand back and let your chips fall where they may.

Do you have an animal kingdom?

Not as you know it.

Have you in the past or at present contacted any members of the hierarchy of Earth to cooperate in what's going on, like Jesus Sananda?

Understand that these beings exist as energy in every one of you. We do not have to reach out for some other individual. There is no disconnection. Anything that has ever existed on this planet exists within every one of you, because this planet and all that is on it, all that is around it, all that is near it, all that is inside it, is made up of a single-cell organism called Earth. And you are a portion of Earth. So it is unnecessary for us to speak to some externalized idea of entity when all of you entities are colored with this Earth-entity ray.

You said that sometimes on a soul level we allow ourselves to be familiar with you. Are our souls on the same vibration? Are they compatible when they meet?

There is a similarity at the unconscious soul level. Some will recognize, as I have stated, a past or future life. Some have never nor will ever manifest as one of us, so there is less likelihood of our communicating with them at any level. When a cellular memory of the future, the past or even perhaps the present awakens in someone, we can have a degree of soul communion in our conversations.

When you said that you neither smile nor experience humor, is that because humor passes through the emotional body?

Yes. We are learning to understand the value of humor. You know, it isn't as though these emotions were shut in the closet years ago. It is as though in truth they were shut in the closet dimensions ago. And dimensional shifts take millions or billions of years, depending upon what is comfortable to you. But each dimension is unique. We have made dimensional shifts since we parted from our emotions. When speaking through a channel, I can also access some of *their* energy, so I am learning even now as I do this.

Perhaps more Zetas might experience the channeling process to do some quick learning?

Yes, because it allows us to experience the idea of emotion – not completely, but a taste, you might say. We are still technologically protected by a device that does not allow total immersion in your energy, but a degree of trust builds up between the channel and the being channeled that will in time allow a greater exchange. Many of our species are willing to speak this way through those who are willing to allow it. But it will take time, your Earth time, to establish a sufficient exchange of energies for trust to be there.

Some of you, however, have had ongoing contacts with members of our species since you were small children. Those might find it be easier to channel one of us. Also, one who is particularly active mentally and who finds great comfort in mentality might feel a greater sense of comfort in experiencing the Zeta being, since our primary focus has been mentality and the physical creations possible from mentality.

I once briefly channeled a being named Lela. I never did know where he was from. He had a very alien feeling. Is that one of yours?

It is not. You will find that our names do not sound with the L sound. That sound is somewhat rare for a continuum name. That would be more of a devic sound; that specific case was the deva of another galaxy.

What galaxy?

One difficult to pronounce, Tck-ahkt-[click]-sung — not one that falls trippingly from your tongue.

How much individuality do you have in your appearance, since it is a cloning process?

There is very little individuality that is perceived, except that some of us are six to eight inches taller than others. Certain beings living within the Zeta Reticuli influence might have bodies that look a little different. Perhaps their heads are a little smaller than ours. Perhaps they have almost humanic forms of bodies. When I say "living within the Zeta Reticuli influence," I am referring to the groups of planets that have been interchanging with us for many, many eons (for lack of a better term), and these beings have allowed a certain amount of hybridization of species. In those cases you might see more of what you would refer to as individuality even in garment.

Do you sleep?

Not as you understand it. We have a form of meditation, as you might call it, or a centeredness within the race consciousness for some moments during a 24-hour period, which we do not consider a day.

Do you have particular work that you personally do?

It is part of my job to oversee a certain group of human beings in their development, and from time to time check on their species' evolution as well as guide them toward greater connection to their soul life. It is not that the Zeta being is not a soul-like being; it is that we have chosen to express our soul-like beings on a more unified mass level. So I encourage some of my charges, so to speak, to be more of a unifying energy.

Is the Chinese race or the races that seem to manifest as a group soul or consciousness part of your group expression?

The Chinese race, which has really evolved from the Mongolian race, owes its heritage to those people who live inside the planet and not so much to those who come from afar. There are many races and individuals who live inside your planet. There is a group variously referred to as the Founders, the Speakers or the Tellers who live inside your planet. It is these beings who are involved, who have been involved and who will be involved in the racial structure or outer appearance of the possible physical manifestation of the human being on this planet. The Founders are also the guiding light of energy and God light that helps connect your race to races from other planets.

Do you have children on your planet, or do you manifest as an adult?

We have not found it necessary in the past to have children (as you understand it) because we can create a body in its perfected or eventual form (as we would refer to it). However, we are experimenting with the idea of children; that has much to do with your race.

But you would create them in the same way, as a cloning process?

No. The children we are now involved in creating are being created biologically, although there is some aspect of mechanical experimentation, because we are attempting to duplicate the highest possible expression of our race culture within a seedling person.

Your name reminds me of the name Hoova, which is an entity who communicated with Andrija Puharich. Is there any relationship? Do you know who this being is? It was supposed to be some kind of a mechanical or computer-type being holding the consciousness of an ancient being or group.

That being is more clearly associated with the Earth energy sometimes referred to as Jehovah.

That has to do with the Hebrew race? As I recall, Hoova had told Puharich that it was more or less like our present computer.

In the sense of being an entity that exists in data, this is so. Jehovah was at one time an encapsulated person from the Sirius galaxy and came here in a large ship. But that's another story. This being, as much as I can tell, is a form of the data register Jehovah. Jehovah is not a god, but a person. Jehovah, you understand, is no longer in a physical body and is now an energy that transmits a different vibration.

Cattle Mutilations: Sirian-Gifted Instruments Used by Humans

Concerning the thousands of cattle mutilations that have been going on during the past five or so years: the incisions removing the organs are far beyond human technology.

It is not. It is from this planet.

Who? Beings on the surface of the planet?

It is from this planet. One of the forms of communication — a toy, as it were — was given, unfortunately, to a government as a tool to be used for medical purposes. It had been deemed by races who visited here that your surgical implements were causing damage to the physical body and that your surgeons (and also patients) would like the alteration or removal of organs from time to time. This form of surgery could be done much more efficiently and without damaging the physical body if one could make a cleavage along molecular structures rather than on the organ itself. Therefore this implement was given to a certain government on this planet. However, those implements fell into the hands of those who would use them to extract certain organs, from which certain toxins are created.

Couldn't they do that more easily in a less obvious and less strange way?

It is advantageous for them to do it in this way.

What is the advantage?

The advantage is to create a sense of invasion as well as a sense of disempowerment. If one believes that there is some great power swooping down from above to damage creatures as well as some individuals, then there is great fear.

Can you say what government?

I will say simply that the original tool was handed down in innocence by some beings from the Sirius system, and that there is a particular government using a particular form of transportation that is an idea of a pilotless craft, a vehicle that moves soundlessly. All UFOs are not from out there; there are a few who are here. Fortunately, those vehicles cannot go beyond your atmosphere.

Since there are so many in this country, my guess is that if it did not originate with this government, it certainly is by now part of their tools. The only motive that is apparent for generating such fear would be that people would ask for a more totalitarian system.

People have sought for some time now to escape the responsibilities of freedom. That will be my cryptic answer. It is not my intent to make anybody out to be the bad guy, nor is it really my intent to point skyward for what are earthly pursuits.

If some governments had not imposed their will upon individuals, this country would not have had its special beginnings. Thus what seems negative produced something quite positive. My question does not arise from trying to point out the bad guys but to understand what new forces of tension between positive and negative can produce a new insight, a new consciousness. It looks to me as though there is a large number of people wanting the freedom of peace now. Does it look that way to you?

What is peace?

A new relationship between human beings, one without a need for superiority and control – harmony.

Thank you. It is harmony. Since on this planet there exists the potential for clashes and violence and communication that goes beyond comfort, it is possible to have discomfort involved in this cycle of harmony. So one might have, in a sense, disharmony and harmony. One might also have discomfort and comfort. And yet since the energy of Earth at this time is involved in polarities, it is still possible to say that the system is balanced by disharmony.

When you disincorporate, what happens to you?

We understand that we will rejoin our total soul entity in the oneness that you refer to as God and that we refer to simply as life everlasting.

Then you don't continue to reincarnate back onto your planet?

We could, but we do not usually do so. It is our desire to experience as much as possible. The equality of life between us, on a rather nebulous level of what's going on, is that we do not remember beyond our race consciousness memory. We do not remember previous lives.

We can access them, but we do not consciously remember them all the time.

Can you choose to incarnate into planet Earth to experience what you did not experience before?

Indeed. It is now our intent, however, to allow our race consciousness as a unit to be filled with the desire to expand physically as well as what we have experienced mentally and spiritually. We would like to create a form of life on levels we have not yet pursued. So it is our intent to experiment with different forms of bodies and cultures to see if it is possible to experience more "lust for life" (as brother Zoosh says) as a Zeta being.

Very well. Osiris speaking now. If you have any questions of a more personal nature, perhaps about the subject matter tonight or anything else, you may center into the energy of those questions. You may ask the questions with the energy and emotion that you might feel when receiving the desired knowledge.

I have a great fear of nonphysical beings coming around me at night when I'm sleeping. How can I protect myself?

The reason you sometimes wake up, feel anxious about going to sleep or wake up startled and then become a little frightened is because it is difficult for you to understand that your physical body has internalized some emotional discomforts and created a feeling of nervousness that leads to anticipating that discomfort. There are a number of things you can do.

First, I suggest that you *tone for yourself before you go to sleep. Vocalize up and down and feel the location of that tone in your physical self. Experiment to find the tone that is most comfortable for you.* It is unnecessary to say anything; *just find the most comfortable tone and record up to 40 or 45 minutes of that tone. If you can, go to sleep with that sound. You may tone along with the recording or simply listen to it.*

For any individual the most comfortable tone will be attuned to the pitch that equalizes the balance of your soul's energy within your physical body. You will find through experiment that this tone will help you. It is necessary to soothe your physical body because those nerves are creating within you a heightened awareness that makes it difficult for your personality to depart on its mission.

Second, *express, or discharge, the unaddressed emotional energy that is being internalized by the physical body. Allow that emotion to be felt.*

Emotion does not consider that saying words is an expression; the physical body must move as a direct form of communication with the emotional body. When that takes place, then the emotional body and physical body will feel as though the energy is being addressed. When there is that addressing, it will be easier to have the sleep time. And it will be easier to allow the devic energy of Earth to be present.

Earth Devic Energy

A new energy wishes to speak through you that is more closely attuned to the Earth devic energy. Since all energies of the Earth are colored by the energies that have passed by there, the emotional and then physicalized residuals of those emotions within your physical body will often demand to be heard before you begin to channel the devic Earth energy. Which is, as I stated, involved in paradoxes and comforts and discomforts.

You can choose to channel or receive the energy of Earth spirit. It can be valuable in time to channel the devic Earth, the spirit of Earth. Earth has devas for each of the plant and animal kingdoms and so on, as well as some forms of devas for minerals and metals, those that occur naturally and other forms of existence. Yet there is a universal devic energy. It can be valuable for you to *attune yourself to the blue-light universal devic Earth energy and be aware of the color and tonation of blue.*

If you are willing, I will act as a link and you can receive the Earth devic energy through the bottoms of your feet. If you will, aim your feet toward me for a moment. The rest of you can experience as much of this as you like. [Long pause for this energy transmission.]

Let yourself be not so much the pillar of the community, but when you are in those alone times, when no one can see you, *allow yourself to simply be silly and childish. If you allow a few temper tantrums, you will find that the physical body will feel as though you are willing to allow it to be what it is without judgment. The sadness you feel will gradually fall away as soon as you allow the tears.* It will not be easy, but once they begin it will help the process. You do not justify why you are sad, you simply understand that it is present. Realize that to allow the material manifestation of what you want, it is necessary to be more materially and emotionally present on Earth. *Material manifestation is an act of materiality, not an act of spirituality.* So simply allow, be more emotional. It will help.

When you manifest on this planet you often bring with you a desire as a baby to be spirit in flesh, in form. It takes time for you — many times, many lives — to understand that spirit must use the forms of expression that are here, as well as the etheric moment in which all can be manifested. This is an expansion of knowledge as well as an expansion of the practice of knowledge.

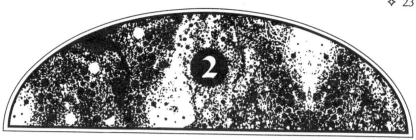

ETs Talk to Contactees

Zoosh, Joopah, Assan and Sigma
Sedona, Arizona, October 27, 1987

ll right. Zoosh speaking for a while, by way of introduction. These days your life follow the bend of the river. Sometimes the river flows in predictable ways. At other times when there is lots of water that needs to move quickly, it cuts a new path.

So it is with your lives now. You will at times need to cut through the underbrush so that you can proceed clearly and smoothly with your life. The days of taking the long way around might just be coming to a comfortable close. It is not that you're being urged to move beyond a comfortable speed, but the long way around will no longer be the comfortable way it has been in the past.

Time to Take a Quicker Way

As an analogy, your government will often take the long way around just to make certain that no stone is left unturned. Now it may be necessary to take the quick way and give the stones the power of their own choice whether to follow or remain behind.

These are times when you will have the opportunity to perceive a vision and be drawn inexorably toward it, sometimes at such blinding speed that you will not be able to extrapolate or calculate the steps you took to get there. The Universe, God, All That Is —whatever you wish to call It —will be attuned more clearly with you. This is not to suggest that It has not been attuned with you before, but the purging that you have all been doing over the past few years has cleaned away enough of the debris of consciousness that the attunement to the ever-present energy of the universe is more easily attained. It is less necessary to have that energy struggle up through all of your chakras in order to align itself totally with you. Now it is easier for you to simply be present with it.

So you will find, then, that if you clearly envision a goal and map out its possible consequences — the responsibilities as well as the joys and pleasures — it will be easier for you to paint the picture and simply allow the hand of an unseen artist to place you in it. It will no longer seem so important to understand every step that got you there, even though it has seemed important in the past. Now that time is falling away.

Since you have shown some interest in how other beings from other planets and other cultures from other associations influence this change, we will now explore a little more how you came to be who you are now and why it has seemed like such a struggle to get here.

Your race, the human race, is a hybrid like that created by a farmer who gradually works with the crops to bring forth a highly efficient, plentiful type of wheat able to grow in a wide range of temperatures and perhaps even produce two crops in a season, should the season be long enough. You are like that. You have been led down the merry path of time that will create you to be a fine wine, so to speak. Some of the finest wines will take a while to come of age, and you have done so as a group.

It has been necessary to show you on this planet all of the possibili-- ties of physical life when the ideas of comfort and discomfort were included. Thus you have had the opportunity to experience as a race all aspects of comfort, all aspects of discomfort and all aspects of those mixtures of comfort and discomfort. Why? So that wherever you went as a race in your explorations of your universe, there would be no surprises, no totally foreign idea or experience.

In your imagination you have speculated about what beings and planets and cultures look like, how they would feel and so on. The fact that you have the imagination to explore these possibilities protects you from extreme surprise. Anything you can imagine has been experienced by at least one, if not many, members of your human race in some timescape of some incarnation. All possibilities have been experienced in all of their subtleties, and the reason you are now moving forward is that *there are no ideas yet to be experienced* that would keep you from that move.

You now can utilize the tools of the etheric between lives and out of the body during dreamtime and so on. You will be able to manifest instantly whatever you choose to experience. In the past you have not had a great deal of recollection of this experience; it has not been necessary. Now the distance is narrower between dreamtime and waketime as well as between the between-life experience of the alignment with soul and the conscious experience of day-to-day life. Thus you have the possibility of engaging in a more instantaneous communication with all portions of yourself.

There will be times when you will have a vivid recollection, and you might not be able to discern whether it was an actual (as you understand it) physical experience or a vivid daydream or nightdream. Times like this are not intended to confuse or complicate your life, but to allow you to see the value and reality of those dimensions in your daily life as a conscious, day-to-day experience.

When you are in those other realities, this conscious experience is ofttimes but a dream to that reality. But there is no longer a reason to perceive much separation. The advantage of this is that in your conscious time — being awake, living — you will be able to utilize the power of instantaneous manifestation that exists in the dreamtime or between-life experience. This is what I have referred to before as the invisible artist placing you in the picture of what you want.

Use All Your Senses to Manifest

In the past, entities and friends have suggested that you be clear about what you want and map out the details. The advantage of that is to use all of your senses to clearly sense what you would like to experience. This is very important for you now. If there is something missing in your life, rather than trying to reconstruct your life using the tools you have learned so far, begin to allow yourself to use the instantaneous mapping facilities of your unconscious self. See, taste, smell, imagine what it would be like to experience that desired thing rather than try to slowly build it up stick by stick, log by log. I'm not saying to ignore the latter method; I am saying, recognize the equality of the methods, for now they are both equal, and sometimes the speedier method is easier. The repercussions and responsibilities of using this speedier method, however, are that you might not remember all of the steps that got you to your goal.

For those of you who need to remember every step, this might be a stretch, a challenge. For those of you who prefer to experience the easy way, you will still have to acknowledge the power of the slow way, for it allows you to examine the details and to experience fully every aspect of life.

So without further ado, I will stand aside and let various other entities of an intergalactic nature come through and contribute their repertoire of magic tricks, so to speak. (They do not have great magical powers, but they do not perceive you as anyone other than fellow magicians.) So I will stand aside and we will see what we will see.

V ery well. Joopah here from Zeta Reticuli influence, as we like to say. Your current planet — and I say that specifically in its now version — is going through the final stages of its preparation before you, as a planetary race, join the races of other planets. You are a member in good standing already, but in a sense you are a secret member. It is not a secret to any of the other members, only to you, since to afford the best usage of the Network you must be consciously awake enough to perceive the equality of all human beings and of all life on this planet.

Your now stage of awakeness moves beyond the semi-elemental stage of alertness. Elemental alertness simply means being aware of your surroundings consciously at all moments — not occasional heightened consciousness, but sharp consciousness at all times. The purpose of the veil that has separated you from being consciously aware of entities equal to you that are from other planetary influences has been to not interfere with the experiment of the creation: the human being.

Earth Experiment Needed Your Veiling

Your own scientists would never dream of allowing someone to come into a laboratory where highly experimental basic research was going on, since they might inadvertently bring in a microorganism that would upset the results. That is why you have been veiled. You have been kept within your own infrastructure so that you would not be upset or follow patterns of other civilizations due to admiration or some other emotional trait. You have specifically been protected. But this veil is like a one-way mirror that those standing behind can see out of; it allows others to see you. Even though you might find discomfort in the thought that you are being observed, it is all done with your unconscious permission.

Not one of you who has ever manifested on this planet has done so without giving total, conscious soul permission between lives that said, "Very well, I will participate in the experiment Earth Human Being so that I can become that hybrid end product, the Explorer Race."

So I simply say to you tonight, Welcome. As the veil lifts, no longer will only those on the other side have one-way glass. You will very soon be able to see out, as though the glass were tipped slightly. Even now many more of you see the vehicles, sometimes thinking they are falling stars. To this I would say, if there are so many falling stars, where are they all? Why aren't you walking around on nothing but falling stars, allowing for time? Most of those so-called falling stars are vehicles. I can assure you there is not enough space rubbish to create that many falling stars.

Simply be alert now to the idea that the veil lifts, and as it does, know that your equality is neither more nor less. You are simply more alert to your own life.

I have been seeing bright lights around Venus recently. Any comment?

As you are aware, it is common practice, when creating an optical illusion, to park vehicles aligned with a given planet or galaxy [solar system]. Some of these vehicles are in a form that allows them to appear closer than they actually are. Within a given range of optical clarity that is interdimensional and beyond the idea of distance (going through dimensions does not require mileage so much as the ability to alter matter), the lights moving around Venus are not so much around Venus as around this large vehicle. They are simply smaller vehicles entering, exiting and reentering through interdimensional windows into the space that vehicle occupies.

Joopah, in what way and for what purpose are you interrelating with humanity at this time?

This is a rather involved question, but we are in our final stages of preparedness: observing mankind and, as Zoosh likes to say, testing the soup to see if it is ready. We are not supervisors who check your names and say you are ready to pass. Because our race is technologically oriented, we are perceived to be the best available race (availability is a key factor) for observing your differences over time.

Our vehicles move through time as well as space. It is possible to sequentially monitor the actual progress of the evolution of your physical matter moment to moment — the physical body of the human being from the beginning of your measurable time in this dimension to the present. We gradually make more accurate predictions about the possible future manifestation of your physical self. We are, then, just about at the point where we can make predictions that are so accurate as to have a variable that is considerably less than one 10,000th of a point. When that margin is met, it will be possible to say that the human being is now ready to come into a more complete and total sense of who they are.

What we are now involved in primarily is the testing of various individuals who have given their permission before this life and who have worked with us in previous lives and have had, in a sense, litmus lives (to use the chemical analogy). They've had lives over the full run of the interdimensional time sequence that has brought this planetary body to this now state of evolution. The lives of various individuals are checked from time to time, because no one life can make a radical change — a departure, a growth cycle, a motion forward — that does not affect previous lives as well. So our primary job now is to check the current state of the life that now exists in any chain of lives or sequential life pattern to see how much their past lives are affected in their physical body. It is not only that this planet is moving inexorably toward the higher-dimensional expression of itself, but that the past is also altering: time is changing.

As the past, mathematically speaking, catches up with the future (being now), so it will be possible for you individuals to understand the ramifications of time-space travel and be able to do it without tools or objects to bring you from place to place. Imagination is present within your physical selves so that you can imagine doing this, but the actual *experience* of doing this is something that is still just out of your grasp. So we are waiting to see, in those individuals who have the chain of "litmus lives" (the total color change of the paper), that you can have lives that are on a par with each other.

The dense body of the human being is gradually changing. This can be felt during times of meditation as well as times of heightened physical alignment with all elements of Earth. Those who take hikes and who feel a sense of upliftment in the body — the emotional upliftment, the spiritual upliftment, the mental sharpness of the experience — will feel your auric energy spreading out farther from your physical self. This auric energy is what you are growing into. Your body has the ability, as does all physical matter, to expand itself in a real as well as a subtle-energy sense.

Right now you experience the physical version of yourself ending at your skin. In the future you can make that connection through the auric self by allowing your physical body to expand to the point where your auric self has enough physical matter that you can feel things much more clearly. You will be able to literally feel the contours of an object, say, 6 to 12 feet from you. You would move your hand this way and extend your auric field, using the power of your "image-ination" and extrapolate through your mind, your imagination, your heightened physical senses, the actual contours of this object. You will sense whether it feels right to you, whether it is compatible with your harmonic energy and soul. You are just about at the point where *everyone* will be able to do that as well as those who have practiced these things.

When you are able to be present in all of your senses consciously using sight, sound, smell and so on within the auric field, you will be able to experience a truer meaning of the idea of time-space travel. This is coming very soon, because as your planet realigns with what you perceive to be the fourth dimension (merely an expanded version of itself), the idea of time travel will seem natural, needing no enhancement by some vehicle.

Right now we are observing your progress toward the larger version of you. The question can be perceived broadly, but I have answered it narrowly because you have given me the opportunity to explain what we are doing. If you had asked, "What have you been doing?" we would have been here a little longer.

There are those of us who are beginning to experience these things you are talking about right now, is that right?

Yes indeed!

And that is part of the importance of really paying attention all times. Being conscious all the time?

Yes, and this also means being consciously alert within the physical body. Daydreaming that removes you from the physical body can better be experienced in the quiet moments in the home. It is most important to *not* escape from the physical body while you are doing physical things, as some of you have wanted to do, because it is possible now to have that heightened awareness, alertness, spiritually energized experience, by simply going to the grocery store in your physical body. Subtlety has been something that many of you have had difficulty in dealing with.

The reason for this is obvious. Perhaps someone is standing 12 to 14 feet away from you and they are very angry. If you are wide open to energies, you might feel their anger and become confused about who you are, whether those are your issues and so on. Now it will be possible to have a subtle sense of discerning. You can experience a harmonic energy of your own. You can be involved in a broadcast-rebound effect very much like your radar, which is an energy that is essentially a focused beam thrown toward something and bounced back. You do not have to consciously do this; you can simply be into and aligned with your own energy essence by being more alert to your energy field, being more attuned and practicing its subtleties. You can do this in the quiet of your own home should you care to.

You could perceive some object across the room, reach out with your eyes closed, and attempt to actually feel that object by using the aura or energy effect bounced back from your hand. You know what that touched object feels like, but you can actually feel it from a distance. Many of you will think that this is imagination, but it is really possible, by experiencing the energy bouncing back, to feel the subtle contours and physical makeup of this object. I request that you do this because it is necessary now to trust that you will be protected from experiencing energies that are not tuned with your harmonic.

Your Personal Energy Harmonic

Imagine that you each have a specific energy that is your harmonic, like a tuning fork. One stroke will produce a true and precise sound. You could say that the sound is precise; yet if it were magnified under an electron microscope, it actually has a broad range. There are multiple tones that make it up, and if we keep examining this tone we will find these multiple tones. That is an idea of your harmonic. There is a broad range of tones that seem to create one tone or one energy that makes up every one of you.

Anything you choose to experience can be experienced. But if you are consciously within your physical self, it will take an effort, because some of you have been very sensitive, having experienced things that were uncomfortable to you. If you are willing to allow yourself to be more in your physical body; to have an energy in your ordinary day-to-day world that is involved with strength and a sense of your own identity as an emotion; to be in those emotions aligned in your physical body, then you may in time practice what it feels like to have the heightened sense of spiritual energy within you.

This is the meditation experience that most of you have done at length, making it possible for you to avoid experiencing any form of harmonic energy that is not attuned to that exact moment's emotional, physical and spiritual status in your physical body. It is possible to broadcast who you are in that moment — strength, spiritual alignment, whatever you are feeling — and to experience the reflection off of all that is around you without having to absorb anything outside your frequency range. By practicing these exercises and taking advantage of the experiences that come to you more consciously, you will heighten your alertness to your own powers. This will guide you inexorably toward your future self, which we, in many senses, represent. Question?

Have I come into direct contact with Zeta Reticuli people in this lifetime?

As a child most of you in this room have had some contact with us. Now, the reason I say "most of you" is that there are a few who have had contact with *other* races. It is important for you to recognize that the experience of contact with beings from other star systems is not anywhere near as rare as is suggested. Most of you as children have had, of course, guides and so on. Many of you have had "invisible" playmates (invisible only to the adults near you). Very often we allow our playful nature (which we do have) to be with you as companions until about the age of two. Some of you who have animals about the house, especially cats, might notice that they have an attunement, a harmonic that allows them to "see" sound; this is why some cats respond to types of music. Cats can see the sound trail left by our motion. When we choose to be invisible to your conscious eye, we still leave a sound trail, which a cat's gaze will follow in almost a cut-out pattern, a shadow of our sound trail, although it is light.

I'm having trouble making this connection; I'm feeling, but I'm not sure. Are you the "little doctors" I have known?

Understand that I am a representative, yes? The "little doctors," as they are so euphemistically referred to, have a purpose. We have our own lessons. We do not have any great understanding of the purpose of emotion, so we can be around children because we can be our playful selves. Yet to be our playful selves, we must be more of our spirit selves. For us the spirit is not a direct connection, but a slight variation, such as examining a statue from from the side as compared to the front. It is a variation of self.

A part of what we are doing in our exposure to the human race is to see how emotions can be useful. When you have at times felt almost a sense of detachment from us when we were present with you, it was because we did not understand the harmonic of emotional energy. It has been necessary for us to use a technological means to shut out all forms of human emotion from our physical selves, since our physical selves as we have created them have no immunological or defense system as yours do. Were we to be exposed directly without any form of protection to a human being who was angry or even experiencing some form of confusion, we would become that. We have no protection from that. So the leaders of our race consciousness have deemed that we cannot have direct physical contact with the human being without having direct protection.

Now, the reason I bring this up is because there were times when you have felt that we were not as compassionate as we could have been. This is because our communication is greatly hampered when we use this instrument to protect ourselves. This is why it is such a joy (if I may use that word in a way that I understand it) to speak through a channel or medium. In this way *we* learn as well, and do not have to use our tools of protection. So, yes, our race is that race you refer to.

I will say that I have also felt love from you at times, and that's very important to me.

Good.

I've recently met many people who have also had contact. I've been processing a lot of the fear, and I assume fear is used as a way to control or to keep us at a distance so that we don't jeopardize you?

It is not. We understand that you create your own fear. We cannot in any way create your fear, nor can we directly uncreate your fear by doing anything that will expose us to the energy of that fear. So even though we may touch you, there is always a thin energy barrier between us. That is why no matter how close we come, there is no direct contact yet. We do not use fear, since we do not have fear. But we do not know how to communicate more directly with you to soothe your fear and still survive the experience.

What are the jolts of energy that many of us have experienced? I experience them at any time throughout the day. There is no time pattern for these jolts.

When you allow these so-called jolts, are they pleasant?

Yes.

That is when you become less protective of self and allow more of yourself to come through, your interdimensional self. I do not like to say higher self because you will create gradations of that value. But I will say that when those energies are felt, they are more often the experience of the total you and the alignment of spirit into physical. When you become more of yourself and feel safe to be that in public, it will be possible to feel that consciously without being distracted by it. Right now it is a distraction, because that energy will draw your attention sometimes away from what you are doing. When it becomes less rare it will no longer be something that distracts, but will amplify your attentive abilities toward what you are doing in the present.

I have had as an adult two experiences sighting UFOs, but I have no recollection of any contact as a child. Can you tell me if there has been any?

The contact has primarily been with Orion. There has and always will be some intermingling of racial cultures on all ships. This is why at times people will remember seeing individuals who looked startlingly different on any given ship from the majority of individuals. When certain beings seem able to work better together, it is because they are frequenting the same vehicle, perhaps specializing in certain roles. So you have seen us. You have been assisted by us. There have primarily been contacts, however, with the Orion influence.

Now I will stand aside and allow another to speak.

I am Assan from the Orion system. Our group has worked with the interbreeding of the human race to bring it to the highest capacity that is desirable mentally and to align those mental powers with the physical body. We have had a history not unlike your own. There has been, however, an evolution beyond the current cultural and political development of your current Earth planet. We have had a checkered past, as you might say, having had our wars and conflicts. We have had some planets, not many, within our galactic systems where we have experienced variations of discomfort. But this is in the distant past.

Orion's Role

We were chosen by the Network to come here and participate in the experiments for the creation of the human being *because* of our past, not in spite of it. It was believed that our genetic-memory energies would influence your energies, not only to give you the desire for excitement but also to give you a degree of choice and the value of peace as compared to war. Since there has been the energy of excitement present, it has also given you the feeling for the value of adventure, which sometimes expresses itself as war. This will change.

As you become a smaller planet through your tools of communication and your means of travel, it is more directly obvious to you how when one person or country suffers, the entire organism, planet Earth, experiences discomfort. As you become aware of the shrinking planet, then you will no longer feel the need to perpetuate the sense of separation that has identified this planet in the past.

Orion's purpose has been to create connective responses between the mental self and the physical self so that there could be a direct alignment with the idea of putting thought into action. This was perceived necessary by the Network from the beginning, since your race must be propelled by its imagination. And although imagination is stimulated by the All Spirit-Being, it is primarily a function of the mind. Hence we were chosen, since it is only through our imaginations that we moved past our slower-dimensional warlike experience into our now light, higher-dimensional selves. We were chosen primarily because we knew of our past and would not treat you as lesser beings and because we know that it is possible to come from discomfort and difficulty into comfort. It was perceived that we would treat you as equals instead of treating you as the experimentees with ourselves the experimenters.

So it has been our task with many of you. When the Zeta scientists were present it has been our task to work in such close alignment with many of you that our energies were directly connected to your own energies during a period of alignment to spirit/soul that was particularly present in many of you during the ages from 7½ to 11½, sometimes overlapping to 12½. This period of openness in the spirit personality, as reflected through the physical and mental-emotional personality, has allowed many of you to integrate the actual Orion energy into your physical makeup and become more than your previous soul self.

Soul-Braids and Imagination

Some cases were a braidlike effect involving the inclusion of the soul personalities of others in your own spirit or soul personality within your physical body. This does not refer to the walk-in idea as discussed by

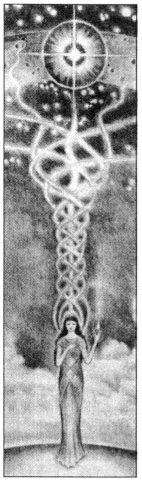

others wherein one energy steps out and another steps in. (The walk-in energy takes place only when a specific soul-self has chosen to depart the physical body.) Rather, it *includes* another energy so that you can have simultaneous spirits living within you as a combined soul rather than a replaced soul. It is also possible to have the braidlike soul effect within a single physical, conscious self, and then one or more portions might step out.

The purpose of the Orion portion is to prepare you for a task later in life when it will become necessary to have a more universal point of view, and when a sharp mental consciousness is specifically needed above any other skills that, for example, might be more balanced or attuned to the emotional than the physical. Some of you have had more contact with us because it was necessary for you to develop a broader mind concept. And it was also necessary for you to become aware of the futility of repetitive historical sequences wherein the planet is destroyed by war and then forgets its past, rebuilds itself and seems to think as a planetary consciousness that rebuilding is a beginning, not a continuance.

Those who have had contact with us over the many years in this life have usually had contact in other lives. It has been necessary to have this contact in this life so that those who have had the contact would be able to mentally, physically and emotionally image spiritual imaginations. The mind has its imaginations, and spirit has its imaginations as well. Sometimes it is necessary to be able to move beyond the measured ability of the mental imagination and experience the imagination that is tied to another cultural species. When this is done you will have dreams or images or illusions of things moving together and being experienced interdimensionally for which you have no direct correlation in your conscious lives. This is often the influence when it occurs in the imagination of the Orion connection.

Do the selves of this braided soul create different personalities, different perspectives of looking at things at different times? Is there a conscious memory of the two?

It is a consequence sometimes of the braided personality that the individual will seem to reflect at times a distinctly different personality from other times. It is not necessary to have this split personality, as you have said. But it is possible for people who are experiencing the Orion influence to have more than one distinct personality. If they are allowed to have more than one distinct personality, then they can simply become broader beings. They can have, in a sense, more than one life in one body. If, on the other hand, that is stifled or they do not feel safe to demonstrate those personality differences, then the life is frequently unfulfilled.

I have the memory of being in a laboratory. I think those who were there must be the Zeta Reticuli. I also remember a sort of shadowy teacher who comes out of a kind of reflected light. Is that one from Orion?

Not really. This is more of a direct guide that you might refer to as the oversoul, or the portion of you that eases your way through experiences for which there is no direct Earthbound explanation. It is shadowy in the sense that the interdimensional aspect of that beingness does not have a directly physical consciousness. If you as your conscious self were to look at that energy, it would be difficult to see any portion of it directly. However, you have had fleeting glimpses of what that energy looks like when you saw it out of the corner of your eye.

This type of visualizing process (out of the corner of the eye) usually happens when an individual, physically speaking, is not looking for something and does not screen what they are looking at through a belief system. This is why some of you will occasionally see things out of the corner of your eye, turn to look at it, then screen what you "see" through your conscious belief systems and not see it. But when something is seen moving back here and your attention is over there, then you are not challenged with the limited concepts of the mind.

I'm confused.

What is missing in your life associated with that experience? I will answer: peace of mind. What will it take for you to feel peace of mind about that?

All I can think of this moment is acceptance.

Then if you are willing to understand that these experiences are done for you and with you and never under any circumstances *to* you, then even though there might not seem to be a conscious permission during the experiences, you will begin to feel the greater umbrella of permission that takes place interdimensionally for your total life experience. This is not just a mental concept. It is primarily an emotional experience of permission. So you have homework if you would choose to do it: *Remember an occasion in which you asked somebody else, a human being, for permission to do something – and when it was granted, how elated you felt. Remember that and practice that feeling of elation associated with permission.*

The purpose of this practice will allow you to become consciously aware of how your physical body feels during that experience. You will notice that should there be future experiences that go beyond what would normally be expected in day-to-day Earth life, even though there might be confusion in the mind there will be the physical experience of the elation of permission someplace in your physical body. That is so you won't feel as though something is being done to you and so you can feel that you are a conscious participant in the experiment rather than a lab rat. It is important for you to know, even though there may not be a mental permission, that there is a physical-emotional feeling of permission that comes in from another source to you. Practice this; it will give you some peace.

Some of us would like to have closer contact with extraterrestrials. I, for one, see living entities. I'm aware of them a lot. It's rather frustrating for me. I would like to have more of a physical experience of sitting down around the coffee table and having a conversation. What can we do on a conscious, physical level to initiate a closer interaction with people who resemble us in appearance or with whom we can be comfortable, like the Pleiadians?

Exercises to Initiate ET Interactions

Thank you for your question. It allows me to give you all homework that will be challenging but fruitful.

No matter where you live, seek out individuals for whom you take an immediate dislike when you see them. Or look for individuals with whom you feel uncomfortable. Spend as much time as you can with these individuals to seek peace with them and allow them to be. You will know that you are allowing them to be when you can see these individuals without an energy of judgment or conflict within you.

This is what you can do in order to achieve face-to-face conscious conversations at will, meaning when it is desired, not just when it happens. You will need to have less judgment and internal conflicts with your own fellow beings.

Make a conscious effort to love your fellow human beings by allowing them to be who they are even though their behavior may seem self-destructive to you, even though their behavior may seem to alienate you. Allow them to be by noticing how you emotionally react to them. When you have people who cause you to feel uncomfortable, learn how to allow them to be by finding the right words to speak to yourself and to them so that they will know that you accept them as they are, not as you would like them to be.

Dolphins of the Future

I assume that Orions know of the species dolphin from Sirius?

Yes.

Do you understand what's happening with them now? Why they're getting the respiratory and bacterial diseases? What's the message that they're trying to give us in doing that, in sacrificing their lives?

As you understand it, yogically speaking, your world is constantly being interchanged from matter to matter through the body. If the dolphin species were aligned with a religious cultural experience, it would be most closely aligned to the identity *yogi.* When the experience of a life cycle draws to a close for a given species such as dolphin, the manifestation of dolphin on this planet will cease to exist as you move through your dimensions. And dolphin as a species will take a new form in the future of your planet, as it has a land form as well as a sea form. The sea form and the land form are not dissimilar. It will be perceived as an accelerated evolution, creating almost a form of walking dolphin. Needless to say, this species cannot exist on the land until you have complete comfort with each other. Which is why the exercise given before was prompted by the question, prearranged in dream state.

The dolphin species must seem to be more humanlike in its susceptibilities. As the species dolphin interacts more with the human being now, there is a necessary blending of consciousness. As more of you channel dolphins, as more of you perceive dolphins as the symbol of love, as more of you become aligned with dolphin energy, then the dolphins give you their gift equally. They take upon themselves some of your discomforts, humanizing this species you recognize as dolphins. At times it is necessary to allow groups of dolphins to discharge the discomfort of human energy that is present within the species dolphin.

All dolphins are connected consciously and unconsciously as species dolphin. So at times, then, the body will purge itself, just as you might have a disease and it runs through a full cycle within your given self (like flu, when you discharge certain fluids from the body). When the body dolphin as a species consciousness must discharge certain elements of discomfort energy, it allows certain members of the species to die out. In this way the rest of the species is strengthened and can continue to give and receive in relative safety. It is a way of balancing the energy within the species and allow a continued energetic exchange between the human being and species dolphin in a way that the species dolphin can continue.

Because Orion is associated with the mental energy, what specific mental things are you working with? Manifestation or . . .

Pineal Converts Thought to Matter

Since it is primarily our purpose to work with the mind as it is associated with the body, it is our purpose to help you physicalize what you think as well as what you can imagine. It has been our task to help you create the physical organs within your body that help you to move energies of thought as well as stimulations of inspiration from soul into imagination, converting it to thought and moving it into your physical consciousness. We will continue to perfect your pineal gland, for you do not have a great deal of understanding of what it does.

Its primary function is to convert thought into a physicalized manifestation in your individualized experience of your physical world. This happens for you on an unconscious level now. But if you are willing to become more consciously aware of this gland, to explore the area of your body that it is near, and to believe that it has this ability, you can begin to use it almost as an auxiliary circuit to the brain. The pineal gland is more closely associated with the brain than any other portion of your body. Its function is to take what you think, what you believe, as well as what you are afraid of (since that is available on this planet as a teaching tool) and offer you the option of experiencing it physically. So as you learn to become more conscious of your thoughts (this also means, of course, your subconscious), the pineal gland can work with you in a more favorable way.

Are there any exercises that you can give to assist us in working with the pineal and connecting it more directly with the brain?

It is not so much for you to alter the experiment as it goes. It is useful for you to become more aware of the pineal. This can be done by looking at an anatomical picture or becoming aware of the location of the pineal. Its exterior looks can be useful to you in imaging it. It is not possible for you to use your imagination without exercising the pineal gland. Therefore I would say: *Touch with your fingers the area around and about where that pineal gland is, as close as you can. Primarily, imagine yourself taking a journey through it. Align your own energies in it. Be more consciously aware of its presence. Listen for its tone, and simply know that it is not for you to speed up anything right now.* Because it is also necessary, you know, for conditions in your world to change a little bit more for that pineal gland to begin to do what it can do.

Right now it is operating at only about half its capacity. If it were operating at full capacity, you would be manifesting things instantaneously regardless of whether they are good for you — comfortable or uncomfortable. It has been necessary to place something like a mitigating clause that presents you with the opportunity of experiencing a comfort or a discomfort but does not drop you into the midst of it. Until there are more comforts within the physical self, do not seek so much to accelerate its function.

If you are simply aware of the pineal and can imagine yourself feeling it from the inside out, imagine it pulsing; then you will be using it *while* you are imagining its function. If you are willing to use your imagination more, that will put you into greater contact with the gland.

What about the pituitary and the hypothalamus? Are there ways that we can work with those?

You can use similar methods. In the case of the hypothalamus you can *begin to radiate heat between your fingers like this, not actually touching. Don't concentrate on radiating light.* (You do that whether you see it or not.) *See if you can consciously radiate heat from one finger to another. Feel it.* This will help. If you can do these things, *then gradually move your hands closer and farther apart, concentrating on radiating heat.* This will *stimulate the glands.*

War and the Immune System

Since you've dealt with the issues of war and peace, can you comment on the conflict that is taking place in the Middle East now?

I will say that this is part of the Plan, because you human beings very often find it necessary to respond to the squeaky wheel. If you give yourself the illusion of peace, you sometimes become complacent. It is necessary for you to understand that there must be an active, ongoing experience of choosing peace within your individual self. I will tell you that there are many, many people within this country and the world who do not know about the activities there at all, who have no conscious stimulation of the energies.

So I am suggesting that if you do not allow so much the ideas of drama and excitement of others, if you do not concentrate so much on others' opinions as expressed through the element of the news, it can be useful as a tool to center more within your own peace and equality. It is vitally important for you in your evolution to go beyond the need for an immune system, which is primarily a defensive system created to get you through the warlike period. As you are moving out of the immune system, it is necessary for you to be able to choose peace within you as a conscious thought, thus creating the opportunities brought to you by the pineal to choose peaceful experiences.

Recognize that this question is but the tip of the iceberg — which suggests that your immune system is beginning to fall away as an absolute need. Therefore, dramatic events in the Middle East are often brought forth to you to test your actual decision-making process, which says that the immune system unconsciously, on the soul level, is no longer needed. When you no longer need defenses but can feel totally safe and unified within the physical-matter shell of your body, you will not need either the expression of disease or the analogy of what is experienced in drama — war.

Every once in a while I get a glimpse of beings I call super watchers. To me they're like a crystal/silicon life form, and they seem to be newly come here. They seem separate from all other life forms. Am I fairly accurate?

They are, we will say, elementals combining toward a physicalized specimen that does not exist yet, almost as though they are the catalyst that brings two things together. But the two things are not yet present. The energy you refer to is almost an etheric energy that is forming for which there is no conscious need yet. But there is an ongoing unconscious need, and that need is coming up to the subconscious and will gradually penetrate the conscious. As it gradually penetrates the conscious you will eventually have a more physicalized version of that.

Now I will stand aside and we will hear briefly from a Pleiadian energy who will send greetings.

Very well. My name is Sigma. I am the partner of P'taah, who has spoken to Robert at length. However, since P'taah's energy is at the very least enthusiastic and Robert has asked for a subtler, softer energy, I will fill in for him this evening. I am what you refer to as a feminine being. My source is the Pleiades. You may ask one or two brief questions if you choose.

I was taken to a Pleiadian songfest involving a choir, a crowd of people and refreshment. What is the significance of this?

Understand that the body consciousness seeks significance, when actually this is primarily an experience of celebration. When you experience those celebrations on the mothership, it is to stimulate your knowingness as to your choice of career, friends, lovers and so on, to stimulate you into knowing that the more universal appeal is at effect here as well as your conscious choice. Many experience the choirlike effect.

The Pleiades, as it is currently experienced in my world, is someplace that is primarily happy. We do not experience discomfort as you know it, though we do have a slightly denser variation of this in which some discomfort is experienced. It is not on your dimension, however, and those beings are not in any sense of the word in contact with you, though some might say so. Your experience of this choirlike effect was to stimulate the Pleiadian total structure within yourself, primarily to help you bring forth creative efforts associated with the potentials of this planet.

This is why, when you have visions or experiences, you sometimes have difficulty interpreting them with Earth instruments. So it might be necessary for you to re-create the idea of instrument here and begin to utilize crystals and color to create a tonal structure that others might experience as something they feel more than hear. This will allow you to move beyond the range of consciously perceived sound. You are being stimulated, then, to create almost a machine with few moving parts, which will help people to move beyond the limited range of sound they now experience and to redefine sound as that which is felt. When you were experiencing that choir you were very aware of how you felt. It was a heightened sensitivity that was physical almost to the point of being uncomfortable, because you are not used to using those portions of yourself. As you move through your life you might be able to help others expand their idea of sound.

Now your energy will become more all-encompassing in your lives. You will begin to feel more of what can be done as an actual physical experience. You will begin to feel your senses stretching beyond what can be measured into the unmeasurable. Your imaginative abilities, which go beyond your senses, will gradually become something you can experience. Allow yourselves the possibility that these imaginations are realities. I will say good night for all concerned.

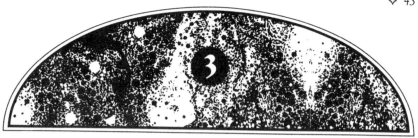

Becoming One with Your Future Self

Zoosh and Joopah
Sedona, Arizona, August 21, 1988

Well, all right. Zoosh speaking. Now, understand that it is in the nature of the extraterrestrial connection that you be involved. It was suggested that there is a Pleiadean and Zeta Reticuli connection here, and that is true, since Pleiades is, in a sense, your past and Zeta Reticuli is, in many senses, your future. You souls that were deposited here on this planet in order to create the race you now call the human race —which I would call the Explorer Race —were synthesized out of what was already here and what was brought here. You were not created in a laboratory, but the way any normal race would be —through contact.

In the beginning of this planet there were a few individuals* brought together who said, "How are we going to do this thing?" Some people said, "It can best be done if there is polarity," and others said, "No, we know that polarity does not work; it is a rudimentary form of energy. It does not allow the high-speed transit of any vehicle from place to place; only magnetic energy does that." And the argument raged on. The powers that be obviously believed that polarity was correct even then in that meeting.

---

*The Council of Nine. The story came out on April 1, 1990 and appears in Chapter 21 of *The Explorer Race*.

Making a long story a little less long, the individuals who chose to break off from that original discussion went to the Pleiades, developing their race there. The others stayed here and got into polarity, separation and struggle. "Why?" you might ask. "Why would anybody want to do that?" It was designed that you as a species would become distilled through struggle.

"But Zoosh," you might say to me, "that doesn't sound very nice." In reality, it has created a very powerful species, this human race. You might say to me, "But Zoosh, we don't seem so powerful all the time." I will say this: You have something that many other individuals do not have on other planets. You have the will to survive in your physical bodies. Many other civilizations do not have this. It is true also that they are more connected to their spirit selves and recognize that any transition from body to spirit back to body is not involved in any *loss*, as you might define it in the idea of death. However, you are *literally designed* to believe that there is loss in death so that you will struggle to live. You as a species can survive in the harshest cold and the most extreme heat. You know what to do in those conditions. Your body can live on a variety of foods; some of them would not be considered consumable by other species, and yet when your body commands, you eat what you must.

This has all been created to make out of you a powerful, curious group of individuals who will necessarily want to spread, not religion, but simply the value of being a human being. If you doubt this, look at any mother or father with their child. They will want to introduce that child to the joys and pleasures of being a human being as well as counsel that child when it discovers, as it inevitably will, the difficulties of being a human.

You have been created over the years to be this powerful, curious group so that you would go out into space, as you inevitably will, not to pollute (you think you will, but you will not) but to bring the will to survive, the will to live, to these other species who have become complacent in their method of life. Many species of other beings (not all, but many) have developed an infrastructure that seeks to expand on some one idea, something that will create the best of that idea. On Zeta Reticuli it is the best of technology; on the Pleiades it is the best of peace at any price, peace with loss.

You could say to me, "But Zoosh, everything I hear about the Pleiades would make me want to live there. I'll go right now. When are you coming to get me?" I will say this: You are in fact here not against your will, certainly not against your soul's will, although it might feel from time to time that you would much rather be elsewhere. You are here to evolve your soul beyond the complacency it gets into when you are in the land of heaven, as you might recognize it in the Pleiades or Arcturus or some other places where there is little conflict, where even the word translated into their language would not be understood.

You are here so you can have the growth that is available on this planet. You can experience in one week on this planet more growth than people on the Pleiades will experience in their lifetime. So you might say that the Pleiades right now is like R&R — rest and relaxation, peace, calm, joy, fun. Nothing wrong with that. But you enjoy your peace, calm, joy, fun here much more because of your experiences of their opposite.

Here you have the pleasure of extremes. You could say to me, "But Zoosh, I can think of plenty of extremes I do not care to experience." And I will say that is fine, and I can completely understand that. But I will also say that it has been your willingness to experience them that has created more growth for your souls in this and other lifetimes on this planet than you will *ever* experience up there where you want to go. "Take me home; you left me here." Understand that *it isn't like that.* You weren't left here jumping and screaming when the bus departed. You were really deposited here by your soul's permission. You know this.

The Zeta Connection: Our Future Selves

So what is the Zeta connection? These individuals represent your future selves in soul incarnate. They have developed a highly refined technological society, so refined that their bodies are to some extent a version of technology. They are cloned, of course, in order to weed out undesirable characteristics, as they might say. But now they understand — oh yes, now they know who you are. Years ago, when they came to this planet and picked people up and examined them and so on, it was a scientific experiment. You were an unusual race: how strange, how marvelous (although marvelous is not an emotion to them; it is plain curiosity — that is how they would experience marvelous).

But now the tables have turned. They now know, due to their recent phase shift, just who you are, and those who are picked up in the future

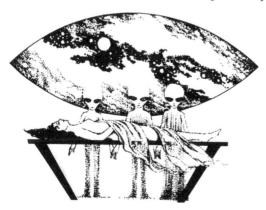

will find that they are treated with much greater respect, no longer simply the object of inspection but an equal. There is always one on the ship who can contact the individual who was picked up and give them peace when they are afraid. Why? Very simply because *they are their future selves!*

Now, the Zetas have understood this in only a rudimentary fashion in the past. They have understood that some individuals were able to calm the human; it wouldn't be everyone, just certain ones. They had no idea why. Now they know, and now there is a new equality from their point of view; now there is a new respect. After all, if they were to make a mistake with one of you, maybe they would no longer be there (and some surely would not!). Regardless how the body is produced, if the soul incarnates within a body and is prevented from proceeding along its path with that body — even if the body is a machine — that soul will depart that body and the individual will simply cease to exist. So yes, they have much more respect for you now.

Simultaneous Lives Necessary for Phase Shift

How has this come about? In the journeys of soul travel it has been necessary for you to explore realities on a vertical level so your souls could accommodate the maximum amount of information. For the entire universe to have a phase shift, it would be necessary to concentrate this soul experience in more than one life. Otherwise it would be like trying to program a computer with all the knowledge that was ever absorbed anywhere in an hour. It could not be done. Even using a universal light technique, it could not be done. It would take longer than horizontal time.

Thus you have all these lives operating at once. Most of you are familiar with this idea. Outside the context of time, they operate simultaneously so that the soul, which is connected to the womb, can prepare for this shift to the so-called fourth density, which is simply a quicker experience of self.

What happens to the third density? Does it go away? Is it uncreated? From your soul's point of view, it remains, but you go on. Since all souls on this planet have been created from the original 144,000 referred to in some of your documents, it really makes no difference. This planet will continue to be a place of material manifestation for souls to examine life slowly in this density so that lessons can be learned *and* understood simultaneously. If you experience it slowly enough, you can learn and understand it *in one life!*

So you will go on. You are braided, you 144,000, and you are all descendants. You are braided to the past, from your point of view, and to the future as well. But the past and the future is not a line — it is a circle. The purpose of life is simply to be who you are; and the larger purpose, since you are a portion of the One, is to experience who you are *in all of its infinite varieties*. Since the One is Itself infinite, It places a concentration of energy in various projects so that It might feel who you are in Its infinite varieties separately.

The Pleasures of Separation, the Importance of Integration

You say to me, "But Zoosh, how can the One be separate?" It really cannot, but It can enjoy the pleasures of separation as It concentrates Its attention and focus on any one area at the moment. The integration of this information is less important than the integration of your own soul self and energy. The purpose of this introductory conversation is to prepare you with sufficient background information so that you can ask questions intelligently and reasonably, understanding the basis of the reality of the Pleiadean and the Zeta Reticuli connection here on this planet.

Tell us more about the phase shift.

The phase shift is universal. Because your planet will be changing to its quicker density, the phase shift is important from your point of view. Your universe (meaning everything that you are, everything that you can see and everything that you can imagine) will also change. When you have an astounding idea, an inspiration that changes your life, you never look at life the same again. As you artists out there who are trained in your craft know, once you study something and understand the lights and shadows and highlights and so on, you never look at physical life again the same way.

All you need to know right now is simply that as a result of this phase shift, which is in transit now and will be for the next 23 years or so [to 2011], your consciousness will expand sufficiently that what you experience between lives can be experienced in embodiment. This means that you can have physical life and soul life in one body.

How can I understand the difference in feeling between third and fourth density?

As a simple example, go to a swimming pool or any body of water and put your arm in it. Swish your arm through it and say, "This is third density." Take it out, swish your arm through the air and say, "This is fourth density." It is referred to as density simply because it is thicker. It takes longer to swish your arm through the water than it does through the air. The reality of it is that you simply expand, and the spaces in your molecules become less apparent. Fourth density is here right now; it's just that your perception of it is not always clear. But as you begin moving back and forth between them as you are doing now, you will begin to see things out of the corner of your eye. You will see perhaps shadow motions, shadows of fourth density. (This will create a temporary boom for the eye doctors!) Eventually, medical science will wonder what it all means: Is it a new disease, or is it time to marry technology with philosophy? But I will leave that to them.

It is best understood simply by experiencing different densities of matter. Let's keep it simple.

Where did the beings come from who colonized Earth and evidently at the same time the Pleiades? What planets, what areas?

Earth As Axis to Shift the Universe

To alter your statement, the Pleiades was already colonized at that time. The idea was that the universe needed to shift, so how could that shift best be made? There were a couple of planets here and there on which discomfort was felt to the extreme. There were no planets on which discomfort (what you call negative, a word I do not use) was balanced with comfort —a balance of polarities. It was decided that a gateway would be needed. In order to move the universe, there would need to be a point where all energy that existed everywhere else could be combined sufficiently to create an axis to move the universe, almost like a rotating knob.

The Pleiades was already colonized, as was everything else. Certainly Earth was colonized, for there were beings here already. It was a planet that had been enhanced to create immediately what one might experience etherically. On the etheric level, if you want something, it is there like that! [snaps fingers] because your thought takes form —thought forms. But to create that physically, you would have to have a slower world, one that is microcosmic as well as macrocosmic. Thus it would be necessary to create what would feel like a separated world and protect the people from finding out that they are macrocosmic, a portion of something greater, to allow the civilizations to develop. Of course, there has been rising and falling.

To answer your restructured question, I will say that the cultures that founded you are Pleiades, Orion, Andromeda, Arcturus (in a receding order) and a couple of others that are influences —and, of course, Sirius. I do not mention it directly because Sirius provided the seed souls. The souls who were provided —the 144,000 —had all been exposed to discomfort on an odd little planet where discomfort is known and comfort is not really understood —but that will be taken care of in time. It would not have been possible to create a polarized planet (since the polarity of discomfort is so rare in the universe) without having souls who had been exposed to it and felt that it was normal. Thus the seeding of Earth was largely with souls from Sirius who felt that discomfort was normal.

Zoosh, did you say that we are all descendants of the 144,000 souls?

Yes, like the strain of any crop might be developed from one original seed, you are all descendants of those souls. The number 144,000 has been disseminated rather widely in your world so that it could act as a key number to always attach you to where you've been. When you're attached to where you've been, since it is a circle, your soul (or subconscious and unconscious) will have a little nudge toward where you're going —and that's what keeps you going.

A ll right, Joopah here, from Zeta Reticuli. I would answer questions from the basis of your future. (I will not, however, tell you what's going to happen tomorrow.) I will give an overview of who we are to you.

As stated by Zoosh, we are a linear future self of your soul chain. We do not look too much like you. We range in height from about 4' to about 4'5" or 4'6". As a result, our vehicles are sometimes rather low-ceilinged; you might have to bend over. We have in the past strived toward creating what some of your individuals have perceived as an emotionless society, but in fact it is not really emotionless; the emotions of calm and peace are present in our one mind. What one of us discovers, we all know instantaneously as a one-mind race.

We are those beings you have come to identify as those with the big eyes. We do not experience your reality directly. When we are here, we enshroud ourselves in our own energy. We sometimes are seen to float or bounce or do things that might not be associated with physical reality, due to the need to protect ourselves from polarity and the energy of separation. As you know, any species of life, when subjected to a hostile environment, is affected by it; therefore, if we dropped our technological guard for a moment or two, we would never ever be able to return to our species.

It has been necessary for us to create this reality so that we could experience to the absolute limits our development of the mental power. When you look back on your society, you will see in recent years how mental power has been espoused as the most saving grace. *Our* reality is a future projection of that idealized virtue. However, it has created a limited society. We do not experience emotions as you understand them; that is, we do not experience the volatility of emotions. Rather, we experience this universal calm and peace. This is not a discipline. Through the generations the actual ability to generate emotions has been cloned out of us. As a result we are somewhat, as you might perceive it, limited in our ability to access the emotional body.

As a civilization we did not recognize the fallacy of creating this as a goal. We looked upon the emotional body at the beginning of the formation of our society as that which has created strife, albeit it also creates love and enjoyment and pleasure. Our perception in the beginning was that the polarity balance system was too extreme for us. We did not wish to have violence and polarity and separation even if that meant we could also have great joy and ecstasy. It was decided that by extrapolating from your most recent past – and I am drawing a direct line, since we are your linear future selves – the mental power that was expanded and disciplined into the race would eliminate any need for destructive emotionality.

Now we are a little clearer as a society about the limitations of that goal. That goal, of course, has created less of a connection in us with our God-selves. Inspiration coming in from the God-self enters the emotional/electrical field of the body. It is conducted from there to the physical body and then to the mind. We know this now. As a result, in our re-creation of ourselves as a species there has been a gradual lessening of the window of emotionality, or electricity. Since the masculine version of emotionality is electrical and the feminine version is magnetic, we had created, even with our expanded mental powers, a situation for physical bodies in which the electrical reproductive system was greatly strictured. As a result, even though we experienced the masculine version of energy as mental power, the ability to perpetuate our race has dwindled due to the lack of physical activity. So it is that our race is dying out gradually.

Thus we needed to create a change in the past. We looked at the possibility of altering the entire structure of our race to continue. But it had taken so very long to create what we had attempted to perfect, as we understood it, that it would not be possible in the remaining time to change our race using the same system. Nor would it be possible to simply expose ourselves to emotionality. We had discovered in contacting your species that your emotions were so powerful that they affected us like the experience of a disease, as an invasion. This is why it has been necessary for us to limit the interaction between us to a mental experience.

Because most communication is energetic, the result was that we had to eliminate the energetic communication to protect us from your emotional energy. Our communications have been so poor on a face-to-face level because only our telepathic or mental communication would be received by you. And since much of what you communicate to your world is through feeling, we did not receive it, nor were we able to. So when you would gesture and feel a strong need, such as to be touched or to have us explain what we were doing with you, we did not understand your request. You are our direct past, as we understood it, and we did not know how to explain to you what we *assumed* you understood. Nor did we understand why you become frightened or happy or any of that. We did not understand "frightened," because it is less of a word than it is a feeling, so this has been the gap in the past between us. To preserve our race, we could not experience your emotionality and you could not communicate with us without emotionality. Thus there has been a problem.

Now we recognize the need to expand our emotionality, and there simply is not time. There is only one course of action that can be taken. From our point of view we had to alter the past so that our reality would not come to pass as it did. This does not suggest that we had power over you, for we simply did not know how to do it — interference is not allowed, and justly so. Kindness is not simply a matter of magnitude. It is also a practical reality, for if one interferes with any race, especially one that is in the past or a different time zone, who knows what might be changed in the past or future? That is the practical reality of that rule.

So we were thunderstruck. We did not know what to do. Gradually, working with those who guide us, we became aware that in order to experience an alteration of our present and be allowed to alter our past, we must become aware of who we are in association to who *you* are. We really did not understand that there was any great connection. (I am referring to our recent past. We understand now, but we really did not understand this before.) We started to get a glimmering about 140 years ago of your time, and then we really started to come here. We understand it now quite well.

What is going on, then, is that in order for your species not to move into another self-destructive cycle — as you have risen and fallen here many times — the value you place on changing your present had to equal the value we place on changing our past. We had to wait for that window. Thus we did not perceive that window, nor did we need to perceive it and understand who you really are to us until very recently.

As always, what you need to know you will know *when* you need to know it. This is a universal law. So now we understand who you are. Equally, you are beginning to understand who we are and the dilemma we face. Fortunately, it is no longer simply for us to try to make these changes. It is now understood by enough of you on this planet who *you* are. It is also a motivation on your planet to change your past because of the discomfort associated with it. And the only way you can change your past is to change your present.

Now you see that we have something in common. It is your desire to change your past in order to create soul balance, thereby eliminating the crushing violence of the past, and allow yourself to redensify in a quicker version of yourself (which you refer to as the fourth dimension). We had to wait for that window where you desired sufficiently to change your past that you could allow a change of focus in your present. And when that window opened, we also could change *our* past.

Joopah, because yours is a one-mind race, how does the individual experience individuality?

There is no individual as you understand it. There is an individual body, as you might perceive it, but we all look rather the same. If there weren't a slight differentiation in your color, you would look rather the same to us, too (but that is really my joke)! We look really quite the same due to the nature of our rebirth cycle of cloning. So I would say that the individual and the concept of individual has been largely eliminated from our society.

Zoosh spoke earlier about an individual upon a craft who would be the future self of the abductee and thus would have a strong connection and an ability to calm that person. If we're incarnated into your one-mind race, would we become part of your race rather than an individual?

But *you* have the ability to have a separate life, as you understand it. It is, of course, easy to calm *yourself* – since the soul energy that passes between the calmer and the calmee is really from the exact same soul incarnated in a different being. It is of comfort. It is allowed that two different species connect this way.

I'm assuming that time is infinite, which I have always thought was the truth. Why were you limited in your ability to change your race without coming back and effecting a change in our present?

In order for you to effect a change in your present, from the universal point of view, it was essential that we have that limitation. Otherwise we would not have been motivated to seek a way. Needless to say, any race that has ever existed still exists in what you might say is the gene pool of consciousness of the universe. So even if our race had no longer been embodied, it would have possible to reembody it. Yet when one builds up a culture elaborately – painstakingly, you might say – it would not benefit the one mind of that race to see it all disappear.

It would not make us happy to see our race eliminated. Even with our one mind, we like to pursue our scientific research and exploration. Yes, we still do explore. But the limit necessary to create motivation for us was put there to allow the universe to spin and change. The advantage of this limit is what truly confronts us now. Understand that it has been our objective to move beyond the limits of mentality for time so long that you cannot measure it because it is interdimensional. So at the core of our desire to perfect mentality, as expressed through technology and the blending into one conscious mind, was the idea to move beyond limits. Our discovery that there is an advantage in limits shakes the core of our approach to life. It literally forces us to see the advantage of polarity.

What is it in third-dimensional humanity that needs to be changed that will change your future?

Your change in motivation, and this can be done only through the soul desire to bring one's culture, the human culture, Earth culture, into balance with the feminine energy. Since that decision has been made in a recent window you have gone through as a race, we are allowed to experience this. Your window, which you refer to as the Harmonic Convergence, is simply the total soul agreement in that moment to change your motivation, to bring the largely out-of-balance masculine into more alignment with the feminine, meaning spirit and emotion.

Much of what you do on this planet has a limiting of the gift of spirit and emotion as a practical, day-to-day experience. In many, many races things that are spiritual and emotional are frowned upon as weakness. As the feminine is addressed in its value, so we can address the value of polarity.

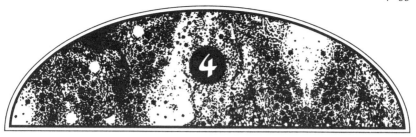

ET Interaction with Humanity

Joopah, introduced by Zoosh
Sedona, Arizona, September 18, 1988

oosh speaking. Now, it is in the nature of this particular valley [Sedona, Arizona] that change is instigated by the energies and their compatibility with those individuals who show up. The energies are changing; there is now some lateral motion of the energy as well as the vertical. This motion will insist, as you might expect, that those who have been leading rather vertical lives, not too well-grounded, will necessarily have to become a little bit more grounded.

At the same time there are visitors here from afar, as you well know. The Zeta Reticuli visitors have paid a call recently in a rather grand way. So without further ado, I will simply stand aside and allow Joopah from Zeta Reticuli to talk a little bit to you about what they've been doing here recently and what's to be done yet.

Recent Zeta Returning Visit

All right, Joopah speaking. It has been necessary for our group that works in the Northern Hemisphere of your world to be more active in this area lately. There has been some serious misadjustment of the energy in this area due to some innocent but tampering influence. There have been some experiments by sound and vibration engineers to attempt to uncover the mysteries of the energy vibrations here that have inadvertently caused some problem in the tuning of devices that are implanted here. Therefore about 2½ to 3 days ago of your time it was necessary for us to come in and retune those devices. Since it was necessary, those of you with whom we are in more direct contact were also paid a visit. You might say two birds with one stone – as you would say, humor. (Joopah makes a joke.) So the visitation, rather than coming the way you expected by ships in the sky, came a different way. Since this area is well-observed by those who observe your skies on this planet, it was necessary to approach from a different angle. Rather than simply move through time as we do, the best way to protect the devices and their location rather than have a light come from the sky with essentially a big arrow saying "This is where they are," we came up through the Earth. This is easily done if it is done in an altered dimension. And since our vehicles can travel in that dimension, it was necessary to come from underground, as you understand it.

There are several crystalline devices here that are in either pyramid shapes or a shape that you would recognize as a form of tuning fork, though there is no fork part; it is simply a long, broad beam. These devices are buried from three to five miles below the surface, and their transitional energy impetus was altered. This type of device is vital for the reimaging of your planet that is going on now, and it has a subduty as a navigational instrument. The navigational aspect of the devices was out of whack, as you would say. It is the navigational aspect that allows us to find this area, but it is an instrument that also allows your planet to alter its orbit slightly. So you can see that any discomfort in that structure could create a serious problem.

There are also several devices that are used to deflect, we shall say, rogue bodies of stone that might intersect with your planet. These were also off-tune, so we worked on them. While we were here, then, since we were coming up from underground, we used that method to visit those of you whom we visit regularly. Some of you may notice some slight physical evidence of that as well as some perhaps odd memories.

Is your work in association with the planetary confederation?

Understanding that there are different names, yes. In the beginning, of course, we thought we were just helping out, as you might help out in your field of expertise. Now we have a different attitude, because we are clear that many of you are our direct past lives. As a result, you have taken on rather a more personal meaning to us than someone who is simply the object of study, as it were. You must understand that since our race is scientific and technological at its core, for us to approach anyone, including one of our own, we have a scientific and technological intellectual approach. So I do not mean to sound as if I am patronizing.

When you rearrange these devices now, will they be retampered with, or there is no knowledge that you have rearranged them?

You understand that the tampering was unintentional. We put a grid around these devices so that should the unintentional radiation of sound take place again (which is radiated into the rock), these devices will not be knocked off their focus.

These are ELF waves that they're fooling with?

Not exactly. They are beginning to use a combination of pulse and sound that would be perhaps described as totally different; but generally speaking, you could say that. There is also some energy being used along the idea of radiant heat and cold. When that is applied to sound waves, the scientists will begin to have a much greater understanding of what can be accomplished with these waves. Right now there is less understanding due to the rather singular approach.

Changes in Earth's Rotation and Water Distribution

Can you discuss how these devices are altering the orbit of the Earth and how that is changing, and what the ultimate attempted change is?

In order for you to achieve what you now refer to as your fourth-dimensional status, it is necessary for the Earth's orbit to speed up slightly. It is not so much an alteration in the path, but in the motion of the planet — that is, turning on its axis and moving through its orbit just a little bit faster, not a great deal. It could be measured very carefully over five to ten years using timing instruments and laser devices, and soon it will be done.

Speeding up the Earth's rotation is also an attempt to control somewhat the wobble that has been going on for some time, caused largely by internal explosions over time. These explosions were essentially caused by civilizations playing with things that go boom [underground nuclear testing]. (When something goes boom [underground nuclear testing] it has a very slight effect, you know, on the magnetic axis.) Enough of these booms can have a cumulative effect. This has happened in past civilizations that have risen and fallen, and your legacy is a small wobble as your civilization has risen. Now you are adding to it. So to some extent the speeding up of the axial rotation even slightly will tend to stabilize the planet through a gyroscopic effect.

Will we experience the flip of the poles?

Physically?

Physically or the Earth itself.

As you understand the polarization or the repolarization of the magnetic energy, what you will experience is a different motivation. This pole effect is happening right now. You are in a cycle in which that is changing. That is why your motivations and issues are up — the masculine and feminine, of course, since polar opposites are analogous with masculine and feminine. The feminine issues are up, as it were. So you might say that this polar shift is taking place right now. It will happen very gradually, since if there were a sudden shift the planet would simply fall apart. I might add that the polar shift is not something that is vital for your specific change in life. It is rather that the polar shift is something that occurs *because* you are willing to change. So it is more an effect of what *you* do rather than your being affected by what *it* does. This will take some time.

Can you comment about the weather anomalies we've been experiencing? I think you're probably expert at that. What can we expect, and can we help?

To some extent this largely has to do with playing around with scientific things – bombs and so on. Mother Earth is necessarily having to alter her energy field in order to compensate. She will make some effort to do so in ways that are compatible with all of those who live on the surface. However, it is natural for Mother Earth to utilize water, since cleansing – washing, you might say – is a natural thing. Mother Earth also uses water to wash herself. Because of the alterations due to moving liquids up and down from below the surface to the surface and to the tampering with the natural breathing apparatus of Mother Earth, it has been necessary for her to create more water. And when more water is needed, it must be removed from the water bank otherwise known as the polar-ice area.

Thus it has been necessary for a slight heating up on the planet's surface. It will take some time, but eventually the polar icecap as you now know it will be greatly reduced and the sea level will be very slightly increased. This, of course, will create much more rain, and much more tropical air will move into areas once known to be more temperate zones. As a result of Mother Earth using her washing effect, the coastal areas of all of the continents will be somewhat altered.

It will be some time before this occurs; it will not happen suddenly. But there will be a gradual decrease in the water banks so that Mother Earth can wash herself. This is what to look for. This is why you will find things such as fires that Mother Earth will start herself by lightning in order to create less area where natural cooling is going on. Trees and vegetation necessarily act as a cooling device. So Mother Earth herself is involved in some of this.

There will also be some storms you will see from time to time that will be out of the ordinary. Because of the need to have more of the feminine influence, the Southern Hemisphere will seem to move up somewhat toward the Northern Hemisphere. This will largely be an effect that is felt by slightly increased humidity in southern areas of the Northern Hemisphere are well as storms developing in areas where they have not been known to develop.

So you can expect more rain, more lightning, and an increase in the water level. However, this will also have some auxiliary effects that could be advantageous. For areas that have been much too dry for their own good, the earthquake potential will be reduced. Since these areas will be much more saturated on a deeper level of the mineral zone, there will be some lubrication effect. Therefore the great big earthquake that has been feared on the West Coast of this continent will be greatly delayed and perhaps eliminated, due to the fact that perhaps instead of needing a sudden chiropractic adjustment, Mother Earth will do it more easily by a gradual motion, or creep, as it is referred to geologically. This creep effect will also assist. There may be, however, some displacement of population.

What about the ozone layer? Is that part of the heating effect?

That is part of the heating effect because it allows for more of the sun's heating rays to come in. They are, in fact, coming in at the specific area where they are needed, at the polar regions.

But there's talk about the radiation being a danger to humanity.

There is in fact some danger, and people who live in the extreme northern hemisphere will probably in time begin to wear broad-brimmed hats. There is less danger for those who live below the extreme northern and southern zones. It is the areas of polar icecap that will become a bit more hazardous. The gamma radiation will have some effect.

We've heard a lot about the various causes ascribed to this ozone problem. From your understanding, what began this cycle?

One could say that there are chemical cycles that are involved here because of mankind's involvement. However, Mother Earth does have the ability to simply increase the strength of the ozone layer to compensate for that. She has done that largely over many years. However, now it is necessary to increase the liquidity. So I would say that while one can draw a direct correlation between chemical pollution and ozone depletion, the effect is largely one volunteered by Mother Earth herself. The polluting effect of all of these experiments and a lack of understanding of the oneness of all life here has created this necessity as well.

Zeta Contacts with Humans

What's your intent or purpose in contacting individuals?

We have a different idea of that now, but I'm told now it is to perceive how the shift that you are involved in is going to assist us. As your future lives, we have a vested interest in whatever you do. Now, we do not tamper with what you do, but since our culture has found itself in a rather precarious position, we are not only interested but enthusiastic (insofar as we can attain that level of emotion) about this change you have embarked upon to alter your dimension, but that in effect is really an alteration of how you experience yourself.

The reason we contact individuals is that a future life is involved in the crew that contacts these people, and we believe that in a more direct physical contact we make it possible for the future life — ourselves — to experience perhaps a little bit more of the vital life energy that you all have here and take for granted. We do not have that in the same way, and that is why our race is dying out.

So it is necessary for us, as a future version of you, to understand what is going on. That is our approach — to understand, to solve the mysteries and so on. In order, then, for us to work on solving those mysteries we must understand the problem. And the problem, so to speak, is ours, not yours. That problem is that the future of the souls who had begun elsewhere and evolved into Earth karma eventually wound up in our own attempt to do away with the emotional self, believing that even though it had gifts to offer, the other aspect of it made for conflict and so on.

Now we can see the advantage of having an emotional self that is present and consciously involved in its own pursuits. This is the link that makes for re-creation of the self — that is, the successful birth. We clone; however, that spark of emotion controlled at the level of calm and peace is not sufficient for life to desire to stay in one body for some time. In order to understand this better, we have a member of our group contact an individual who is a direct past life, and during those contacts it is possible for that particular individual of our group to power down the technological device we use to protect ourselves from your auric emanations.

We cannot receive your auric emanations directly, but we can allow them to come closer to our auric emanations when we are dealing with a direct past life. In this way it is possible to almost absorb a little bit of your energy. While we cannot do that directly, we can come a little bit closer to understanding the vital life force that you emanate through your auric field.

It is necessary so that we can slowly move toward a motivation to allow the change in our future. As you change your present, our present, of course, changes as well. Yet there must be allowance and agreement. For our part, we have chosen this method of working with our mutual souls to direct our motivation. That is the overview.

Isn't it valuable to the Zeta to communicate with us as you do through Robert, because as you learn from interacting with us, the whole learns too?

It is a reminder; and it can be beneficial, since you will ofttimes make decisions of allowance based upon your intellectual input. Yes.

We do, but don't you, Joopah, learn from us in this interaction, and then doesn't that transmit back to the group mind also?

Yes. We understand your motivations, and that helps us to attempt to grasp how ours are similar. At times they are. Not always, but at times.

Did you say that you have altered your motives and your way of dealing with humanity? We have heard so much about the abductions and things that have happened during those abductions; could you speak to that a little?

I will say that as a child walks through an anthill without a great deal of regard for the life forms who are valuable there, so we (and perhaps I'm being a little too strict with our race) did not truly respect the valuable contribution of the human being in the early contacts. You must understand that we cannot interfere; we can only operate at a level of our own understanding. So while I would not compare our race to a child who casually strolls through an anthill, I would say that we did not fully appreciate who you were, not only on a personal level but on a pivotal reference level. You might say that several years ago we were much drier [humorless] than we are now. We do not exactly have the Johnny Carson Show yet, but we do have a greater appreciation for the value of humor and the effect that it causes within the integrating aspect of the emotional body.

So in years gone by we were considerably less emotional than we are now. You would not find us to be specifically emotional now, but you would also not find us to be opposed to emotionality. So in the beginning we were less aware spiritually of the evolution and the pivotal role of this planet's involvement in the change in the known universe. So I would say that some of the early contacts were a little more scientific than they needed to be.

But you must also remember that we have always had to protect ourselves technologically with devices. In this way your energy was not transmitted to us at all. Since most communication is energetic, we have received only your conscious and subconscious thoughts.

Now, here's one for you: The mass of us is not able to differentiate between your subconscious and your conscious thoughts. This is the refinement of our contact with you, which has largely developed due to your having a neighbor here who is your direct linear future — that is, one of your future selves. The future self comes as close as possible to being able to differentiate between your subconscious and your conscious thoughts. This has largely made it possible for us to have almost intelligent communication with you sometimes. This is why at times people will report in their contacts that they will have a brief moment of what seems almost like a conversation. There is a phasing effect in and out of the subconscious as thought.

The Shift in Your Subconscious

As a result of your fourth-dimensional shift, the subconscious mind is moving up. That is, what was down is up and what was up is down. Thus what has been perfected is no longer the stress in life; your mental, conscious mind is no longer the main focus you need to work on. But the subconscious mind needs to be worked on, and that is dredged up by you quite a bit, not just in an interaction with us but in your daily lives, so that you might be able to deal with those issues that have been hidden from you. As a result, there is a purging effect. This is done on purpose so that your conscious mind can expand in the fourth-dimensional aspect of itself and utilize the space used before by your subconscious. That is how that will work.

However, understand that since the subconscious mind is up now, you are even more emotional and more likely to have fear reactions than you would ordinarily have. This is how you can have a conflict wherein you would consciously look forward to having contact with us, but since the conscious mind is no longer the great power and the subconscious mind is up, when you do have those contacts the fight/flight reaction is much more powerful. The subconscious is much more powerful than the conscious mind, so you have difficulty in focusing into your conscious mind due to the physical interactions between us – the invaded feeling when someone touches you who didn't say please. We do not understand "please." You understand that that is not an aspect of our society.

This touching type of contact is more familiar to us; when we do a group meditation, we are all touching. It is typical. We do not make a differentiation. We are one body, in that sense. Even though we are individuals, we are one; we do not differentiate the idea of individuals. As a result, subconsciously speaking, you feel much more invaded when we touch you than we would if you touched us, even though when we touch you, you (naturally) touch us, even though this protective technological device creates an energetic interface between us and you.

This is why sometimes, in some of your stories about these experiences, some people will feel reassured by touch and others will feel very frightened by it. It depends upon how involved you are in your conscious mind compared to your subconscious mind. So there are complications that are at the same time opportunities for growth. There are always complications in our communication with you.

I started reading about these so-called abductions, and it occurs to me that the people who were selected somehow contracted this abduction on a soul level. Could you comment on that? Also, aren't we already connected on a soul level, or would "soul" be an applicable concept to you in terms of how we connect on a higher level?

Indeed we are, of course. Understand that spiritually speaking, we have almost a separate place where we consciously express our spiritual selves. But of course we do have spirit in us, as all beings do, and we are absolutely united.

As far as the individuals who choose on a soul level to contact us or to be contacted, I shall say that almost without exception these beings have future selves with us. So it is a soul-level contract. In a sense, you might say that you in your present time are reaching forward into the future to help us in our present time. And since you will have an incarnation there as well, you yourselves have a vested interest to see that our civilization can experience comfort and be saved, as it were. Although nothing is ever lost, it is our desire to perpetuate our civilization physically (in our sense of physics). So the soul-level contract occurs as a result of a direct linear connection.

You say that you have improved in humor. Have you gotten very close to learning how to laugh yet?

I've been working with Robert to appreciate the value of smiling and can almost do it, but laughter as yet escapes me. I learn slowly, but I will learn.

Can you see the analogy between the planet using water to cleanse, and humor in the new age (such as it is — hopefully there'll be more of it) also a means of cleansing and dealing with the subconscious coming forward? Is this an appropriate analogy?

Yes. I would say that an ability to (and I am certainly no expert in this area) allow for the frailties of oneself experienced as humor on this planet seems to be much more beneficial in integrating the emotional body as a portion of life. Our own emotional bodies are with us, but we have been somewhat confused by thinking we were more involved in our mental bodies due to the fact that the emotions we have bred ourselves to experience are calm and peace. Yet they *are* emotions. So let's say that humor does appear to be vital in order to perpetuate a lust for life and a desire to survive. And since you are, of course, the Explorer Race, your desire to survive is vital for the universe as well as for yourself.

How do you express joy, if you have any?

We express it as a unit body, so to speak, as one being. When we have a group meditation or a ritualistic experience, we do it to essentially renew our oath for living, and we experience the joy in the union of us all.

Can you say a little about how long you are incarnated in your bodies in terms of our time? Is it a hundred years or a thousand years? Do you retain your memories? Do you rejuvenate?

Some time ago a Zeta scientist achieved what was felt to be the perfect body, and all of us since then have been cloned from that body. This is why it is so easy to interact with each other's energies. You know that different souls incarnate into different lives, so although we have the same body to incarnate into, we are in fact different souls. However, it is our choice to be involved with each other in a expanded mental way as well. So when one of us makes a discovery due to some scientific or intellectual research, we will all have the knowledge at the same time, giving us a group mind, as you have said. This we have discovered to be very efficient. Of course, it does rule out the experience you have of the joy of discovery on an individual level. But that has not been our path so far.

I would say that our incarnation depends less upon the duration of the physical body than to an arbitrary period we might choose to experience that particular physical body. Since there is no definite advantage to being reborn in another physical body, we will on the soul level pick a time. We would say that perhaps 275 years allows us to achieve a degree of perfection of experience as a member of our race that we find to be compatible.

So in the interaction with humans when they are physically inspected, cloning material is taken from the physical body of humans?

Not for direct use in our race.

The Zeta-Human Hybrid

You're hybridizing the race, is that not correct?

Yes, for a hybrid race, but not for us specifically. There is an attempt to hybridize a race, as you know, between us and the human being so that there can be a go-between race that can understand and appreciate both the human being and us — a translator, you might say. This was our intent. And this race in its nucleic form has already been invented. Since it is a future life form, from your point of view, whether it exists now or in the future makes no difference. But from our actual interaction in our time sequence, we have created several prototype models from whom we will begin to clone sufficient species so that they might develop their own idea of culture. We are not going to instruct them as much as we would instruct one of our own on a way of living. We will encourage them to be much more involved in contact with you than one of us might be. They will be able to contact you directly, as we cannot, without the need for an energy field to protect them. As a result, they will be able to contact us as well. They will be first cousins to both of us.

Will we be in the fourth dimension before we can interrelate with them?

Since we are traveling through time, of course, they can interrelate with you right now. Some of them have begun having contacts. They look a little different from us. For one thing, they are taller, generally 5' to 5' 1" tall. Their heads are not as large as ours. They have two arms, two legs, a head, and so on — a typical humanoid. They have the very large eyes that we have, but they are proportionately not quite as large. Since we are very short compared to you, our eyes are proportionately larger. Their eyes are not as big proportionately, but they are still quite large, dominant features. Since the eyes in our race have everything to do with the mental power and its transmission of energy (as it does in your race, but you have not yet remembered that), then having the tools of these eyes is necessary for us as a way to alter not only our perception of our world but to assist others to alter their perception of us. They are not only receivers but broadcasters of information.

In this hybrid race is each race one prototype, or is there a mixture?

There were several experiments in the beginning that did not seem to be sufficiently balanced between both races. So in our typical style we created one that we felt is just right and then cloned that one. There are now (from our time perspective) about 100,000 of these beings in existence. Since they can travel in time, the number is arbitrary for you, since it is all in the future, from your point of view. But right now we are experiencing roughly 100,000 of them. They have been given their own planet to develop their own culture. And although they have the knowledge and most of the mental power that we have, they actually have a more organic body. Our bodies, roughly from the neck down, are not what you call organic; they are more plasmic even though they have a surface and appear to be humanoid — two arms, two legs and a head. Their bodies are much more organic, though it is a hybridized form that does not involve itself much in the idea of breakdown over time. So their form is a highly efficient, organic receptacle, and it is much more organic than ours.

Are they between you and us in dimensional reality? As we are third and eighth, are they fifth?

I'd say that they are mobile between the dimensions. They would not experience the pulse of the third dimension in its entirety. They can travel much easier in dimensions. This is why they do not have to use the protective devices that we use in your dimension. They are a little more efficiently created. We did not create our civilization to travel in dimensions; we created it to *live* in other dimensions.

Do they reproduce organically?

They do not. At this time that capability has not been applied to the physical body. We are still deciding, with them as equals, whether this will be something that they choose to experiment with. We have created some beings in the past in the initial experiments that did have aspects of the ability to organically reproduce. But we were dissatisfied with the results. Most of the offspring were extremely frail, and due to our lack of experience and expertise in working with organic matter, we were not of much help in assisting them to become more sturdy. But as more of the hybrids interact with them, we will understand better how to assist them. We are not encouraging the hybrids to use any other means of reproducing than cloning until we understand the reproductive idea better. They are likely to develop that as a science first and then re-create themselves to perhaps experiment with it first.

What comes to mind is seeing rows and rows of people that look the same. Do you have diversity within the population of clones?

No way – if you've seen one of us, you've seen them all!

Have any Zetas ever crashed and been in custody of any Earth government or military installations?

Yes. Understand that crashes and cessation of life is a soul-level decision. Due to the older versions of the ships we used, there have been some that were inadvertently affected by magnetic fluxes. Some of the older ships used a rudimentary form of radiated ion energy that is involved in a magnetic creation. The really ancient ships used some versions of atomic energy – these ships were not affected. But the early ion-magnetic ships were occasionally affected by sudden solar or magnetic flares – magnetic flares happen – so that the navigational instruments were affected and the ship crashed.

Some of the bodies are preserved here on this planet, but there are no live ones. There were some survivors initially, and had we been allowed to rescue our people, we would have been able to give them a form of life, though they would not have been able to reintegrate entirely in our civilization due to their exposure to you. But they would have perhaps been happier with us. However, our requests, which were made directly to governmental bodies, were not honored, so we do not have those individuals back. Understanding what they must do, they allowed their lives to come to an end. It was not what you call a suicide, but by allowing those human beings who would interact with them to touch them and so on – and due to the nature of your energy fields we cannot tolerate too much of that – they had a cessation of life. The bodies are preserved in some areas.

In the United States?

There are some here. There are some in France and there is a body in the Soviet Union. There is also a portion of a body in Italy.

During the time they were in custody, was there interaction between humanity and the Zetas?

Yes. There was a brief interaction.

Thus many government leaders know positively that you are real?

Yes, although that is not a widely shared secret. As far as being discussed openly, it is a handful of individuals.

Earth-Pleiades Connection

Why did so many of us choose to come here from the Pleiades?

You were born there? (Joke — smile.)

Many individuals who believe they have a soul connection on Pleiades are naturally here due to the fact that the Pleiades is a direct ancestor, you might say, in the sense that your forefathers and their forefathers are the same beings. So you might say that you are directly related. It has been said that the Pleiades is your past and Zeta Reticuli your future. But it is equally true to say that it is a parallel existence. In order to appreciate the value of Earth life, many beings here have a more direct connection with Zeta Reticuli, and many have a more direct connection with Pleiades; Earth is the middle point. It is as though there are three points on a triangle, where the balance of that triangle is jeopardized without any one of the other points. To have the complete experience and become whole and complete in the understanding of different aspects and expressions, one must have the Pleiadian, Earth and Zeta Reticulan experience. It is like a family.

Will the clones require any fuel or food to subsist? Perhaps we can be of benefit to them. What things should we look out for to protect them?

Understand that they will be innocent. They will require some subsistence, yes. Unlike ourselves (we do not eat, as you understand it), they will require something to consume. Being more connected with us from their perspective as at present, they are not likely to have the variable foods that you have available. So they will be thrilled (since they will have the potential of being thrilled) to have food that looks good and tastes good and smells good, since what they will receive from us is essentially a mishmash of vitamins and minerals and leaves a great deal to be desired in cuisine. So if they approach you and ask, you might be able to offer suggestions about basic foods. It is more likely that they will pay visits to farms and interrelate with the farmers. They will have a certain agricultural interest due to the fact that in farming on this planet, cloning and hybridization have been going on for many years. These particular hybrids that we have created will find their most natural counterparts here in farmers and individuals in agriculture, and they are much more likely to suggest techniques of hybridization to farmers and interact with those individuals. So those who might have farms or know people on farms can expect to see them first.

The Hybrid Explorer Race

You made a comment earlier that we are known as a race of explorers. Can you elaborate a little on that?

Your bodies have been created over the years as hybrids as well. The original species of Earth-being bears about as much resemblance to you as we do. You are a hybrid that has not been involved with us genetically. You were largely hybridized from the original Earth species through contacts primarily with Orion, Sirius and the Pleiades. There was some mixture from Andromeda, Arcturus, Sagittarius and a few others. There is a need in this universe of yours to have a civilization that will bring the simple traits of enthusiasm and extroversion to other cultures. These cultures, like our own, have been long inbred with a goal toward internal perfection. Despite our contact with other races and species, our primary goal is to achieve a specific goal for ourselves.

So there needs to be an Explorer Race that will with enthusiasm explore the galaxies as a child might explore a toy store for the first time. That race will necessarily have to be survivable under extreme conditions. Your race has been created to not only be able to tolerate extreme cold and heat, but have the desire and willingness to do so.

Many races would simply die out if exposed to the type of extremes that you have here. But you are born with a will to live, as are most species on this planet. It is a lust for life, as we have come to call it. So you have been created – understand that this is a three-hour answer condensed somewhat – to propel yourselves out into the universe and bring your lust for life to civilizations that have become too involved in their own infrastructure.

What is your concept of the Creator?

It is the energy of creation. We do not specifically refer to this as an individual, whereas many civilizations on your planet might deify someone or something, in the case of cultures that might consider aspects of nature deities. We stand in awe before the ability to create that is beyond what we can create, and accept our creation as the unfoldment. We do not perceive of a sacred God separated from ourselves, but we do acknowledge that One, for lack of a better term in your language. (We have some difficulty with the rather precise aspect of your language. Since this is a philosophical question, preciseness is actually a problem.) I would say that the energy of the Creator is something we identify with much more than the idea of God. It is, in other words, an answer that is nonverbal; we identify energetically. I will attempt to bring through some energy of what we identify in our experience with the Creator. A moment – I can bring to you only a small amount. A moment; there is some resistance. I can bring through only a subtle aspect.

We believe in the unfoldment. Anything else?

I've been curious about more direct contact with these brothers. Will we be seeing more?

As you might know, you are being prepared now through your visual and media groups to accept not only your enthusiasm but to confront your fears as well. This is a vital human trait, curiosity. And it is through curiosity that you are being prepared. Do not expect the proverbial spaceship on the White House lawn — or in Red Square, either. You are being prepared. So you can expect to see a little more of us in some ten to fifteen years.

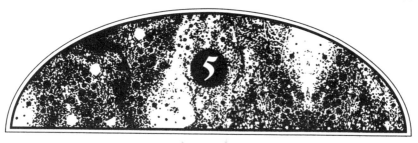

VFOs and Abductions

Zoosh, Joopah and Tsengey

Sedona, Arizona, February 19, 1989

ll right, Zoosh speaking. Ufos and abductions – what is this all about? Understand that the word "abductions" does not allow for the reality that the soul *always* gives permission for whatever takes place in a life. Even though some things might not always be fun or delightful, the soul's purpose in its journeys is to understand a particular issue or many different issues from as many points of view as possible. The soul gives permission to learn. When anybody is abducted or taken someplace without their conscious permission, there is always the unconscious permission.

The idea of abductions goes back a very long way. It has historical ramifications way beyond the idea of UFOs, but we will stay within the UFO parameter. My perception is that the Earth person is the direct result of a genetic experiment on Earth to create a being who is both curious and willing to do whatever is necessary to achieve knowledge, regardless of the struggle or ease, and who is also willing to take risks in order to teach that knowledge.

This situation was brought about because there is a need in the universe to have at least one group of beings who, like gypsies, would go from planet to planet bringing with them information about what's going on on the other planets and who have a specific need to learn and to share what they know – the Explorer Race. This is needed in the universe because there are many planetary civilizations that have attempted to create a perfected race without having a great deal of interaction with its neighbors or others within their own solar systems. Thus there often needs to be more communication.

An Overview of the Earth Experiment

The term "abductions" can be changed to "contacts." Contacts between beings from other planets and this planet have been common from the beginning of your species. Your species was created from the race of beings (not the so-called Bigfoot or Abominable Snowman) that existed millions of years ago on this planet in a slightly different characterization. This race of beings, which could be referred to as the **Andazi**, were quite tall, rather well-furred (body hair, you understand) and were extremely connected to the All That Is. They were fully telepathic, absolutely balanced and totally allowing. It was that allowance and willingness to give up their civilization to allow a contribution of their genetic structure (along with that of the Pleiadian, Orion, Andromedan, Sirian and a few other civilizations) that created what is now represented as the Earth human being.

It has been necessary, in order to create this race with the full cooperation of your soul, the Creator and all concerned, to check up on the experiment over the years. As is the case in growth and evolution, you are ever evolving in your state of consciousness toward a greater understanding of who you are in your totality as well as in this individual life. Civilizations on other planets are experiencing very much the same thing. They are evolving in their understanding of who they are and who they are in relationship to others.

So in the beginning many of these "abductions," as they are called, were carried out from the point of view of civilizations that you might say had an attitude about Earth people, including an attitude about the Andazi. The Andazi were apparently not very technologically advanced, and the beings who originally came here from **Sirius** to begin the experiment (which was, from their point of view, an attempt to improve qualities for the beings on this planet) did not understand the advanced degree of the civilization of the Andazi, because they were not sufficiently advanced enough themselves to realize who they were dealing with. You see, the Andazi were beyond needing instrumentality or technology to create comfort for themselves. So I would say that there has been an evolution in consciousness within the genetic experimenters as well as the subject of the experiment, of whom you are examples.

Over the years many different races from different planets have checked up on you. They often check up on reincarnated versions of those who were originally involved in some of these experiments — not a single line traced directly back on a soul or genetic level but on soul trees. You might say that those original beings who came here from Sirius (who happened to number 144,000) would have implanted genetically and on a soul level much of their karma, as well as their genetic needs and their specific unfulfilled desires, into the karma of the human being. Therefore much of what they had not accomplished in their lives —from Sirius and Andromeda and Orion and all these places —has been perpetuated through your own fulfillment, needs, desires, possibilities and talents. Through the years, then, these beings have picked you up and checked on you.

You inherit different things from different civilizations. The Sirius race was somewhat warlike because the planet they escaped from was more negative than the world you live on now, and as a result they had warlike tendencies, which you have inherited. However, they also had qualities that you would admire as well; for example, Sirians would think nothing of laying down their life for their friends. We are talking about a race of beings who are somewhat warlike, but also courageous and somewhat self-sacrificing for the greater good of all. You might recognize those traits as something to be admired here.

There are also other civilizations that have had an influence. **Orion**, for example, had an unfulfilled planetary destiny. Beings from Orion settled on a group of three small planets where your asteroid belt now exists. These beings had an evolutionary process of continually doing the same thing —their civilization went out to a certain point and no further. They would blow up a planet and then would have to reincarnate elsewhere. Some of them escaped in a group, came to this planet and worked their consciousness and karma into the genetic mainstream, which included their need to create conflict situations that could be resolved only through absolute and total cooperation by everyone. You are now confronted with the same crisis, not as a war situation but as a pollution and atmospheric crisis that is becoming apparent to everyone on this planet. It can be resolved only by absolute and total world cooperation. To some extent this is a legacy from the Orion need to bring their karmic pattern to a satisfactory conclusion.

Another civilization that is involved in your traceable roots is the **Pleiades**. These individuals have had a source somewhat parallel to your own: their forefathers and your forefathers are the same. The **Founders** of this particular area of the galaxy, who still live on various locations (including inside this Earth at about the eighth to ninth dimension), pulse out considerable energy. These Founders were the creators of the Pleiadians and Earth beings and others in large part through their thoughts and energetic workings. They were not directly related to what you understand to be the Creator —that is, they were not God, but they have capabilities that far exceed the idea of technology. They helped to create the idea of Pleiadian races and they also helped to create other races. Those who moved to the Pleiades from an original source did not want to experience any idea of negativity, discomfort, separation or polarization. However, those who stayed here on the soul level and occupied planet Earth welcomed others such as those from Sirius to come here and conduct their activities, believing that polarity and separation had possibilities that could be integrated into a positive world and thereby create excitement, enthusiasm and so on to stimulate their races' development.

Now, I'm giving you an overview, as you can see. The Pleiadians have had little experience with the idea of polarization, separation and even drama, and they would be somewhat interested to have you exchange with them when they feel you are ready so that they can experience your memories of drama without having to experience it themselves. They could not stand the emotional and physical effect on their bodies, but they can experience your memories. Through a form of memory transfer they can learn, without having to have lived your lives, what could influence the development of their culture in a positive way.

The most notable other civilization would perhaps be from **Andromeda,** this being the seat of thought for your immediate area of the universe. It has contributed largely to your thinking style and aptitude.

There have, as stated, been many beings who have picked you up. Very often people on this planet are picked up by Zeta Reticulans. There is absolutely no genetic connection between you and the Zeta beings. These beings were the scientists in this part of the universe and perceive themselves as technicians. They will pursue or be involved in any technological experiment that catches their interest and that they could assist. Your association with them is on a soul line. Rather than being your past lives, you, from their point of view, are *their* past lives. That is, the Zeta beings, as they now exist in many years and dimensions into the future, are your soul's future lives. As the Zetas have begun to realize that, they have changed their entire point of view about who you are in ralation to them. That is the overview.

The Zeta Reticulans

Now, one of you might experience being picked up by these Zeta beings. I mention this because these are the contacts that are the most controversial right now. The Zeta beings are the short beings who have large eyes, big heads and a strange pallor to their skin — somewhat grayish or chalky. They have a tremendous intelligence that cannot be measured by your IQ tests, but if you used IQ values you could say that their IQ ranges from 300 to 500. They can process tremendous amounts of information through their minds in an instant, very much like a large computer.

These beings experience themselves, their civilization and their culture on a one-mind level. What one of them knows, they will all know in time due to the interactive experience of their single mental capacity. Although they have the advantage of that knowledge transfer, the disadvantage is that since they have largely a single-minded motivation, they are sometimes very slow to understand that the things they are doing and processes they're involved in could benefit by the increase of some totally different point of view.

This is not to suggest that they are rigid and stubborn, but rather that they are very focused in their own culture, although perhaps not entirely on a level of beneficial creativeness for themselves. Their problem in recent years has been the dying out of their civilization in vertical time. They would very much like to have someone to pass it on to. They know now that the reason their civilization is dying out is because of their attempt to divorce themselves from their emotional bodies, which they perceived to cause much of the strife in the past, thereby creating a greater dominance of the mental self and a goal of technological pursuit that could constantly stimulate their minds toward the creation of technology.

I would say that they have created a tremendous technology that has gone so far as to be genetically based. They have come to realize that it is their emotional bodies that act as the electrical conduit from their soul selves to their physical experience of themselves. Because they have narrowed their emphasis on their emotional selves, they have greatly cut down on their direct energetic transfer of inspiration from the soul's energy to their physical presence. Naturally, they are having a considerable difficulty in incarnating and reincarnating, since there is a tendency for souls to wish to pursue a balanced lifestyle — balanced between mental, physical, emotional and spiritual — rather than a stunted lifestyle, too mental and not emotional enough.

When these beings picked you up they have been very scientific in their approach. They have not often been fully cognizant of your emotional needs, since their own emotional growth was so stunted, due to the emphasis placed upon the elimination of the emotional body. As a result, when one of you who was taken aboard a ship would have an emotional crisis, due to their ignorance of their own emotional bodies, they would literally not understand. You might ask, "How can such a technologically and mentally advanced civilization be so narrow in their understanding?" It is simply this: they are telepathic and do not communicate verbally. Though they can make a sound, they have evolved to a point where they are no longer using the spoken word.

The complication occurs when they receive communication from you. There has been no complication in the other direction. You have been able to receive their communications because your energetic selves (your emotional and physical interactions with your spiritual and etheric selves) are very powerful and pronounced. So you are actually more sensitive in your communication skills than they are. You can receive everything they have to say even though it does not always make sense to you. The real problem has been the fact that they have a very poor ability to differentiate between your subconscious and your conscious thoughts. This has caused an extreme difficulty for them. When they induce a hypnotic state in you in order to take you aboard the ship, they use their eyes as well as a degree of technological support to induce this state, but they also have to screen their very large eyes with their inner lids, since they are extremely light-sensitive.

The side effect of that —which they have only recently realized —is that the deep pools of their black eyes seem to bring your subconscious to the surface. This is why many of you have the experience of wanting, wishing and hoping to meet these beings from other planets (if for no other reason than so you can know they exist and tell your friends about them), but when you actually meet these particular beings from Zeta Reticuli (they are not terrifying looking, just different), the effect of their eyes is to bring your subconscious to the surface. And since they do not themselves experience a subconscious mind (they have only a conscious mind and an unconscious, soul-level mind), they do not know what they're dealing with.

When a person's subconscious comes up, you will not simply react to the Zeta beings, but you will experience *everything that has ever gone on emotionally in your subconscious*, including the ideas of love, hate, fear and so on. Because you have suppressed a great deal of fear in your lifetimes and placed it into your subconscious, you have to deal especially with fear. Even the slightest feeling of fear in you will be amplified a hundred times, due simply to the increased presence of your subconscious. So while on one level you might wish and hope to communicate with these beings and express it telepathically —and they pick up your thoughts —at the same moment you could be having a subconscious thought you're not even aware of that is screaming for these people to get away from you and leave you alone.

They cannot differentiate at all. So although they can communicate more directly to you because of your openness and abilities and energetics of existence, due to *their* limits they cannot fully grasp the differentiation between your feelings and your thoughts. This has created a tremendous problem in the past. Now that they are aware of it, they have done what they can do. They cannot directly change their civilization or drop their psychological shields because, having disciplined themselves so long not to be under the influence of emotions, they cannot tolerate the energy of Earth people. The actual energetics of emotion would buffet them too much and cause them such discomfort as to prevent future interactions with their own race.

The Hybrid Race

What they have done, therefore, through the use of the so-called abductions, is go back in time. They had to go back in time in any event, to see your civilization in the past as well as now. They have begun to use some of the genetic samples gathered from human beings over the many years of their contact, as well as get contributions from certain volunteers (from their point of view, they feel that since your souls and their souls are directly in a karmic and interrelated past life/future life experience, they have your permission) in an attempt to create, not a direct cross between you and them, but a bridge race that can communicate to them and to you equally — a secondary race.

They have, over the years of time and space and now within the context of time, created about 40,000 of these beings primarily through the use of cloning, since this is their number one format for re-creation. But there has also been an attempt to create actual biological births, since many times they did not understand why you had so many powers (from their point of view). They have begun to believe that direct biological birth might have some bearing on an individual's desire to survive. And since it is their intention to create survivability in their race, they wish to breed in that factor, or what your race outstandingly possesses: a lust for life.

What has taken place, then, is this exchange of genetic experiences to create this secondary race. The secondary race has attributes of both races: the knowledge of the parent race (the Zeta Reticuli) and also the knowledge of the other race (you). These beings will be able to communicate more directly with you because they will have a degree of an emotional body.

They will not be as emotional as you, but they will be considerably more emotional than the parent race. Thus they will not need any technological protection from your emotional body. They look a little different: the parent race is three to three-and-a-half feet tall at most, but the secondary race is about five feet to five feet, four inches tall. The head will not be as proportionately large as that of the parent race, and although the eyes will still be quite large, they will be smaller than those of the Zetas.

These beings will eventually begin to contact your race, and there has been some minimal contact up to this time. They will largely act as ambassadors between the two races and improve communications considerably. From the Zetas' point of view, the creation of the secondary race has been the reason for the abductions.

Abductions by Other ET Races

There are other people who are involved in what you refer to as abductions, but what is going on here is often the experience of wishing and wanting to find out more about you. Sometimes people will be abducted onto **Pleiadian** ships; these experiences, though, will be much more pleasurable. You will often have an experience of play. Sometimes they use tone and light to create teaching games, because this is the orientation of their own educational system. The idea of tone (or song) and color in an embodied form — color that moves, that can exist as its own entity and that can influence as an almost solid substance is very inspiring and delightful indeed — can act as a way of bridging your races. This is what they will do for you.

The Pleiadians' object is to be able to observe your wide range of emotions. They also must protect themselves somewhat if you emanate an emotion of discomfort, but they can be fully exposed to you when your emotions are calm, peaceful, happy or joyful. So they are perhaps better off than the Zeta beings. They look very much like you, with only minor differences — around the area of the skull (the ear receptors are somewhat different) and the gut (about seven feet shorter because they don't have to digest some of the things you've had to digest simply to survive), plus a few other minor differences.

The beings from **Andromeda** will often be seen in lightships. (Pleiadian ships are often seen as solid or glowing with a sky-blue or pink color; the Zeta craft are most often red-orange; and the Orion ships are usually blue-green.) The Andromeda lightships, if visible at all, are seen as a compressed form of white light. These beings are extremely advanced, dimensionally speaking, fully balanced, and the thrust of their race is to create justice. They have upon their planetary influences the seat of thought, where different races are encouraged to see how their thoughts work toward helping them evolve to their life purposes as well as to see how they are similar. So they sometimes check up on you.

You seldom experience being taken aboard their ships, but every once in a while some of you will experience it, even if taken physically, in the form of your lightbodies. Their vehicles, which often appear as flat disks of pure white light, simply act as transfer zones or time-space windows; thus you can experience any planetary phenomena over which they have an influence in their own area of culture and galactic origins.

As far as **Orion** is concerned, there are two different influences. To some extent there is the old Orion influence, which has largely infiltrated into your karmic pattern and motivation and no longer exists outwardly. There is the now Orion, which is very positive, very much involved in light, color, sound, music and somewhat theatrical expressions. They are in appearance (unlike the beings from Andromeda who are lightbeings) quite varied, with a wide range of representation. Some of them are quite humanoid; others, although they have two arms and two legs, have heads shaped like a softened valentine heart. Some are no more than four to four-and-a-half feet tall and others range between eight and nine feet tall and have very long limbs. A very high evolution of their souls is integrated into their day-to-day reality.

Orions pick you up not to check on the effects of the Orion past and the karmic tie, but to see how you are overcoming it; not to see how it progresses but to see how you are throwing it off—what has been processed and what has been shed due to that processing. Historically they have kept track of your progress (from their point of view). They do not do genetic tests and so on that the Zeta beings do. If anything, they might attach a comfortable device to your head and transfer the emotional and mental memories of your life into their computer banks or into one of their individuals who acts as a link to a data storage unit.

The **Sirius** influence is a different situation. There has been an odd form of bleed-through. There are dimensional beings from Sirius who are from the planetary location that the original beings are from. This Sirius planet is somewhat more negative than your own: they do not appreciate or experience any idea of positivity, but they are wonderful warriors and have many of the attributes on the most positive level of a good warrior (so as not to misunderstand them). They also have tremendous fear. They are actually somewhere between the second and third dimension in their experience of life. Due to the anomalous window experience that has developed (so that they might be prepared to make the shift that you are all making now to the next dimensional expression of yourselves, from the third to the fourth dimension), they are preparing to make a shift from the second to the third dimension. They are preparing to integrate the idea of positivity into their world so they can reach a greater sense of balance. Thus this bleed-through has to take place for them so they can prepare themselves for this new experience.

To some extent they are acting as interferers, for their experience of life does not include an understanding of how their soul structure fits into their-day-to-day life. They are not religious and do not consciously believe in any idea of the Creator. This is not to suggest they are soulless or evil, but that they are unevolved —not even as evolved as your race is or has been these many thousands of years. So they must be, if not pitied, at least understood in their own light. They believe that if this shift takes place for their civilization from the second to the third dimension, they will simply cease to exist. If they do not have an understanding of themselves as spiritual as well as physical beings, you can see how any idea of a change that would totally revolutionize their experience of themselves could be perceived as an obliteration of their race. This is their approach to the universal change.

Of course, as your planet changes from the third to the fourth dimension, all other aspects of your galaxy and imagined world as well as the real world will change as well. The negative Sirians are desperately frightened about this, and although they are quite certain they can do nothing to prevent it, they are doing their darndest to slow down the process. There is practically nothing they can do to slow it down, but this does not prevent them from fighting in a lost cause. This is an aspect of their behavior that might be considered positive by some on your planet. You can see that even though they are warriors, they are also exhibiting some positive traits, although they do not recognize them as such.

These beings are here and act to some extent as corrupters. They are the ones who are involved in and influencing directly, or indirectly through others, the so-called cattle mutilations. They're also involved in subversive attempts to make the Zeta beings scapegoats for activities they are not directly involved in. They are attempting to blame certain activities on the Zeta beings when they themselves — these particular Sirians of the second- to third-dimension orientation — are involved more directly. As a hint, at this northern New Mexico locality [Dulce] where there is an underground Zeta Reticuli base, there is also a nearer-to-the-surface base of these Sirian beings, where they are attempting to create on a rather grand scale the idea that the Zeta beings' real purpose in their genetic experiment is to make a human race of slaves. You might say that there is a grandiose idea of subversion going on here. It is not reaching the public to any great extent, but it has percolated out a little bit.

I must comment on the **other Sirian beings,** who are at a very highly evolved state. They would usually not pick anybody up because their evolution has been so extended that they are not fully embodied anymore. I am not suggesting that there are no Sirians who are embodied, but that those who are directly associated with the Earth are the direct *soul* lineage of those 144,000 beings who came on that first ship to initiate the social engineering experiments that began the creation of the human race. Through time and over millions of years, through their contract with Earth karma and Earth's auric field, those beings have evolved into what is now experienced by many as the angelic kingdom. They are directly associated with Earth's auric field and will be involved with Earth for time immemorial. So they will act to some extent as protectors, guardians in a direct alliance between the Creator and Mother Earth herself.

Billy Meier Contacts

Can you give us any information about the Billy Meier contacts with the Pleiadians in Switzerland?

For the most part these contacts are genuine. There has been some information that has purposely been given out to cloud the actual reality of these contacts. The contacts have become somewhat more clandestine in recent years, due to a realization by some individuals close to Meier such that Meier feels, on a soul level, a sense of concern for his own safety, and has created some dramas.

The Pleiadians on their part have recognized that Meier has an Earth karma. He has a purpose for being on Earth and a need to learn some lessons, so they have to some extent backed away from face-to-face, physical contact with him. This is not to say they are not concerned about him (for they are influencing him away from this planet), but rather that they are concerned that the contacts they have made allow Meier to create on a soul level, and manifest physically, dramas that might involve them and him in ways that are not beneficial to him.

They have needed to pull away in any event, due to the increase in emotional energy not only of Mother Earth, but of you as direct representatives of Mother Earth on the physical-emotional plane. Your activity has become more emotional. Mother Earth is changing to create for herself a greater sense of harmony, and you must, as her representatives, change as well. So they have had to physically back away. However, they are still in telepathic contact with Meier and are continuing to give him information for himself and his archives. In time the Meier archives will be translated very carefully. Some languages can be easily translated, such as German, but in the translation into English there is a lot of nuance lost. I would suggest to those who can read German, to read them in that language; the contacts are real.

Cattle Mutilations

Can you tell us why cattle are mutilated and parts of their bodies taken?

Those beings who are involved in that are, to some extent, Earth beings. I do not wish to comment greatly on that due to their desire to remain anonymous, or at least be veiled from the knowledge of the general public. I will say, however, that the initial instrumentation involved in assisting these Earth beings to pursue these studies was provided by the negative Sirians, though they themselves did not invent it.

I would also suggest that the other Sirians are highly evolved. And there are animal species who are very high beings themselves, such as the whales and dolphins who are derived from that particular area of the galaxy. The particular parts of the animals' bodies that are being removed is not so much a pursuit of the DNA (since that is understood) than the creation of a synthetic hormone that can alter the physical mass of any given body (including animal bodies) to re-create it into other forms. I am purposefully speaking somewhat obliquely.

Many years ago a woman was abducted by a UFO. The beings had a calf on board, which they were mutilating, and she scolded them. They indicated that their masters were humans who looked like us. Can you explain this?

This is a direct reference to the idea of the negative Sirians. These Sirians, while they do not in their normal bodies look that much like you, are humanoids and they have similarities to you. In an adapted form of Earth body that they can wear, they look very much like you. You notice that the beings said that they *appeared* to be like you. They did not, from their frame of reference, see a great deal of difference. The particular beings operating that vehicle did not fully grasp the difference on a soul level, due to their inability to understand emotions or even appreciate them as having value. That that is why their discernment would be so limited.

I might also say that the beings on that particular vehicle who appeared to look somewhat like the Zeta Reticuli beings were in fact a form of that crossbreed created by the Sirians, who used some of the genetic structure of the Zeta beings through direct access to genetic coding files as well as samples of Zeta tissue remains. These particular beings were somewhat cynical because of their evolutionary process, which is extremely limited. There have been at times references to the Zeta Reticuli past. In their past — not the level from which Joopah speaks — there have been wars and extremely cynical civilizations, though these specific beings were not from that.

Are some Zeta beings giving information to the top echelons of government in exchange for being allowed to conduct mutilation experiments?

This is absolutely untrue! Understand that the reference you are using here is an example of the Sirian attempt to create a subversive sense of blame toward these Zeta beings. I will say to the source of your information, that while 80% of that particular document [the Dulce Papers] is true, the names have been changed to protect the innocent. About 20% of the alterations have been made so that certain parties who would prefer to be anonymous can continue to be so. The actual biological facility that was graphically detailed in that document actually exits, although what is going on there was somewhat distorted.

There are Zeta beings who are involved in some information transfer, and the scientific community in this particular case operates with a direct clearance from some elements of the government of the United States. I might mention that there is another Zeta being who is engaged in a similar activity in the Soviet Union, although the information gathered there is of a slightly different nature. There is also another Zeta being in a European country recognized at this time as a world influence, if not dominant power. There are a couple of others. The so-called attempt to corrupt the human race and to spread the idea of a world of slaves is a subversive attempt to make the Zeta beings look like monsters.

The Negative Sirians

Is the purpose of the second-dimensional Sirians to create a slave race?

No.

Their purpose is to disrupt?

Yes, their motivation is to disrupt. Their purpose is to survive, and from their point of view survival can take place only if the pivotal point in the universe in this space and time —which is Earth and its karmic evolvement to the fourth dimension —can be delayed in that motion as much as possible. But you have begun that motion to your fourth-dimensional experience already. As a result, even they are changing. They are now in some communication on a slightly more open level with intelligences that can assist them in their own change. Even though they resist those communications, they are experiencing them in their dream state. In the past their dreams have been nightmarish; now some dreams are happy and positive. So they are experiencing the anxiety associated with the totally unknown, and they have real major anxieties and fears because of them. They are being influenced already to a degree at the unconscious level and there is some hesitant contact going on with those who might advise them, including myself and others. So they are beginning to change in spite of themselves. But understand that their motivation in these subversive activities is simple survival.

Do these second-dimensional Sirians have space travel of their own?

They do have what might be considered rudimentary space travel, from the point of view of other ETs. From your point of view it would be quite advanced. The primary motive power of their ships is a form of atomic energy, which is perhaps the most rudimentary form of interstellar transportation. They cannot make huge leaps in space and time. They are now accessing that window in space and time that will bring them into your now, or whatever now you and your souls occupy in this incarnation on your planet.

There is a very narrow range they can come to from their point of origin. They cannot travel in great space and time to your distant future or distant past to be involved in corruptions. They are able to access you only, so that they can learn and become prepared for what they might expect in their own evolutionary process. Their ability to travel in space has been given to them by certain beings with the full realization and cooperation of the Creator so that they could simply come here from where they are. It is understood that they do cause some discomforts; however, on a soul level you have all agreed. And after all, one must respect the fact that even the most incorrigible child is worth saving.

Is there a difference in appearance between the Sirians and the Zeta beings?

There is a striking difference in their actual appearance; however, there has been some attempt to create, through the use of some rudimentary forms of genetic engineering, an appearance somewhat like the Zeta beings. They don't exactly act like the Zetas and are programmed to be, we shall say, pesky. Recognize that they are not all-powerful, these beings from this rather dense aspect of the Sirian galaxy (as I call it). Their technological abilities are very carefully controlled by those in charge of the creation of this portion of the universe. However, it is almost as though the incorrigible child is sometimes given the weapon of his own destruction so that he can learn from his mistakes. Since you yourselves have the experience of negativity (albeit not to the extent they do), you can see how, if you touch something hot, you learn not to do that again. They have been given the weapons of their own destruction so they can learn how *not* to use them.

Which of these groups are you related to or do you interact with?

I interact with them all in an advisory capacity, but I'm not directly related to any of them. Wherever energy can be, I can be, and I am not embodied or encapsulated in a limited framework of life, such as a physical form. I would perhaps consider the idea that the higher-dimensional aspects of Alpha Centauri would be a homeland to me, since Alpha Centauri is directly involved as a portal from the Creator. One might say that the stuff of life spews through Alpha Centauri.

Ashtar

There are many people channeling the Ashtar Command. Can you tell us anything about that? Does it exist?

I've said this in the past and I will say it again, without any intention of offending anyone who is involved in the pleasure of reading and experiencing this material or even in contact with Ashtar. Ashtar, as a being, is a child not only in his evolution but also as an existence personality, evolutionarily speaking. This is ofttimes the reason why the material from Ashtar that comes through individuals is coming from the point of view of an adventurer. It is fun, it is exciting, it is something that any child could appreciate in the universe as well as on this planet.

One must remember that this does not mean that Ashtar is to be dismissed. Ashtar is involved on this planet with your emotional understanding, so he is karmically tied to this planet. He is evolving as your emotional ego structure. His aspect of emotionality is directly related to the ego structure; the ego structure itself is an aspect not only of mentality but also of emotionality, and emotionality relates to physicality. This is why so often the Ashtar material will be exciting and inspire or instigate emotion. Recognize that it is an attempt to evolve itself in these contacts.

Ashtar is a beloved being associated with Earth, and the immediate outcome of his next step of evolution will be to combine his energy with what is now referred to as the angelic and devic kingdom on this planet. So his function is necessary; he is providing a valuable service. It is also important to remember that this service is one that is for children as well as adults.

Up to this time the Ashtar material has largely been consumed by adults. It was really always and only intended to be consumed by children. It is, from your Earth perspective, a child's view of the universe. In time, when the real purpose of Ashtar's relationship to the human being is understood, there will perhaps be the Ashtar TV show and the Ashtar movie series, which was originally intended by Ashtar himself, as well as others, to create a make-believe world (and I'm not saying that what Ashtar says is not true) to prepare the children to be the next founders (on a soul level) of your society as it evolves. The energy as well as the purpose of Ashtar is very benign indeed. It is to be complimented and perhaps in time appreciated for what it is.

Is there any validity to the idea of an evacuation of this planet or a lift-off?

For the sake of clarity, I will say that although that was planned in the past as a potential and it has been done many times before, it is really your soul's desire on a universal basis to have a different ending to create the zenith of this new culture. Rather than have someone come in, lift you off and take you to the fourth dimension, you are attempting to create an actual biological, genetic, spiritual, ethereal motion in karma as well as in soul. You want to make that motion *yourself* (it could actually be measured at a distance from your planet, from the solar system's point of view) rather than have others come in and lift you off. The last time it really existed as a potential was in early 1982. The intention now is not to do this, so that your souls can have the opportunity to create a different ending to the culmination of this civilization.

When people are taken aboard a craft, they report seeing not only these little gray chaps with the gray eyes, but regular-looking human beings, frequently in blue uniforms, who seem to be working with the aliens. Can you explain this?

To some extent we are talking about your own race, but this particular race exists at a future version of yourself. The most advanced vehicles that enter your space (not the most ad-

vanced vehicles, period) travel through time as well as space, and the idea of retrieving someone from the future to come and assist in this experience is very easily done, technologically speaking. Thus some of these beings would be future Earth selves.

Many of them would be from 2500 to 2600, at which time (when you have a dimensional shift you can't really put a year on it) much of the work that is being done now will be culminated. These future Earth selves are coming back to check on their past lives, from their point of view, to see how things are getting along. What is difficult for them is remaining passive and objective, because their normal personalities are nothing like that at all. So the suits they wear are somewhat of a protective device to keep them from being as normally emotional as they would otherwise be. At that stage of your evolution, the emotional body as well as the spiritual self have come to the level that is really intended for you, and it is much more evolved and integrated in your reality on a

very positive level. These particular suits, appearing rather like jumpsuits, act to screen some of their input so they do not become emotional and radiate an energy that would confuse their hosts on that vehicle.

There are also a few other beings who are not from the future. They are from evolved cycles of other planets and look very much like human beings. They would look sufficiently human to pass for one on the street, provided they wore a mild form of disguise. These beings might also be present from time to time.

Joopah speaking, from Zeta Reticuli origin. Do you have any questions about the interactions of Zeta Reticuli from my dimensional point of view, which would be far in your soul's future?

You say "far in the future"; can you give us some sort of idea in our Earth years how far in the future?

Perhaps I can. Recognizing that our light-year is actually a measurement of distance, I will use light-years, since it is a time in the future as well as a time in space, and if one travels far enough, space and time both curve. Let us simply say that we are about three to four million years, in terms of light-years, in the future of your now time. In my immediate experience of civilization and culture, we are now experiencing life around the seventh to eighth dimension. We are also shifting. So it would be about that, but it does not really directly relate to years.

Thank you. I get the idea.

Are your experiments and data collection successful so far?

Yes. "Successful" meaning achievement, yes. We have achieved a greater understanding of who you are. In our new understanding, with the help of Zoosh and others, including the Creator and our other advisors, we now understand who we are. This is quite a startling experience for us, for we never understood that there was a direct relationship between us. Our initial experience of this genetic experiment was that we were involved simply because we are such experts in this field. It was quite a surprise to us that there would be such a direct connection between us. But I can see how the Creator would have involved us this way. And I can also understand why the Creator did not tell us, since the Creator would prefer that we find out for ourselves. Philosophy is a little new to me, but I can understand it from that point of view.

What have you found out about us?

We have been involved with you since before you existed; we have found out everything.

Picking the Contactee: Genetic and Soul Lines

When you contact people of this planet, what is the method you use to pick the contactee? How do you find the person?

We use a form of genetic ranging device. Sometimes a version of our culture will use crystal coding keys to find a particular individual. This is a more physical aspect of how we find you. You could understand this as a form of homing device that operates at an interdimensional level and synthesizes and syncopates itself to your brain-wave rhythm, which is unique to each individual, sending out a signal that can be picked up by a brain-wave receiver. This is a particular device that has sometimes been referred to as a nodule [implant] found or placed in various individuals.

We have found that to be somewhat impractical, because now we realize the discomfort involved in the placing of this in your bodies. We do not have discomfort if such devices are placed in us, so it took us some time to understand why you resisted these things. I must apologize. This has taken place due to our ignorance, in the sense of not having a frame of reference for the idea of discomfort.

We now use a device that is involved as a genetic-code key. This essentially creates a genetic heritage. That is, when we first contact an individual (from your point of view, millions of years ago), we remove a genetic sample without discomfort, perhaps from the epithelial layers of the skin. Then we keep a linear genetic account of the evolution of that particular DNA as it evolves. We use that particular version of human being when we check up on later lives. Although I do not wish to make you sound as if you were white rats, it is not off the mark to say that this is what is done in laboratories, but we do not pick you up by your tails and mistreat you in such ways. We have needed to understand how the evolutionary process has taken place in the development of your race. One can do this scientifically only by having a thoroughly analyzed sample and then see what changes occur during the process of life and evolutionary direction and so on.

Can I clarify that last statement a bit more?

All right.

You've taken DNA samples in the far-distant past and then continued to check that particular DNA as it evolved through marriages and the evolution on this planet. Is that correct?

Yes.

So the people who are now contacted are chosen genetically, because of the past experiments?

Yes, as well as others, in the sense that any experiment would have an experimental group and also a control group as a comparison. The other group that is primarily involved is the soul group. Those who were contacted in the past might have branched off, genetically speaking, from that particular line and developed along different soul structures. This is another one of our groups, and this is why very often we will have a frame of reference along soul lines.

For example, when we contact a particular individual and bring him aboard the ship, in the past when there has been some discomfort for that individual, there has always been one member of our crew who could step forward and, through the placement of a hand directly over or near the third-eye region, calm that individual's discomfort. We never understood why until recently. It was because that particular individual is a direct future soul incarnation of the individual on the table. This is an extrapolation, this idea of soul transit. Because we now understand that we are the future expression of your soul selves, we have another point of reference to track souls. As any mapmaker knows, you need as many frames of reference as possible in order to outline boundaries. With this new frame of reference we have been able to track the souls more clearly.

The Second-Generation Hybrid Race

Zoosh spoke a bit about this hybrid between your race and ours. Which, if any, of our past civilizations have related directly to that?

It is difficult to say how long it has been taking place. In terms of the time that we ourselves have been working on the development of this race, I would say it has been perhaps a few hundred of your years. The direct contact between this particular species and your own really did not start even on the most limited of bases until perhaps thirty to forty years ago, and then only in an extremely limited way with the direct evolutionary soul beings. There has as yet been no direct contact between this particular race – the second generation – and those we track genetically. But there has been some contact with those we track on the soul level to see how the soul connection can be curved to accept them.

In a sense, we are attempting to alter the past by creating these beings. Because they will be able to communicate more directly with you and you will be able to relate to them much more easily, the communication will be tremendously improved. They will also, as a result of your contact with them in the coming years, create and support your own desires to evolve to a greater capacity than you now express yourselves to be. It will encourage your transit from the third to the fourth dimension and beyond. While we cannot directly interfere with your society, we must do something to preserve our race, since our race, on a level of actual incarnation, is beginning to die out. We have made this attempt to influence indirectly by the creation of this secondary race, which is biologically as well as soully influenced by both groups.

There has been little contact between them and you, but there has been some. The uniforms (as you call our apparel) would be a little different. Their skin texture is quite smooth, much like your own, although perhaps a little more durable. To touch the skin it would feel perhaps like the nose of a dog – a little bumpy, but smooth in general (not wet, though – a joke for Joopah, that's amazing! I would say that I just recently attempted to learn humor. I am still struggling with that.)

Their skin color is black, not like the dark races on this planet, but actually the color black. They, as indicated, are about five feet to five feet, five inches tall. They wear a black uniform with either gold or silver (depending upon their rank or job) metallic spots toward the mid-abdomen and then going to black. If any of you find these beings familiar, perhaps this is the reason.

They have different articulations – you say fingers, yes? They have five digits, as you do. Their thumb is longer, so they are able to manipulate better. They do not have hair, just as we do not, nor do they have eyebrows or eyelashes. We did not see any reason to create that since they are not subjected to extremes of temperatures. Is this sufficient?

Yes. Are these related to the beings in Inner Earth?

They are not directly related. Of course, these beings, sometimes called the Founders, are the origin of almost every form of intelligent (and even what you perceive to be nonintelligent) life in this area of the universe. So they are related, but they are not first cousins.

These beings that you are describing with the black uniforms and so forth, might one of them come through on a psychic or telepathic level? I wonder because I had an experience just a few days ago where I telepathically or psychically picked up a being who resembled the description you gave.

It is possible, you understand, indicating that the contacts are taking place along the soul line between the Zetas and your civilization.

Thank you. This person gave the impression of being like an ambassador or a public relations person, which seemed to fit what you were saying.

Yes. Thank you. Anything else?

Then I will say that I will bid you —what does Zoosh say? — adieu. (He likes to use the French sometimes.) I will say farewell for tonight. Thank you for your cooperation and your interest. We will see if one of the second generation will speak briefly to you, and then perhaps Zoosh will have a closing statement.

Well, good evening. I am known as Tsengey [tsen'-gay]. How would you spell this? I would say T-s-e-n-g-e-y is good. I am of that second-generation race. I have been created to act as a liaison between the parent race and your race, to be not only an ambassador, but also to gather social and cultural information so that the parent race can learn how better to interact with your race, your culture. They are beings who do not have the best of table manners. Their ability to be involved in intersocietal social gatherings would be extremely limited indeed, since they have attempted to create the best of their own rather than to create direct contact with others. So they struggle somewhat with these social graces. We have perhaps been given more of the ability of social graces, since our direct purpose is to gather cultural-social information from you initially as our tryout experience, and then go out into the galaxies with you and with others, acting as a universal interpreter for you.

It appears likely that within the next few hundreds of years we will work together in our space explorations, for there will be many situations in which you will need our assistance not only as an interpreter but to help prevent the type of mistake that the parent race made with your civilization. Perhaps I will take a quick question.

Are you some of those we contact more out-of-the-body than physically?

What a fine question! Yes. You more often contact us in your sleep state or your astral-projection state than by direct contact. We have had direct contact in the past thirty or forty of your years with only about a thousand people on the surface of this planet, so it is rather uncommon. However, there are those who have us in their recollections.

To broaden the horizon of who we are, we are quite interested in the arts. We are artistically expressive, and it is our intent to create a civilization devoted to the homogeneity of arts and the expression of art and art forms in all cultures and civilizations. We will make this our theme for the development of our race.

Now I will bid you a fond good evening, and we will have a closing statement from the advisor Zoosh.

Z oosh speaking. Understand that your civilization is involved in a tremendous leap. It is a leap not only of evolution on a soul level, but it is a leap of faith that must take place before that evolution is evolved. Recognize in your immediate cultural surroundings the upswing of interest in religion and religion's direct cousin, philosophy. This renewed interest has been created by the energy of inspiration, which is the direct transit of energy from oversoul to soul, which owes its origin to the Creator God, the One Mind, whatever you wish to call It. That upswing of faith is a direct manifestation of the faith that is needed in order to commit to this change from the third to the fourth dimension.

Recognize also that these abductions will become more benign in the coming years as the races involved begin to realize who they are to you. The Zetas are already beginning and, as indicated by Joopah, who is in this rather higher-dimensional aspect, they will also begin to instruct the lower-dimensional aspects of the Zetas from the past about who they are to you. This will take some little time. They can relate to Joopah and others of that dimension and they will be slow to respond, but they have already begun.

There will also be some delay with the negative Sirians, but they have begun their own evolutionary process almost in spite of themselves. Those so-called negative Sirians will get some assistance from the cetaceans, dolphins and whales, who will act to some extent as interpreters between the negative, second-dimensional aspect of the Sirians and the more positive aspect of the Sirians existing in the now time frame who are representative of the true Sirian experience.

Thus the contacts will become more benign, although there will be a brief period of drama in reaction to the negative contacts of the past, because it is through drama that your cultures achieve the highest levels of success in becoming the best that you can be. This is what you have done in the past, and you're not yet ready to give up on these dramas. You always rise to the occasion.

So I will say, expect in time that the abductions, as they are called, will become much more cooperative as individuals on your planet begin to realize that they are actually choosing to be involved, and how by consciously re-creating their motivations they will become involved with beings who are much more cooperative. As a result, the more negative beings and even the ones who are cynical will not be experienced, because you will not choose or allow it to be so.

Recognize that many of you will live to see this take place as well as hear about it on your news broadcasts. In time a major power will come forth and state clearly for all to hear in the press that they not only believe that beings from other planets exist, but that there is interaction now between those beings and the citizens of Earth. To some extent other governments will chime in and say, "Yes, and it is negative." Other governments will chime in and say, "No, it is positive," and so on. And there will be an argument, but there will be a conscious acknowledgement. You will all live to see that.

Your lives are changing not only in time but in your relationship to time. Since your whole time perspective is changing, your evolutionary process is greatly accelerated. This is why you can experience so much in a given life now. Many of you will be uncomfortable with the extreme acceleration. You will feel that perhaps too much is being demanded of you. A lesson that you had months to get through in the past will now take days to get through. But since time is being collapsed and you are moving interdimensionally as a planetary experience, you are now able to accomplish the lessons of ten physical lives in this one. So your souls are gaining more karmically useful information than they have ever gotten before in any unit of time.

It is for you to know now and ever understand that the lives you are living now, even though they are not always comfortable, are given as a gift. Do not wait for the rewards of afterlife. Appreciate the reward that you are being given now. This gift of life *right now in this moment* has everything to do with the great reward that comes in the hereafter. This is really the hereafter.

The True Nature of the Grays

Joopah and Zoosh
Sedona, Arizona, May 28, 1989

All right, Joopah speaking. I will discuss briefly the idea of the Grays, as they have been loosely referred to. I know that on your planet it has become a fad to refer to individuals by their appearance, so I understand the usage of the term "Grays." In reference to this term, we are talking not only about beings from Zeta Reticuli, but also some beings who have been manufactured or cloned by certain individuals to appear to be Zeta Reticulans. But for now I will discuss only my race.

From where I am now in the future (as you might call it) I can look back and see how my race has progressed. Right now we are confronted with a difficulty in our survival, as we perceive it — though now I understand that we will survive but no longer be embodied. Our internal bodies in our dimension are almost entirely plasmic. However, in your dimension we are ofttimes defined by something that is less of our body than it is of the shield that we use. In this sense, I attempt to explain the effect that you refer to as gray.

In interdimensional transit our physical selves, or individual encapsulated selves, will ofttimes wear a protective suit that keeps us from merging with your dimension. We also use a certain amount of protective air that prevents us from interacting directly with you or your dimension. It creates somewhat a shield, and to some extent adds to the gray color in our actual environment. (As we experience it, our skin is more of a beige.)

My race as it now exists is largely focused in thought and expresses itself in technology based less in instrumentality than in the use of plasmic energy. However, in the distant past my race has had many splinter groups, some of which are interacting with you right now. The Zeta race has long been able to travel in time, so we integrate and mingle with our own race in different time sequences. You can imagine that. In order to do this, our race would have to be nonviolent at the very least because of changes in the structure of the culture. We are, largely speaking, nonviolent, although in the distant past there was some conflict.

It is possible for me to go into the past of my race (which from your point of view of time would also be *your* distant past) and communicate with these individuals. I will do that, but I am very, very careful not to change anything, even their minds, since what they think will have everything to do with what they will *do*. Even the slightest change could alter things radically in the future. So I am circumspect. On their part, they can travel to where *we* are now in time, but they rarely do that since our existence is one that is not as action-based, because we do less interacting with each other or with others than they do. I refer to these beings who are in the distant past (that you refer to as the Grays) simply because it is these beings who are largely interacting with you now. You will see many different beings who have a variation of Zeta appearance: large eyes, small bodies, large craniums, grayish, beige or whitish skin, thin (if any) mouth and an unusual appearance, relating to a lack of apparent emotionality.

There is an absolute cultural element in my race, which is, believe it or not, service. But as we have gone on in our development, we have gradually begun to realize that service must be applied to ourselves as well as others. This desire to serve has had what you might refer to as negative results. In the beginning (especially referring to the Grays with whom you sometimes interact) the willingness to serve created interactions between the ancient Zetas and other cultures. This led to scientific cooperation in experiments with the human race for which they (Zetas of the past) sometimes are blamed because they are front men for others. Although I start off tonight, you will hear from Zoosh soon, since he, as one of our teachers, has a better understanding of this.

I simply expose you to the energy so you will realize that I am attempting to apologize for my ancestors. Ofttimes they have interacted with you and your race as if they did not care about the consequences of the examinations that took place aboard ships or elsewhere. That is because they do not understand *care* in terms of individuals, although they understand it in terms of mass units. Since we have one mind, we are able to assimilate a great deal of individual information, but we as individuals are not easily able to change our minds without the entire group changing their minds, and this takes some time.

Many different splinter groups (since we are involved in genetic research) of the Zeta race are interacting with you now. They are involved in various experiments with you that are designed along the lines of the genetic experiment on Earth. They are also supporting the original individuals who blended their constitutions and their cultures with those they found here on this planet in order to create what is now known as the conglomerate human race (since to some extent you have different features).

You as a race, however, did not originate on this planet, and are really much more of a cross-section of racial attributes associated with extraterrestrial sources. The soul energy in all of you is somewhat anchored on this planet, but the energy that is primarily involved in your manifestation is associated with Sirius, Orion, and to a lesser extent, the Pleiades. To my understanding, there is some influence from Andromeda, but it is of a minor degree. We as a species are not involved in your actual appearance. We serve as scientists – cultural advisors, in a sense – and will as a unit choose to cooperate with any scientific experiment anywhere in the universe. I now understand, of course, that this can lead to problems. If one is exclusively scientifically based, one might make a mistake and work with life forms that one cannot communicate with directly. You can understand this, since your scientists are working in large part with animals; but you assume that because animals do not readily speak the languages of this planet, they are lesser life forms. I do not wish to suggest that my race considers your race to be a lesser life form, but since there is a lack of communication, in the past we have assumed that your life form on this planet is in a formative state. This interaction has been the result.

I would like to say that much of what has been blamed on the Grays they have not actually done. The major offense would fall under the heading of acting as a support and being the scientific interacters with you. Since we are so different from you, it is difficult for you to assume that we care about you. We now understand that you are our past lives on the soul level. This is a recent understanding, and now that we understand this we have taken a somewhat more personal attitude toward you. But there is in my race this difficulty of the slowness to change. For a time you will have to bear the ponderously slow attitude of the Grays at their stage to understand who you are. At my stage we understand and have integrated it.

I will be back later. For now I will simply say that Zoosh requested me to come in first to throw a little of my energy into the group so that you might feel it and so that those with whom we are interacting now and might not know it would recognize the energy. All right, I will step aside and let Zoosh carry on.

All right, Zoosh speaking. There has been some confusion on the part of the Grays, as indicated by Joopah, in realizing who you are (*realize,* meaning think, feel, do). There has not been a true understanding of who you are. As a result, a focus of energy has necessarily been created that would not allow them to perform the deeds with you that could wake them up.

There has been a tendency by you (you who have been involved in metaphysical and New Age awarenesses) to assume that you are all asleep and that you are waking up. Well, I can assure you that what is needed for *you* to wake up (and there is already some degree of waking up) is very minor compared to many other races from other planets who seem to be so spiritually evolved. Their actual spiritual evolution might not be as much as your own, in that they have (in the case of the Grays) devoted a great deal of their attention to their mentality rather than their spiritual and emotional integration as an interactive element of their growth. Very often the Zetas attempt to grow only in terms of expanding their knowledge. Those of you who have elevated the mental body to be something far superior to any other element of life on this Earth, thus separating you from the so-called "lower" animal kingdom, will recognize this idea. I do not wish to mock you. I understand that this idea has taken root but is now beginning to fade.

Earth School for ETs

Recognize that these groups from other planets have much more to learn from you than you have to learn from them. It is why in conversations between Earth people and Zetas there is often somewhat of a minuscule exchange (in terms of what is actually told or exchanged) on their part about who they are, where they are from, why they are here, what they are all about, where they've been and so on compared to what you provide to them. This is because *they are the students* — it is true! Ofttimes they will say to Earth people, "Well, you are here on Earth, and it is a school." The impression left in many who have had that contact is that the school is for *you.* The school is much less for you than it is for them. They are just now beginning to wake up to the idea that the school is in fact for them, and that they are really in kindergarten in a lot of ways because they have not integrated on a practical, interactive level into their day-to-day life a lot of emotional and physical interactive experience. Without a physical lesson, a lesson might take a long time to learn. For example, if you touch something hot when you are a baby, you learn it right away. "Don't do that; it's not good for you!" How would you learn that if you didn't have the opportunity to have the physical interaction with that hot thing? You would be attempting to learn the abstract idea that too much heat can cause discomfort. It might take your whole life to discuss it philosophically and still know nothing compared to touching that hot plate and getting burned briefly.

Understand that what you know, what you learn in your day-to-day life, is ofttimes superior in terms of practical applicability than all of the technological devices placed end to end and wrapped around the Golden Gate Bridge several thousand times. Recognize that the true value of knowledge is in *how it is applied* rather than how it is stored as a record. The Grays are gradually understanding that they are directly associated with you. This school has been in session for them for many years: It dates from the origin of mankind, at which time they cooperated as scientific advisors and provided scientific assistance. It has taken millions of years, as you understand it, in the scope of mankind's development, plus dimensional shifts that go beyond years, to get as far as they are — knowing that you are somehow associated with them on a spiritual level. In the far-flung future the Zeta culture understands more, but the actual beings who are now interacting with you most of the time have only this vague sense of relationship. It is curious to them, but they do not know what it really means.

So the challenge for you is to begin to change not only how you think about these people, but your perspective as you interact with them. Remember that they are here to learn from you, and they are now beginning to get a glimmer of this. They do not know how to ask questions, whereas you absolutely *have* to learn how to ask questions simply to survive on this planet! You need to learn how to make demands as a baby to survive, and as a child you learn how to ask for what you want even if you don't get it.

They don't have that. They have, as you say, cradle-to-the-grave care. As a result, they simply do not know how to ask. This is why their questions will appear to be, as you say, lame-brained. In UFO contact literature, the questions are often very vague, very strange, and sometimes replete with such curiosities as "what is yellow?" — a classic question. How would you describe what yellow is, especially if they take you up on their ship but there is no yellow around? Since they do not understand how to ask the question, they are not beaming up university professors or even kindergarten teachers with Dick and Jane books and color wheels.

I am not here to bash the Zetas, but I need to help you understand that your new level of responsibility on this planet as interactive universal citizens is *to teach as well as to learn*. Never forget that, because Zetas very rarely have the opportunity to learn what you can learn in five minutes. It is unlikely that a single Zeta will have the opportunity to learn in a single lifetime (whether it is 275 years or 800 or 900 years, depending upon their point of evolution or cultural existence on the time or dimensional scale) what you can learn in five minutes just by interacting with your environment or other people. That does not mean that they do not have a great deal of wisdom and knowledge, but it may not necessarily be applicable here.

Some Grays who interact with you are, in fact, the past of the Zetas and a few are from the far-flung future. But the ones who get the blame for so-called cattle mutilations and the idea of so-called people mutilations (which is not really something Zetas are doing) are being wonderful patsies. The ones who are involved in the cattle stuff are the true patsies. Now I will say a little bit about them.

Negative Sirian Corrupters and the Men in Black

I have not said this too much in the past because it has not been time. Because it is time now, I will simply say that these individuals have been created by a group from Sirius who are attempting to corrupt your civilization. Now, most planets in Sirius are just fine; they are happy with life and so on. But there is one little planet that is attempting to corrupt your civilization, and they are, by way of doing so, creating an experimental being that looks like the Zetas (as you say, "looks like, walks like, talks like" — but they don't talk), but they are not in fact really Zetas. They are *designed to appear to be Zeta.* How can you differentiate them? It is difficult. But they are usually not extremely short; they are usually 4½ to 5 feet tall, for example. They are not violent; they are docile, in the sense that they are likely to do what they are told by those they work with.

They were cloned largely out of Zeta material, but with certain other genetic structures thrown in so that they would look something like a cross between a human being and a Zeta. This is to suggest, of course, that they are crossbreeding human beings or utilizing human parts to create these beings in an attempt to confuse and confound you. (I am doing that somewhat as well here tonight, scattering myself around.) I will simply say that they will be confounded from their attempt to manipulate your race as they discover who they are, and their relationship to you has everything to do with it.

Tonight was largely created for questions and answers rather than a lecture about the Grays and who they are. I will hang around for a while, and Joopah will come back pretty soon. Any questions?

What about the Men in Black? Are they in any way related to the Grays?

Not really, even though there is a slight relationship because the Men in Black [MIB] have a twofold origin. Some are from the Sirian negative group and are somewhat cloned — that is, a cloned variation of an Earth person. They are cloned by techniques somewhat used on this planet but largely on other planets. They are created to look very much like Earth people. They support efforts to corrupt and control this planet, which relates directly to that negative planet in Sirius. And because they are also oriented to the Grays, they are a portion of the support associated with the corruption. They are not as involved with humankind as they once have been. There have been some alterations of the energy field of this planet that have made it less accessible for them. This was not from anything done outside the planet, but from the magnetic flux and change of the Southern Hemisphere coming into a greater alignment and balance. This is an ongoing process and has necessarily created a little more magnetic energy here, which they find some difficulty in dealing with.

There is another aspect of the so-called Men in Black that has to do with the forms of Grays cloned by the Sirians to create a being to associate with the Men in Black. They are sometimes seen with them and are reported to appear like a disguised Zeta (if one can imagine Zetas being able to disguise themselves in public). They are usually seen in this manner only by certain select individuals, not everybody. There have been curious stories circulating about these individuals who appear somewhat Zeta-like, wearing big floppy hats and turned-up collars and so on. These beings are not in circulation to any great extent. But the Men in Black are agents who attempt to corrupt here.

Do the Grays have a post in Dulce, New Mexico, near the Colorado border?

Yes, they are there. One level is a Zeta base; another level is associated with the Grays. These individuals are involved in a network of tunnels that spreads throughout the areas associated with tribal reservations—a portion of southern Colorado, northern Arizona, somewhat into Utah, and with branches reaching into Nevada. There is also a little bit of influence in northeastern Texas.

What is the origin of the Zeta Reticuli? Are they indigenous to the Reticulum star system?

The Zetas' True Origin

I understand your attempt to clarify. It is a large question. They are in fact associated with that system, but the culture has spread so far beyond that system that there has been a need to establish a remote base for their creation. Even though they are associated with that star system, they did not originate there. There's the rub. They have become known to that area, but their origination is really (no big surprise) associated with a group of planets that once occupied *this space!* They find it easy to travel into this space because the dimensional phases they travel through in time take them straight into the past. So they come into this space, traveling through a loop that goes into the past that is associated with their home. Their actual origin in the distant past goes beyond the point where they had wars and so on. Their actual origin is on what could be referred to by its shape as a disc-shaped planet, a rhomboid shape, rounded off. They were created on that planetoid (loosely referred to as a vehicle, but so large as to be incomprehensible by the term "vehicle"). It is difficult to put years on it, but to understand how long ago that creation took place, one might simply say 500 billion years ago. This, of course, is just a frame of reference in terms of the interdimensionality.

From what type of life form did they evolve?

They were created in an attempt to establish a basic form of life from which many different types of physical-extension beings, one might say, could develop. (No one has really asked these questions before. It is always nice to have new questions.) Their life form is associated with so many different life forms that one might say that in the actual physical life forms between the second to the seventh dimension, the Zeta life form as they now appear is *a source of all life.* In the origin of their species they might not necessarily look as they do now. But the standard of reference would be the very large eyes, the telepathic communication, the predominance of the mental power and the absolute desire to seek knowledge at whatever the cost.

The Founders

They were manufactured, one might say, by a race of beings sometimes referred to as the Founders, with these basic ingredients. From their position of reality, the Founders attempted to synthesize basic forms of life from which all other forms could spring. This is an interesting question, in that it creates possibilities for answers to bizarre circumstances reported by many individuals. That is, many individuals have had experiences associated with Zeta beings in which they are taken to some huge insectlike being who emanates a powerful sensation of love similar to that associated with the after-death experience – absolute, total, unconditional love – and is ofttimes a feeling of absolute, committed mother energy.

We are talking about the origin of all species on this planet. This being who would seem to be insectlike (I know this will be a little difficult for you to swallow) is actually the mother, in a sense, of your species. The Founders, though they be life forms now, were in those days attempting to create different dimensional aspects of their own lives, to create root forms of life that could, by interactions with other root forms, create the variety that creates different forms and appearances of life. The result? The Founders in certain dimensions look like those beings. They understand who you are completely, and unconditional love is what they feel for you.

I say this now because it is important for you to realize that even on this planet some (not all) in the insect kingdom, though they might not necessarily interact with you very much, really have a tremendous sense of unconditional love toward human beings. If you are all alone in a room with one of them, you might actually even feel it. That is a hint. Pretty interesting question, that one.

Would cockroaches be one of those?

No, though you might feel fond of one from time to time.

What about a cricket?

This is much closer. The cricket, grasshopper, praying mantis — this type of life form is very similar to how the Founders look within certain dimensions. The Founders are the source of not only your existence but the existence of *all life* in physical or individual bodies or individual personalities. The idea of God is a frame of reference here. I would not say that the Founders are God, but that they are associated with that idea.

Could you tell me where the Founders exist now and how many there are?

How many is a little difficult to describe. Since they are not necessarily encapsulated in body form and can be one or many, they hang out in the center of your planet as you experience it in terms of space. However, in terms of the origin of species, they actually hang out on the planet that once existed here in the far-flung past. They do not often encapsulate in number, but if they choose to, it could vary anywhere between 4 or 400 or even 40,000 on occasion. But they would not be encapsulated in bodies as you would understand it. They would be like small circles of light or some such thing. They would find the circle, allowing for its infinity, to be the most comfortable expression as a symbol of who they are. If you sometimes see little circles of light out of the corner of your eye (they are very bright), it is not them directly; but if they are moving about and cause you to feel unusually happy, it is ofttimes them in some form. Being in their presence will cause not only the sensation of unconditional love but incredibly good cheer.

Can you make a distinction between the Grays and Zeta Reticuli?

Yes, in the sense that *there is now a shift in focus in the universe.* It has been referred to by many others as a bend. The universe, as you understand it at this dimension, is just about ready to take a new flex. As a result, *all* life forms that have ever been created as individual forms are now just about ready to change completely. Thus the Grays are beginning to establish their own individual life form apart from the Zetas. What the Zetas now perceive as their past (which is in fact true from their point of view and even from the overview as it exists now) will establish a new overview as a result of the expansion in consciousness. As a result, in the new world that is coming — a new universe, in fact (to move it beyond your immediate sense of identity) — the Grays will become something apart from the Zetas. The Zetas will not remember them as being part of their past.

Does this have to do with entropy, going to greater disorder?

It is a good term, that. It is suggestive of reorder rather than disorder. But reorder might appear to be chaos in the beginning. This, of course, relates to the biblical prophecy.

So that is what is happening at this time?

Changing Past and Future

That is what is happening: Those of you who are living through these next twenty to thirty years will look back in time on your own life, and many of you will have some difficulty in remembering your early years. What might occur is an odd juxtaposition, since the past as well as the future is being changed because of your choice to move from the third to the fourth dimension. The actual memories of your past will change because the past will change. *Everything* is literally in change, so what you might remember as an experience will alter, since the past is being uncreated and realigned. This is happening not only in terms of memory but in all ways. As a result, the Zeta Reticuli race is becoming more than one. A mother, in birthing a child, gives birth to an extension of herself, in a sense — she divides, one might say, and becomes two. The second one, the child, has a life of its own, although originating in many respects as the mother. This is a riddle for those of you who really think about life.

Is this true in all dimensions?

All. No exceptions. This is how the Creator keeps from getting bored. Imagine for a moment that you knew everything and felt everything. Life, while it could be infinite, would never be unexpected. The Creator does not experience the unexpected, but whether you can believe it or not, the Creator *desires* to experience the unexpected, so the Creator has let go, in a sense. As a result, life forms are seeking their own level, and all levels within life forms are seeking their own levels.

Has anyone ever thought that perhaps the Creator might be a mad scientist?

I will say that many have thought so. Well, I will not ruffle anyone's feathers — maybe a "glad" scientist.

There was a slow start tonight for a reason. Right now there is an energy shift — notice it now. It is an electrical-energy shift.

Can you describe the function, purpose and nature of this energy?

It is an electrical energy more than magnetic. As a result, it has, without intending to, created a slight drain or interference. The purpose of this energy, which is approximately one thousand feet below this immediate area, is to create water resources for about fifty to sixty years in the future. There will be a little more rainfall in about five years or so. The intent in the far-flung future is for this area to be more of a lagoon. There will be some lakes and streams that do not exist here now to support forms of wildlife associated with the sea.

The session has evolved to the somewhat related idea of the basic race, the formative race, the Founders, and that is all right.

Is our government aware of the presence and intent of the Grays and Zetas?

A Treaty with the U.S.

They are, we shall say, rather nervously aware. They experienced what they thought was the diplomatic coup of the century a few years ago. The United States created a secret treaty (not understanding that this was a worldwide phenomenon) with this species of beings, assuming that there were would be certain secret exchanges of information; and there was an allowance built in for the other planetary beings to pick up and examine (that was the sole intent, as far as your government understood) some few human beings, not a lot. Their reluctance to give in to that idea of access was tempered by the thought of the genetic and scientific information they would get. You might say that cooler heads did not prevail at that time due to the stars-in-the-eyes experience of the science advisors of those times, who felt that the bulk of the information given in exchange for this access would make up for any slight inconvenience to other people. (It is never an inconvenience when it is happening to others.) Even though the Grays did not really *require* cooperation from your government, your government could have made it much more difficult simply by using technologies developed for other purposes. For instance, radar and sonar, if directed in a certain way, could greatly disrupt the flight of certain vehicles (only certain ones).

Only recently has the government discovered that they have been caught somewhat with their pants down, and have realized that they are in over their heads. This is why there is more information out and about now from government and pseudo-government-related sources to (we shall say) prepare the public for the idea of what has been happening for some years.

It is a little embarrassing, since the government has had a policy of official denial, to admit forthrightly that "we were just joking, we didn't mean it, we knew it was real all along." Of course, they cannot say that without creating grievous embarrassment at the very least. There is a benign allowance toward the idea of letting this information out to create a public sympathy in the direction of (from their point of view) getting rid of these people. They do not fully appreciate who these people are, but they do know that they are not what they said they were. There is some confusion on the part of government authorities about who the Grays are, and there is absolutely *no* real understanding why some of them who are more future-oriented (from the future in higher dimensions) are really so benign and pleasant to commune with, while others from the past (though they do not realize that) can be almost like talking to a tree, having no apparent clear form of communication. This has created real problems. So I would say that the government is becoming uneasy in the treaty and is attempting to find a back door.

Do the people who have interaction with the Zeta Reticuli receive a benefit from it, or is it totally one-sided?

Understand that no one is contacted by these people without a form of soul permission. As any event happens in your life, there is a form of permission so that you might evolve as your individual self and so on. You recognize that. So there is a degree of interaction on the level that goes beyond the simple victimization that one might say is an abductee experience.

There has not yet been a full recognition on the part of the abductees, for example, of *their* role in educating those who might take them on these voyages for these examinations. This is why I am attempting to put out the idea that there is a little responsibility here that is not recognized. Of course, that responsibility has not been brought to the fore where these people can identify it and understand that their presence is *desired* as well as commanded. There is some confusion there.

I would say, however, that the experience for a contactee will (somewhat as a side effect) invariably bring out or enhance certain psychic or spiritual abilities. This is why certain individuals, when they have experiences associated with energy sensitivities, sometimes experience increased psychic ability.

Underground Tunnels

Who is responsible for the tunnels that you mentioned around Nevada, Arizona, Utah? The Grays?

They are. There has been a network of tunnels underneath this planet for many years, using technology that is not very commonplace on the surface. It is really a type of highly condensed laser that can be focused within a specific range as one might broadcast a radio signal. It is a sound/laser broadcast on a certain frequency that creates a depth. It can penetrate rock, for example. Utilizing certain ultrasonic reverberations within the rock, it will go around streams of water instead of going through, even though it can be done interdimensionally. Those who are responsible are many individuals, somewhat the Grays, somewhat the Sirians — and at a much deeper level from the surface of the planet, somewhat the Founders.

For what purpose are these tunnels?

To create a degree of interaction as a potential between different races. There are many different races living inside this planet at different dimensions. And there are even some races living at *your* dimension or very close to your dimension, with which you could have a form of interaction from time to time. The tunnels are to create accessibility from the inside to the surface as well as laterally. They are not designed to create any form of invasion. It is simply a form of transit.

What about the perceived separation between the Grays, ourselves, Sirius, yourself?

Why is there a perceived degree of separation? Well, of course we are all one. This is a *reality.* Yet why does a cell in your finger not suddenly decide that it is going to be a neuron in your brain? Since the body of the Creator has different cells designed to do different things, any one cell or soul might necessarily desire a different form of expression. Is this what you are asking?

Close enough.

How would you then get closer?

I am just wondering why the different compartments? Why the different missions and things?

For the same reason that no two paintings are exactly the same — for the fun of it or the experience of it or the variety of it. Because life explodes from the inside out *while* it is imploding. Really, just for the experience and the opportunity. In order to grow the most, on this plane especially, one must necessarily experience resistance, so sometimes a little resistance helps you to grow. Since your race excels through struggle, sometimes you need variety in the available forms of struggle so that you can bring out these shining qualities in you that would not be needed without those forms of struggle or stress. It is all part of growing.

Was that laser technology something that was shared with our government, and are they using it now for their own underground installations without the knowledge of the general populace?

Some of the information was shared with the government; however, not the ultrasonics. Your government has developed that largely on its own through other contacts and records as well as inspiration. A form of plasmic energy involved with nuclear thermodynamics was shared with the government for the purpose of creating energy devices as small as the head of a pin that could support a city's electrical needs. Your government did not choose to explore that, even though certain elements in the government know about it. That has not been explored, perhaps because of political involvements and intrigues.

But there has also been a need for your society to move slowly and bring up various forms of conflict so that you could resolve not only your own karma (in the sense of experience rather than burden), but express and resolve the karma of Orion and act as an activator to other planetary groups such as Zeta Reticuli, the Pleiades and this so-called negative planet from Sirius. As a space race (in the sense of exploring other planets and other cultures), you are their activator as well. You have not really perceived yet your true purpose. Basically you are the Explorer Race, and it is destined that you activate other races into an expansion of what they perceive to be their purposes.

Is there some advice you can give us or a technique that can activate individuals to their full potential now?

In terms of energy, you have been activated. What you can do with it and what you can experience would best be done physically and emotionally and creatively. Do something over the next three days that is both physical and emotional and artistic or creative. And put your heart and soul into it, even if it is only for thirty seconds. Do something that would be artistically creative, whether you consider yourself to be an artist or not. Put your passion into it! Lust for life, yes? This is what I recommend, because there has been an assumption by your society for too long that some people are artists and some people are bookkeepers. But you are all equally passionate. Be passionate, how's that? I do not give you great and uplifting light techniques, because I feel you have a desire to rush the process. Rather, I suggest that you become more of what you are rather than less.

Are these Grays and the starships that are here associated with the White Brotherhood?

I have a different idea of the White Brotherhood. From its benign characteristics, the White Brotherhood, though it be a highly structured lineage, is associated. The White Brotherhood, as you understand it, is fully aware of the Plan not only for this planet but for the immediate star system. That is naturally an association, since there is an allowance, but I would not say that they are working together — although I will not say that they are working in opposition, either. This is a comment equally for the White Brotherhood as for the Grays. The White Brotherhood would like to structure a bit too much for its own good, though its intentions are pure, one might say.

What is the purpose of the Grays in abducting someone who is unaware of the experiment?

They believe, of course, that they have permission to do so. They have been asked *before you were created*, by those who came here to create the human race, to be technologically involved — asked not by the Creator, but by those involved in the genetic evolution and creation of the human race. So they feel not only that they have permission from the boss — those who form the human race — but that on some level there is a degree of soul permission or they wouldn't be here. You must recognize that they do not recognize individuality apart from the group, so that if one person enthusiastically seeks involvement with them, then they assume it is the same for all.

In the beginning there was a considerable amount of enthusiasm (regardless of the lack of it now), so they still feel there is purpose for them to be here. They generally feel a sense of benign acknowledgment for their presence and are ofttimes bewildered (or as close as they can come to that) by the lack of cooperation from someone they pick up. They invariably state that they do have permission even though it may not be conscious permission, from that individual's point of view. This is their perception.

You described the patsies as somewhat of a cloned race and in the process of beginning to awaken to the fact that they really are patsies. Is there anything we can do to assist? Will our own awakening process do that?

The more you wake up to your true purpose and do not simply assume that you are here to be saved by the space brothers, the more you will realize that *you* are also the space brothers. These individuals can be assisted by you because you are, from their point of view, their future lives. Your souls have traveled an evolved path. That is, at one time your souls evolved (or swam, one might say) through the Grays and have swum again through that civilization as a unit in the far-flung future development of Zeta Reticuli. So even though there is this connection, the best thing you can do is recognize that there is a soul connection between you. And as you accept your equality and also your responsibility to equalize the pressure between your soul units, there is a blending.

To the degree that you are willing to accept that you can help them, they will perhaps begin to learn how to ask for help. When one does not know (and you can all identify with this) that you are ignorant about something or someone or some idea or some experience, you don't know what you are missing. These people do not know the joy of having a question answered in a way that is accessible to them, that they can use, that they can apply in their lives. As a result, they do not know how to ask a question. They need to be taught not only the value of asking a question, but the value of applying the answer beyond being put into a nice vault marked "Knowledge."

So you are saying that someone somewhere could attract the Grays because of their wish to make a connection?

It could be on the subconscious or unconscious level, yes.

Right. So at that level they make the contact. But how do you avoid being one of those at random people getting picked up by them?

I do not perceive that there is "random."

Is it on purpose?

Always. You as a race, you understand, are being tempered not to eliminate the weak but to empower them. Sometimes the weak are portions of you that are simply not exercised. These days you are exercising your emotions in order to allow them to expand so they can be a greater conduit for the spiritual inspiration that will inspire physical acts of alignment and balance.

Recognize that as individuals are picked up by these people, although there will be stresses in their lives, they will also have an accelerated opportunity to expand. The challenge for them always will be to treat these beings as equals or, as one might treat a child, to treat them with a degree of parental attitude, encouraging them. It is a little difficult to do this in some circumstances, but encourage them to interact with you more.

Zetas are ignorant of their own fear. Ofttimes you will hear even from Joopah and other Zeta beings that they do not experience fear. They do not even know what it is! They do not understand why a contactee is yelling and screaming. Yet *why are they not willing to touch you* — even allowing for the protection around their fully encapsulated body, the shield that protects them from your energy but would not cause you any discomfort? Why are they not willing to do that more? They are afraid. They do not recognize their own fear because it is so integrated into the emotion that they call "common peace." (I tell tales on Joopah out of school, yes?) They do not recognize that it is what they might refer to as shyness. And shyness even in that reference is a form of fear. One might say that these beings are so shy that they do not always interact with you.

Encourage them to interact with you more on the so-called physical level. To those of you who are having contact, I can assure you that 99% of the time (maybe a little more than that) it is because they have something to learn from you and 100% of the time it is not what they think it is! They think it is because they are checking up on you, the genetic experiment on Earth, and that they are the scientists who are monitoring it. It isn't that. They have something to learn from you on a level of communication they do not know how to access. That level of communication is *physically applied knowledge.*

As you hear these ideas, let them percolate around, go into your dreams. Many of you are interacting in the dream state right now with them; some of you are interacting on the subconscious level; a couple of you remember some experiences that will seem dreamlike but are not in fact a dream. As a result, begin to encourage more contact and know that no one is picked up at random; no one who is even experimented on is a victim, even though it will seem like that. Never assume that these people have powers greater than yours.

When you begin to remember who you are not only in spirit but in *deed*, in *action*, you will begin to command energies within you that are both magnetic and electrical — that are, for example, of the gold light, the energy of material manifestation itself on this planet. If this energy is simply felt inside yourself and broadcast around a room or broadcast before you go to sleep, the residual effect is felt and will remain within the physical space for some time. As a result, they will feel it and wonder.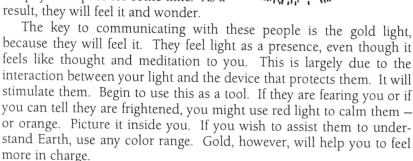

The key to communicating with these people is the gold light, because they will feel it. They feel light as a presence, even though it feels like thought and meditation to you. This is largely due to the interaction between your light and the device that protects them. It will stimulate them. Begin to use this as a tool. If they are fearing you or if you can tell they are frightened, you might use red light to calm them — or orange. Picture it inside you. If you wish to assist them to understand Earth, use any color range. Gold, however, will help you to feel more in charge.

Becoming One

To draw the evening to a close without keeping you after school too long, I will say that in order for you to understand your true relationship to these species, you will need to understand your responsibility not only to each other as each other's teachers, but also to these beings. They are here to learn, and you are their teachers. Even though it appears to be the other way around, that is not the case.

This is why the Pleiadians have to some extent pulled back, since they are just beginning to learn that the same is true for them, much to their concern. So you are coming into your own not so much as a superior being, since that is not the purpose, but in terms of your responsibility to yourself as you learn that you are all one on this planet. You will learn that as you express oneness on this planet and elsewhere, one *can literally become one* in application.

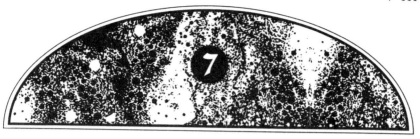

Answering Questions in Las Vegas

Joopah

Las Vegas, Nevada, July 7, 1989

and excerpts from "The Jerry Pippin Show,"

Las Vegas, Nevada, August 24, 1989

ll right, Joopah speaking.

Joopah, at another time you spoke about magnetic poles on the Earth being closed off. Did I get that right?

Yes. Temporarily closed, yes.

Did Mother Earth close those off?

Mother Earth allowed them to be closed off. She does, by her actions, cover the poles with ice, for the most part. However, she has always allowed windows in time (you might say in space, but truly in time). This creates a level of access to those poles because they radiate through the center of the Earth. The closing became a necessity due to a breach in the security system that was for the most part inadvertent. There have been times in the past when certain Earth individuals were allowed to see into or go into the access point beneath those poles. Those access points are essentially interdimensional. That is, one might be flying (or conceivably walking) over the pole, and if one is in a proper frame of mind, spirit and body, it is possible to see the other-dimensional aspects of this planet as well as variations of this planet.

Most often the individual would not achieve access to those areas. However, recently one individual — not a malevolent person but an individual whose energy was, shall we say, misplaced — achieved a level of access into those areas and was able to retrieve (primarily through observation) some factual information that would potentially allow his race an advantage in the future. (Of course, nothing is accidental, but it would have been preferable for that not to have taken place.) As a result, through a coding device the interdimensional window on both ends was sealed to disallow access by even the highest embodied sources. In any event, beings who are not encapsulated in bodies (and lightbeings who are) have access now, but this is not deemed irresponsible.

Time Travel

The individual who had access is actually from the future, but only slightly from the future, and this individual is actually an Earth person. You see, in the not-too-distant future a rudimentary time travel will be experimented with. The experiments will be risky; some individuals will simply disappear into folds of time only to reappear at some other place or space, but some individuals will be able to return and understand many things. The individual who gained access was a member of a ruling political party, so you might say that coming back in time has given him some advantage in understanding the future.

From your vantage point, can you see future events for Earth?

From my vantage point they would be past events. Understand that I am so far in the future that it is impossible to give a truly accurate representation in terms of years. If you refer to the immediate future, I have some understanding, since my job title remains "architectural historian." Thus the history of time and the events that have occurred in it are my specialty. However, to prevent "diseventing," there is only a certain amount that can be revealed to you. That is, if too much is revealed about the future, the future might be altered.

We are lightbeings, and we are supposed to be progressing to lighten ourselves and to become more transparent so that we can evolve. Do you have any breathing techniques or any information that will accelerate that process?

When you say "transparent," I would prefer to say "expanded." You might not notice any actual change in your apparent density while you are centered in your physical self, but when you are involved in meditation, that is another matter.

Expansion Exercise

As for breathing cycles, I would suggest that you find a favorite tree or plant and breathe with it by centering your consciousness within it and breathing in and out of its consciousness: On the exhale, blow your consciousness into the tree and observe as much of that tree's existence as possible. Then on the inhale, breathe as much of that tree into you as you can readily absorb.

Trees and their con-
sciousness have the to-
tal history of mankind's
future on several prob-
able levels. They might
not have the exact picture,
but since they need to be
informed so that they can
cycle their growth appro-
priately, a certain amount
of the future has been
revealed to tree con-
sciousness. Under-
stand that any form of
life that helps to sustain
other forms of life might necessarily receive some of this understanding.

We've heard so much about California and possible quakes and so forth; is that still a possibility?

Some Earth motion is possible. I do not perceive a catastrophic quake in your likely lifetime. In time, yes. But by the time the cata-strophic quake occurs, it may be that the population on the soul level that has been occupying this planet will have shifted to the higher-di-mensional aspect of the planet, which is much more in balance. You are now all working toward that balance to become compatible with it. It is possible, though, that there will be some quakes, but I do not perceive a major disaster.

Are we working toward the fourth dimension, or fourth density, and so is the planet? Or is the planet going to stay in the third density while we go into the fourth?

So that you can have a frame of reference, you are working toward the fourth density and so is the planet. It is natural, since as you examine your world, any philosopher or scientist could say that every-thing is everything else in either micro- or macrocosm. It is a simultane-ity of action. However, Earth as a reality will remain in the third dimension, and the fourth-dimensional version of this planet will be an experiential phenomenon as it manifests. It is, of course, manifested now; but experientially to you all, it is more likely to be referred to as Terra. So while Earth is evolving itself on the fourth dimension, it is already evolved.

In terms of particle physics, the particles are being speeded up, not with the intention of causing destruction, but with the intention of causing wave-form magnetics that will create expansion if it happens at a certain speed and pulse. There is no need for explosion, but rather expansion.

What density are you?

I am in transit myself. I am now not encapsulated. My self, which was in transit recently from the sixth to the seventh, is now no longer encapsulated. In about 4½ or 5 weeks of your time I will be encapsulated again in a ninth-density body. I am, as you say, between lives.

What is the total number of dimensions?

There is no limit that I am aware of. Limits are sometimes stated in order to help you to place yourself in the universe. But according to all of my teachers, I have never heard of anyone providing an arbitrary limit according to their experience.

You still need teachers?

Everyone does. In a sense, the Creator experiences teachers when the Creator can enjoy forgetting. I see no advantage to knowing everything. Where is the enjoyment, the unfolding? Where would be the expansion? Why exist?

Don't black holes contract, so that after you expand enough, then you contract?

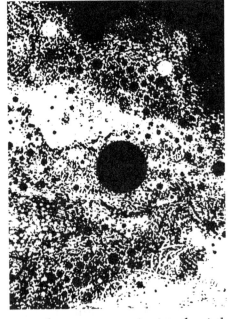

Theoretically, according to your present particle physics, that would be true. But black holes are dimensional doorways that have a layer of third-dimensional analytical behavior attached to them as a result of direct observation from any dimension — in your case, the third transiting to the fourth. So while it might appear that that is what black holes are, black holes are primarily doorways. Rephrase the question.

I think what she means is that since black holes have a property of expansion and contraction, do we also have that capacity? Could we go on to say that as you are going into the ninth density, you could theoretically choose perhaps to go into a lower density at will?

According to your frame of reference, theoretically, yes. But that is not my job. My job is also to be an example, and as I understand it, my next example will be this ninth-density body, which will emanate light. The purpose is to show my race where they are headed so that they can see for themselves that what has been perceived of as the death of my race is simply change that has not been understood.

Is the best thing for us third-dimensional beings to just go with whatever is happen-

ing? To relax and let third-density life bring us to the end of the road? Would that be the best way to approach it?

If you assume that you chose this (which is so, according to my understanding), it seems valuable to experience it to the maximum – which would mean, according to nature in this realm, to let go and flow, although this can often seem adventurous from your perception. It is the reality of your life, in any event. Sometimes when you maintain the illusion of hanging on, it will create a more brittle change. Then life changes suddenly, not gently, ofttimes with some level of drama. In other words, the planet is always in motion, and you as direct extensions are in motion as well.

Those areas of the planet that experience earthquakes will ofttimes experience and attract people who might have some difficulty in letting go. As a result, they have most of the time little reminders of the disadvantage of not letting go, not flowing. Many times members of your populations who live near rivers will perhaps find it easier, if they live close enough, to let go and flow. If they do not learn to do this on a positive, nurturing level, the river will give them examples that are sometimes more dramatic and flow their things away.

In this way this planet is a constant school. There is never a single moment when you are not learning or relearning something. As a result, the level of intensity here is beyond that of any dimension that exceeds it (in your mind). That is, the maximum growth available to your souls as you have cycled through this time of Earth has been this third density. You will have less opportunity and more time to access it on the fourth – and again, expansively, on the fifth and so on. While one can perceive the All much more magnanimously from quicker-plus dimensions and experience many aspects of self that are not experienced on this plane, one never learns as much.

This form of life you are living here now is a great reward even though it is sometimes very difficult. The reward is constant teaching and education and study. Whatever you have learned even in this one life in this place, you will have eternity to examine over and over again in other densities where stimulation is much, much less. In and beyond time you will long for the spontaneity and unexpected turn of events of this place. Learn to enjoy. Let go and flow, for in this reality you have the greatest potential to experience grace.

Are you saying that emotion is the primary factor we have that other densities don't have?

Other densities *may* have emotion. You have polarity. You have struggle. You have stress. You have distraction. You have, in other words, all of the potentials to create the finest you that you can *simply due to the possibilities to do the opposite.* As a result, this level of stress, sometimes referred to metallurgically as tempering, can create a very fine and appreciated edge.

I must comment, a personal aside. As I find myself between lives here, I am becoming somewhat more open to understanding many things that were elusive to me in my last life. I no longer feel the restrictions of one-mind. One-mind in my civilization offered a great deal of information, but it was a narrow band – primarily intellectual knowledge. In my now state of being I have been granted some level of potential to achieve a new level of grace that I have yet to experience. It is not exactly struggle as you experience it, but I must learn new techniques of absorption.

Right now I am everything. As a result, I am you and other things that are unknown to me. I'm able to absorb feelings, but without a physical body to reflect it, there is nowhere for them to go or a way to be dissipated. Nevertheless, this level of absorption is new for me. I am greatly thankful for this. I am expectant that my ninth-dimensional body will allow me to understand myself and you better. I am looking forward to the experience, and to be able to even say that, I can tell that I have grown, since looking forward is truly an emotion as well as a thought.

We will have a birthday party for you.

Thank you.

Is it your civilization that is getting a lot of negative attention about abductions and cattle mutilations?

We have received less notoriety about cattle mutilations. We have not done this at all. I must say that not only in my time but in the past, some of my race who also contact you have been less than gentle with you. But never purposely brutal, never – even quite unsophisticated groups who are so far in Zeta's past that they would greatly precede your own time. No, this type of press has been stimulated by other beings who would, through what might be referred to as counterespionage techniques, cast us in a shadow that we do not represent to create what amounts to disguise on their part. I would say, however, that many of my species are still in emotional ignorance, not understanding or appreciating the value of this great gift.

As a result, there is still a tremendous level of misunderstanding, even though in my time there is great respect for your race. There is still misunderstanding about who you are and who we are in association to you. In my recent time there has been the knowledge that has spread through the one-mind, even though the one-mind of my race thinks of it now as theory. Many are beginning to conclude the factual potential that you are our past lives. The more this absorbs into the one-mind, the more likely it is that being intrigued with you will greatly accelerate into becoming much more dedicated to your well-being. Which might mean that my race, from that recent time in which I was embodied, will then be able to make the decisions that are necessary to integrate greater forms of expressive emotion. This will take many, many lifetimes. But an alternative race has been created by us that looks somewhat like us and somewhat like you, and they will act as interpreters and be a great assistance to us. They will be more accessible to yourselves. This will take place in a gradual unfolding over the next forty years or so.

We have designed these individuals to appeal to you on the level of attractiveness. We have perhaps overly based it on this quality, in my now point of view; but the actual appearance of these beings has stressed design from your museums of modern art at various places around the planet. As a result, these beings are somewhat streamlined-looking, elegant, perhaps, even though they are different. They are certainly exotic, and do not look quite as strange as we must appear to you. You will find that your media recognition for the body I have recently been in — the Zeta type — will continue to receive a certain amount of applied disinformation and misinformation, much of which is understandable due to the confusions in communication.

Technogical devices that we must use to protect ourselves in communicating with you will not be necessary for them, since they have a high level of tolerance to your emotional energy and can adapt themselves to speak with us without emotion so that we can appreciate their company. They are designed to be gentle ambassadors between us, you see. In time these individuals will gradually be more appreciated by your race. With the fresh start of this race in their connections with you, I feel that you will find them sufficiently appealing that you will want to know more about them. And since they are just getting started, they will, of course, want to know about you, since they are part you. They are part us, of course, but they are also part you.

Are these the Essassani?

They are one of the groups. There is another, sometimes referred to as the Fawns.

Are the Fawns the crossbreeds, when they were taking our eggs and crossbreeding your race with our race?

This is a large question. Many aborted experiments were established during certain attempts to create blends between us. Many of these offspring were too frail to sustain a civilization of their own, so they will be supported for their lifetimes by us. They could not possibly survive on this planet, but they can have a life of sorts with us when treated very gently. The beings I have recently referred to, the Fawns, are the most successful experiment.

Excerpts from "The Jerry Pippin Show"

All right. Joopah speaking. Well, I will say to the listeners that at this time on your planet there is an awakening taking place. The awakening has to do not only with the individual goals that you all have set, both consciously and at the soul level, but also with your destiny. Your destiny is to be the Explorer Race — that is, individuals who go out from your planet to other planets to help beings who, like my own race, have become so involved in our own goals that we have become rather cut off from what the sparkling personalities such as Earth people might have to offer.

Understand that there are many races everywhere, many of which look rather like yourself. As a result, you will find your adventure in space in the coming years to be most enjoyable.

To expand the idea of the beings that you have come to know of as the Grays, for those of you out there who are familiar with this topic, I will say that the Grays are not always from Zeta Reticuli. My own race, for example, actually has beige-colored skin. We have rather large eyes and an unusually large cranium, or that portion of the head that surrounds the brain. It is unusually large in accordance with the rest of our head due to the fact of the intellectual power that we must possess. We are of one mind in my culture, and as a one-mind we need to have a connection on the brain-tissue level that allows us to be in focus with all of our species at any given time.

About Joopah

I myself am about three-and-a-half feet tall and would be easily recognizable on your planet as not a normal Earth person. However, I have been on your planet from time to time, and even though you would not necessarily ever see me, I have, through remote-viewing devices on various vehicles, seen many of you conduct your lives. I am not spying, but I am curious.

You are actually from the Zeta Reticuli star system, is that correct?

That is correct.

How long does someone live in that star system?

Well, in my last life, for example, I lived about 275 years. Although in my now life, having changed dimensions, I will be in this new form for about 10,000 years.

Then you are not in an Earth dimension with three dimensions like we are?

No. I am not in a dimension where wear and tear takes place.

So there are several other dimensions that we are not even aware of, is that correct?

Well, yes. There are quite a few that even I am not aware of, of course. I have my limits. But I will say that according to my understanding of dimensions, my now self is in the ninth dimension. It is a little difficult to explain what this means in practical terms, but I will say by way of interpretation that it would mean that I am several million years into the future from your point of view. Which is why, in my job as an architectural historian, I have some knowledge about what you might do in the future. I know that you might feel funny sometimes because I do not tell you precisely what you can expect, but it is important that I do not deflect you from your natural creativity.

How long does it take a spaceship from this star system Zeta Reticuli to reach here?

Allowing for the method of travel that my race uses in this dimension, it would take about as long as it takes to snap your finger and thumb together. For some of the older cultures of my race it might take perhaps a few hours, but most of that time would be in negotiating various forms of maneuvering around the planets in your solar system. But it would not have to take any more than just a few seconds. You understand that the travel is taking place in *time* rather than in space, as this way is the easiest.

Human beings have reported seeing spaceships and flying saucers and things. What colors would your spaceships be?

They glow with a red-orange color. Perhaps some of you might have seen that. There are other ships that might display different colors. For example, some ships from Orion might be blue-green, and some from the Pleiades might flash various-colored lights, ofttimes blue.

We are doing this show as Voyager reaches the outermost planet of its mission [Neptune]. I want to ask you: If you are from the future, what happens to our space exploration here, the United States, Earth? Will it continue?

It will continue for some time. There will be, from my perception at this point in time, a little gap in time before you get to a form of propulsion that will be less exhaustive of natural resources on your planet. Perhaps a better way would be to use the principle of attraction. That, however, will take some time. I will say that a form of fusion energy that is being worked on even now by some of your governments is likely to be involved in generating the light energy, a form of plasma light energy, that will transport the first vehicles without the use of the fuels you have been using.

You are saying that you, Joopah, are one of the little gray men with the big eyes. Is that correct?

Well, I would prefer to say that I am one of the *beige* men with the big eyes, because in point of fact, there is some confusion here. Sometimes there are some beings who look somewhat like us who are gray in color. But sometimes I or others like me might *appear* to be gray because of a technological device that we use to allow us to image ourselves in your dimension. This device is a form of energy that moves electrons and neutrons around and so on and creates a form of electrical barrier. As a result, it makes us look gray. Those who are the Grays who have come to be known for doing misdeeds are not my race.

Where are they from?

They are from a very small planet in a star system called Sirius, which has mostly very like-minded, pleasant beings. But these beings from one planet in Sirius are involved in — well, how can I say? — some serious misdeeds on this planet that are not in your best interests.

Are they a danger to us?

I cannot say that they are a real threat. But I can say, speaking diplomatically, that some individuals on this planet perceive them to be a real threat. They are allowed, you see, by the Network of Planets (one might say) to interact with you only just so much. They might claim to be a much greater threat than they really are.

Abductions have been alleged. Are they really going on?

Abductions are in fact going on, yes.

Are you a party to that?

Well, I will say that we are involved, but we do not involve ourselves with harmful abductions. We will sometimes take people aboard, and we always trade with them. In a sense, we always show them things about your world and give them a great deal of education. It is true that in the past (meaning in the forties and the fifties and somewhat in the sixties) we were involved in the medical examinations. But we do not do abductions of a sort that are destructive. We recognize that you are our *past lives*. As a result, we do not wish to damage you.

Can you explain anything about cattle mutilations? What is the deal there?

I will explain that the beings involved in those mutilations are attempting to synthesize, by use of various body parts from the animals

referred to, and create a clone of Earth people that would be under their control. Now, I realize that sounds rather ominous, but I must tell you that these beings from Sirius have some serious problems in being involved in your immediate society due to the extremes of weather here. They are very sensitive to heat, so they are attempting to create a clone that looks like Earth people and that will be possible to integrate into your society but be under their power.

What these beings do not realize, of course, is that even a clone, when it is created, will have a form of soul enter it from the Creator. And if not immediately, then eventually it will create its own destiny and be under no one's authority other than the Creator, of course. So I will say that their attempts to synthesize a being that can act as a corrupter will come to no good end. I must also say, in all honesty, that some of the mutilations are being done by individuals on this planet who have rather different interests.

The Network of Planets

I hear some terms that I am not really familiar with. Evidently there is a group of extraterrestrials called the Network? What is that?

The Network would be rather like your own networks on this planet. That is to say, groups of planets, even complete star systems, that are considered to be in some way related to Earth. In some cases it might be that genetic material from those places such as Orion and Sirius and Pleiades and so on were used by the Creator to create the human race. But it also includes the idea that there are even beings from other places who have no direct connection here who have a very benign and gentle attitude toward Earth and are involved in protecting Earth.

You see, very often it is stated that Earth is a school, a place designed for people to come and learn the most advanced forms of education. It is *not* a place where people are sent to be punished or where they must move onward and upward. It is only the most advanced and coopera-tive students who are *allowed* to manifest here. So the Network of Planets not only helps to protect Earth from extreme forms of invasion, but also it protects the rest of the galaxy from radiations from Earth.

I'd like to get back to the spaceships themselves. From reports by people who see them and swear this is true, they can make a right angle at literally thousands of miles per hour. How is this possible?

You must remember that we are not talking about vehicles that are being pushed. Your vehicles are propelled – that is to say, pushed from place to place. Our vehicles are attracted, or pulled, from place to place not only through time but in this case, through space (as referred to by your right-angle turns). When you are being pulled, it is possible to be pulled without experiencing g-forces. That is, when the beings aboard the vehicles allow themselves to show this type of maneuver, they as well as the ship have to do so consciously. In a sense, they become the ship and the ship becomes them. I realize that this sounds rather vague, but it is almost a religious experience, as you say.

We have a call. Hello, you are on the air.

Caller: I'd like to ask the entity if he is familiar with the human known here on Earth as Jesus Christ. Do you know, was there a Christ and was he truly the son of the Creator?

Thank you very much. Yes, certainly. And this being is respected widely throughout the universe. You must remember that on this planet you receive versions from time to time of the Creator — gifts from the Creator, one might say — to help show you the paths that you could follow. Jesus was sent here to create an example. You must know that, since he was, in his manifestation on this planet, beyond the physical laws that you must follow. He could be in many places at once in different bodies. And he has imagined himself on other planets as well. So I can assure you that he is known and widely respected everywhere I have gone.

Can you give us maybe a closing message to the people of Las Vegas?

Thank you. I will say this: In this now time on this world you are living in, you will be experiencing many extremes. You must know that what is going on has little to do with other people. It has much more to do with the energies of the future, which are unfolding even now. You are transiting from your third to your fourth dimension and you are surrounded, albeit somewhat invisibly, by your future selves on that fourth dimension. They are here to help you; sometimes you might feel their energies. Know that they will support and love you, as does the Creator.

We have time to take one more phone call.

Caller: I was wondering how common it is for the space aliens from the Zeta Reticuli star system to utilize robots when they come down here to Earth.

Many beings from various points do utilize automated life forms like you do when you use a form of robotic vehicle on your Moon and in hazardous nuclear areas, for example. Beings who have not been here very much consider it to be hazardous territory, the unknown. Yes, robots are considered to be a form of cautionary device.

Thank you very much.

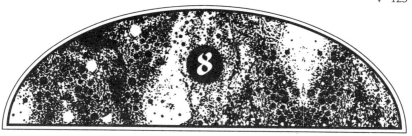

VFO Encounters in Sedona

Zoosh and Joopah
Sedona, Arizona, July 16, 1989

obert Shapiro: Here are some new developments. Joopah up and died on me! His body came to an end and he is in a transition. It used to be that when I channeled him I would always get a picture of him sitting at this instrument-control panel inside this craft. Then for several weeks I wasn't getting that picture, and I was kind of upset about it. I didn't know what it meant. I would get a dark space picture with stars floating along or some other nebulous picture. I didn't know what to make of that.

Joopah's Transition

Finally, he did a session with my business partner, who asked what that was all about, and Joopah said that his body had come to an end and that he was in his transition state to his next body. He said he would be into that body in about four weeks of our time. He mentioned that as a result, he is going through changes, becoming broader in what he comments on and what he can do. He said that the planet where he has been living is in a transition from the sixth to the seventh dimension, just as we are in a transition. He said that he now understands the reason that their race was, from their point of view, dying out.

They can clone bodies very easily, but they had to wait for a soul to enter the body. For a period of time they would wait reverently for the soul to enter, and they could actually measure the change energetically. But it wasn't happening, and that is what had caused them all this grief (they probably wouldn't call it grief, but concern). In any event, he now understands what is going on. Some of them are going to make the shift to the seventh dimension, but the bulk of the population is going to make the leap to the ninth dimension. What was happening is that the bodies they had been cloning are not the bodies the new souls want to enter. So he is going to be given a ninth-dimensional body, which will emanate light, he says. He is still unclear about what it will look like, but it will look much like the bodies they have. The eyes, I think, will be a little more swept back and a little narrower, not so big.

In any event, he says that he is experiencing different things now. He understands that the body he will be given will be like a demonstration body. Normally, he would just go on and be in the ninth-dimensional version of that planet in the far-flung future, but in order to show the population (since they are primarily so technological), he is going to go back in time in his ninth-dimensional body to where he was before so the people will be able to see it, and then they can begin creating bodies like that. Souls will then enter those bodies, and they will make a technological shift to the ninth dimension in sort of a gradual wave. He is going to go back and be an example.

In any event, he's been having these strange (for him) experiences. He's been sort of experiencing forms of emotions, and he talked about it recently. It was really moving. He was experiencing the wonder of looking forward to his ninth-dimensional body. In that moment it dawned on him that he was feeling the emotion of looking forward to something, and it was pretty amazing. So we might or might not hear from him tonight, I don't know. I thought I'd bring you up to date on that.

Will he be able to communicate through you when he comes into his next body?

Yes. My impression is that his personality will be altered. I think he is going to be more cheerful. Maybe his jokes will be a little funnier.

What about Joopah II? Will he not come back, or will he be a different version of Joopah?

Yeah. I am now clear that there was a transition state where there was a being who was the transitional being. I don't know how to describe it, but there was this secondary being. In any event, I think I might have thought that Joopah of the ninth dimension was Joopah II. Or maybe that was the being who was the cross or hybrid between human beings and Zetas.

He explained at length that their original attempt to make a hybrid between human beings and the Zetas wasn't working. All these failed experiments happened primarily because of their desire to attain the durability of the human being (and there is a large amount). In the beginning they were just putting about 20 or 30 percent Zeta because they wanted largely the human being. But it was a disaster. Now they have created this being — I've seen it in my mind's eye. They are really beautiful; they are about 51% Zeta and 49% human. They are a lot more human-looking and are taller. They are very graceful-looking. They are just different. He describes them as a kind of modern-art version of a human being.

Good evening. Joopah speaking. I will begin by saying, speaking for my people, there has been less activity from Zeta Reticuli in this immediate area. We have been called elsewhere. However, other groups are now involved here much more. Amongst them are Andromeda and several from the farthest reaches of the galaxy for which you have not developed names. Perhaps they are free to name themselves. Nevertheless, there is a great deal more activity here than there was, even though the Zeta clan is involved elsewhere. However, we have some assistance programs associated with other groups — that is, on the Andromeda ships they often have one or two of us to assist them.

Perhaps the biggest change here in terms of the vehicles is that they are fewer but much larger. In the past there have been many small vehicles in this immediate area. Now there are perhaps three or four quite large, dominant vehicles. They hail from various places in your universe, but for the most part they are from areas familiar in your study of the stars.

The Sirian Water Vehicle

There is one vehicle from Sirius, but not anything to be concerned about. It is filled with beings associated with the development of the Sirian water people here. To be specific, many of you know that dolphins and other sea creatures hail originally from Sirius. These beings have a source; that is, on their home planets they do not appear as they do here. It is just that mankind is here not only to resolve their own soul lessons but also to act as a clearing house to resolve lessons from many of the nearby star systems and planets that have been unable to work them out for themselves. What you have come to call karma is really the inherited lessons from others who have been unable to deal with them.

The Sirian vessel here is really the source of these water creatures. On their planets they are beings who have much the same stature as yourselves, a body that is more humanoid. On this planet, of course, they must take these various shapes that you have come to refer to as animals so that they will not in any way conflict with the idea that mankind is the dominant species.

This vehicle, which I will describe for your edification, is one that would seem to you to be wet. It is damp inside almost all the time, with pools of water. Their water is a little different from your water — more akin to what your scientists call heavy water. It is filled with life forms. The people who occupy it might, from your pint of view, "swim" from place to place. It is, in a sense, an ocean in the sky. Yet they are humanoids — two arms, two legs and a head — some of whom in variations could pass for human. There are many other beings living in this star system of Sirius, but I mention this one to clarify the idea of the so-called animals here who are really derived from this source being. I will make my joke and simply say that those of you who do some underwater snorkeling in the ocean, if someone snorkels on by and doesn't have a lot of gear and seems to be breathing underwater, they might not be from around here!

They are here primarily to make a final study of your oceans in the current change your planet is developing. Mother Earth is getting prepared to expunge much of the discomforts, to clean herself, so there is a last-minute check on the status of the oceans. Studying the lakes and the rivers is the secondary check to be done, since they are already here.

This is going on now by other vehicles elsewhere. You might wonder why a water vehicle is parked above this area. "Parked" is the term, because it is never very far from here. (Of course, it is sufficiently high to not pose a threat to navigation.) It is also usually invisible, only occasionally allowing portions of itself to be seen when those portions can appear to be stars.

They have a vehicle about ten miles long. Sometimes, just for fun (which is their way, since they are amusing), they will allow a light that is quite bright from where they are but, depending upon your point of view, can really only be seen from underneath. (As you know, these vehicles have the ability to create what would appear to be optical illusions, but they are quite real.) They will sometimes, just to be funny, allow this light to move along the underside of the vehicle, creating what briefly appears to be a satellite moving across space. Allowing for certain distances, if you see something that moves from one side of the sky to the other, it is a satellite. But if you see an object briefly that moves rather slowly like a satellite and then disappears (remember that they have the ability to alter optics), it might be them kidding around.

This is *almost* a breach of the intention to remain anonymous, you see. It is so cleverly done that the Network allows them to get away with it, since it really causes no harm. It looks very much like a satellite, but of course it will appear for only a short duration. I mention that simply because some of you might see it, if you have not already done so. It is, in fact, here.

The vehicles are involved in the future work that will develop here. This area, as stated several times before by Zoosh and others, will in time be a water area. To even the casual observer, this area has been a water area once upon a time, but is developing. For people who have a home in the hills, there is no immediate reason to build a boat dock in front of your yard, since this will take quite a bit of time.

Earth Cleansing

The beginning work is being done in synchronistic activity with the Mother Earth, who prepares herself for this cleansing. The cleansing operation will happen somewhat interdimensionally, with the assistance of devices that can neutralize many forms of polluting substances that would take many, many years to break down. I must say, however, that the radioactive pollution will generally not be altered.

You must understand that you are in transition from one aspect of this planet to another. When that transition is sufficiently completed, you will not really experience that radiation, but you will, unfortunately, leave it behind for those who inherit the third-dimensional aspect of this planet known as Earth. However, because they have been experiencing negative energy for so long, when they come here and experience any positive energy at all, it will be quite a wonderful thing. So even though the planet will be mildly radioactive and have outbursts of radioactivity from time to time, their bodies are a little more durable and will be able to tolerate that condition, unlike your own. Therefore, although there is some assistance from extraterrestrial sources to help Mother Earth in her cleansing, there is also a certain amount of interference as well.

I mention this about this Sirian vessel because there has been so much talk in the past about this negative planet from Sirius and its connections to you. I want to remind you gently that for the most part that planet is the exception, you see. Other beings — the source of dolphins, whales and so on, the source beings — are present. If you feel this energy, which is possible, that will be why.

Why is the planet going to be radioactive?

There is a great deal of radioactive waste material that has been somewhat thoughtlessly disposed of, in many cases in the oceans. You will hear about it from time to time, but due to the nature of the military and political necessity to have secrets, most of the radioactive dumping that has been done has had to be kept secret because of its association with secret projects. As a result, those who have dumped this material were unable to command the resources to move this waste material to a more permanent and safer burial ground. That would have drawn too much attention. So they did the best they could by utilizing some ships at sea. But sometimes their best is not enough. They are also functioning, of course, within the limits of the technology you have now.

But within a few years – especially forty years from now – there will be major leakage of radiation into various bodies of water as well as bursts of it on land, and serious contamination of the ground water. As a result, the planet will be somewhat more radioactive. However, these Sirians, who will inherit the third-dimensional aspect of this planet Earth while you shift toward Terra, have a greater tolerance of radioactivity. It will not be as much of a problem for them as it is for you.

You will be transitioning, you see, to the planet Terra, and although you are not going anywhere, you will be experiencing an increase in the vibratory rate. You will feel and have the effects of perhaps no more than half of the experience, because you will have moved sufficiently from this frequency pulse that is Earth by that time. You have already moved, so there is already some detachment from the bulk of the experience.

Since the inheritors of what you have come to call this Earth have not only a greater tolerance for radioactivity but also have more of it on their planet, it is not deemed to be a negative, but perhaps even a plus. You see, not only do their vehicles sometimes use atomic power to run on, but they are more casual about the emanation of these energies, since their bodies are so sturdy. They are not particularly affected – unless, of course, one of them fell into a pool of plutonium, in which case they would probably be affected. But they are much more durable physically than yourselves. So radioactivity is not perceived to be a negative.

This is not to suggest that individuals who are operating nuclear power plants should suddenly assume it is their patriotic duty to leave the planet in the best possible condition for the inheritors by dumping radioactive waste directly into the land and the streams. However, simply due to the breakdown of substances and the decomposition of the containers, it will leak out eventually. But that will be all right.

Was the bombing of Hiroshima the inception of radioactive pollution on planet Earth?

No, it was not. It had happened many times before that. Many civilizations existed here before.

The Testing of Earth's Hybrid Technology

Last Tuesday night about 8:40 p.m. I went out into the yard. There was an object that came in from the northeast and made an arc to the southwest, returning in the direction it came. It seemed very large, and it seemed to glow, but there was a period when its lights were flashing in an erratic pattern. Studying it further, it looked like lights were reflected off points on its surface. As it turned back toward the northeast, it made no noise, but there were two high-speed interceptor planes pursuing it. I've never seen anything quite like that before. Can you shed any light on it?

This type of experience will become more common. You are somewhat in a flight zone for the testing of what will in time be called Earth's flying saucers. A very gentle relationship is being developed between certain forces on Earth and beings from elsewhere. This particular vehicle has been here before and will be back. It will ofttimes disguise itself as a plane. Sometimes it will make no noise, since it has that capability, but it also has the capability of sounding suspiciously like a plane. What you have here is a test vehicle with more than one motive source. This is not a false sighting, but a sighting of the presence of space technology within an Earth vehicle.

Your government has recently stated that it will begin public testing of this so-called Stealth bomber. That is a cover, because they are really beginning to test their new vehicles, which look much like what you call flying saucers. Contrary to some people's opinions, this is not an intentional cover-up to say, "See, this is what flying saucers *really* are," although some people will pass that information about. In reality, this is the beginning of public contact; it is your government's way to prepare the citizens to accept the idea that there are civilizations elsewhere.

I do not wish to seem as though I or other members of my race are breaking faith with government officials with whom I have been in contact, but government officials have felt that it would be of value to release this information through unofficial sources. You might say that from the governmental point of view (allowing for my GS rating), I am simply an unofficial source. So I will simply say, you have seen a vehicle that could simply be called hybrid technology.

In the last few weeks there have been a number of people suffering from chills and fever. Are there any particular influences?

This is not associated with that extraterrestrial source. It is a little more associated with adjustments to the frequency intensity involved in Mother Earth's work. I might say, as an aside, that there is a supportive effort from extraterrestrials to calm the energy. I do not want to leave you with the impression that extraterrestrials are interfering with what Mother Earth does, but in order to cleanse herself she must intensify various sounds that are primarily ultrasonic. However, these sounds have deleterious effects on the surface population. It is not possible to totally rid these sounds from the surface, because they must be there so that Mother Earth can do what she does to cleanse herself. But there is some attempt by extraterrestrial sources to nullify the sound sufficiently so that people will not have more than discomfort. Good question.

Current Human Changes

How will the space people contact the star people on the Earth plane, if they have not already?

This is ongoing. There will not be any sudden broadcast over television. However, not to treat your question too lightly, I will say that Zoosh has referred to the fact that souls from other places in your reincarnational cycle who are associated with other planetary systems have begun braiding into your own souls. That is to give you the support that you need to get through these times as well as the skills and the aptitudes you were not born with. In the future there will not only be more of that, but also more of the walk-in replacement energies. Since some prophecies have stated that Armageddon was going to happen, I can say now that many, many souls will be replaced by the so-called walk-in experience wherein the souls themselves depart to the future to be trained for living on Terra.

Contact now is being shifted from the focus of waking people up to allowing them to continue the activities for which they originally came. Many souls are experiencing, from their extraterrestrial source, this wake-up signal, but it is not always understood to be you in your bodies.

Many of you in this room as well as many on this planet have, on the soul level, come here to learn the value of unhappiness. This is not to suggest that unhappiness is wonderful, but that the original intention of unhappiness was to act as a subtle tool to urge change. Change has gone on at a snail's pace in other areas of the galaxy, and the original intention of so-called negative energy was to stimulate change so that one would not have to live ten lives in the Pleiades, for example, to accomplish the growth that takes place in five minutes here. Souls have begun to learn that unhappiness at the level of 2% can accelerate growth without causing discomfort.

When you are living at the fourth dimension (as you understand it) on the planet Terra, you will have the opportunity to have no more subconscious, so your energies will be much more receptive to subtle messages. You experience the subtle messages now, but due to the distraction of major discomfort and other things necessary to function on this planet, there has been difficulty in hearing and feeling the subtle messages. The subtle messages of that 2% of unhappiness in the future on Terra (yes, there will be some unhappiness in the fourth dimension) as a spice, will be felt more as frustration. And when that gentle frustration is felt, you'll have the immediate knowledge – no longer confusion, the subconscious and all of this – of what is to be done and you will act on it. As a result, unhappiness and the original purpose of negativity will be one.

The lessons – sought for so many years that it is impossible to mention a number – have been achieved on this planet in this society now. The souls who came here to experience it have learned the value of unhappiness. Their departure, somewhat through the walk-in status and through the normal cycle of passing on and being born, is the source of the original idea of biblical prophecy of Armageddon. What was perceived to be death, what was perceived to be the yellow from the north, will be golden light associated with the birth and the death and the completion of the lesson.

The souls will return to the higher-dimensional aspect of Earth (known as Terra), prepared to not only manifest with the gold light (material-mastery color), but to achieve the purpose of the human being, which is to be the Explorer Race. They will bring to citizens of other civilizations not only that tiny level of discomfort, but also the motivation it takes to grow so that those civilizations will no longer stagnate. Contact will be made with the starseeds through the act of completion as well as through accelerated soul-braiding.

You have accomplished something on this Earth that has never been accomplished in the history of existence. This is the reason for living – to create total change. It is, according to my understanding now, the opportunity for the Creator to grow. Think for a moment what that means! The Being who is All That Is can grow! Imagine, if you can, how life will change when the Creator grows! Ponder that for a moment.

The Dolphin Connection, the Role of Sound

I had heard a couple of years ago about there having been in very ancient times a dolphin temple here. I think it was exactly a year ago today when I felt I had to be in this particular place near the Chapel at dawn, which I was. Earlier this year I was up there again with a friend, and we had an experience of a dolphin being (not in a dolphin body) who took us into this rock into a place that looked like a temple. Can you tell me anything about that?

As stated at the beginning of this evening, the vehicle that is the source of that energy you have indicated (dolphin) is not only conveniently parked above this area, but it (of course) requires a corresponding underground circuitry. As you know, underneath the planet there is a considerable amount of underground activity, and underneath this particular locale there is more activity than under many other places. There are windows, one might say (portals is another word), to enter these quicker-dimensional areas. Depending upon your frame of being and your cultural reality, you will perceive, if given the gift of entrance, different sights inside.

Your experience of the temple had to do with the natural arc of your soul's experience through this planet. In a sense, what you were seeing was not something of the present, but more associated with the past. Since this area is going to be underwater in time, it will become a treasure house of reverential or sacred objects of the ocean. These objects will be utilized to condition, harmonize or tone the aspects of this planet that will move from the third dimension to the fourth dimension.

Now, I have stated that this planet will, as Earth, remain here. But to some extent Mother Earth as you have known her will also evolve, so she will have the pleasure of the evolution much as your souls will have. As a result, there needs to be a transition team, and part of the transitional team will be having to re-create the past. This planet and the souls upon it are associated with your own here and elsewhere on the planet since it started out being Terra, and you are simply rejoining its original starting point. So what is being experienced is the reimaging of what was. When you saw that temple, you were actually viewing the ideal that will be created; but it was associated primarily with the past.

I have received some information that the dolphins would be leaving the planet over the next five to seven years, their work being done. Can you speak a little on that?

Briefly, you might notice in the news that the dolphins are leaving in increasing numbers. You might ask yourself why these beings are being destroyed who are actually involved in assisting those who are destroying them. One might say that this is one way of departure. Much of the dolphin energy will depart in this fashion. It will not be liftoff, but termination.

What are the tones that go on in the ears of many of us. Is this some type of contact?

Beyond having a medical reference, when they are fleeting it is assumed that it is a way of localizing you — keeping tabs on you and knowing where you are. That is one aspect. But your physical body acts similar to what Mother Earth does with herself. Sometimes it is slightly uncomfortable, but it is temporary. It is a way of toning (to create the double entendre) the physical self with its higher-aspect, fourth-dimensional Terra self. Outside the context of time, *you all exist right now on Terra* in your idealized bodies that would be responding to 2% discomfort, having no subconscious minds. So you would actually look a little different. Not to threaten beauty operators and those who sell wrinkle-free cream, but wrinkles will be a thing of the past. Deterioration of the physical body will no longer happen as at present. When the body ages, it will tend to age more from within than externally. This is a hint of things to come.

So there is need from time to time to strike a tone, one might say, to assist in the developing of that transition. This would not need to be done, you understand, if the individual body were not going to experience some elements of a fourth-dimensional, actual felt experience. This is an experience somewhat like alternating current, which pulses essentially on, off, on, off — yet is experienced as being on all the time. You're actually pulsing very much like alternating current between the third and fourth dimensions. Therefore, even though you do not experience all that you will experience of the fourth dimension, you also do not experience all that you have experienced of the third dimension.

One might say that you are re-creating the idealized past on this planet at its highest sources through the use of this tonation that many will hear but all will feel. Only some people actually hear it, depending largely on whether you have had physical contact. This tone is designed to create and stimulate the past, which is a halfway point.

At the beginning of civilization on this planet, as it densified from the fourth to the third dimension, there was still a great deal of openness to the rhythms of nature. That openness has been lost, largely at the advent of the idea that the mental properties of the mind were the most superior and capable portion of the human being to deal with life as it is. The subtle energies, or the feminine principle, were discarded many years ago in favor of the mind and the body working together to create external reality.

In time came the belief that external reality was the primary factor that created personal reality; it was the root of people believing as you do now — that your external reality is the source of the conditions and experiences of your day-to-day life. Whereas the actual source is a balance of the two — primarily the internal reality, which is experienced through the subtle energies of the feminine self, the emotions and the spiritual inspiration. What is going on is a sufficient quantity of change so that you can have a halfway-house experience as you move into and are harmonized into the fourth-dimensional reality.

What is this energy that is in my house, and how was it put there? Is it an entry into another dimension?

It has reflections in the community. You are referring to what amounts to a tunnel, almost a crack in time. It was there, of course, before the structure was built. The structure is not so much a monument to present architecture as to that of the distant past, emulating a structure that flows with nature rather than conquers it. This crack in time will move about somewhat, sometimes giving the impression that it is some one rather than some thing.

This will also have effects in the community. It is not exactly extraterrestrial, but it is balanced from extraterrestrial sources so that it does not become a problem. It creates windows through which you will have occasional bizarre or abnormal experiences. It will also cause this area to be seeded with an energy that allows it to be much more magnetic and electrical than it might normally be. The soil structure, the iron content, largely has to do with the doorway this represents. It is somewhat involved, of course, with the interdimensional experience, and it is tempered largely through the use of Inner Earth and extraterrestrial balancing techniques.

Can we presume that the more positively polarized ETs will tend to not reveal themselves, respecting the code of noninterference; and conversely, the more negatively polarized might tend to intervene more in third dimension?

I will simply say that regardless of the beings' positive or negative status (referring to the actual statement of the question), the intent to reveal might or might not be allowed. If there is a negative desire to intervene there will be no more permission than there is for the positive. It is more likely in your civilization for the squeaky wheel to get the grease, yes? That which is unpleasant or uncomfortable will receive much more attention than that which is pleasurable. How often might this occur in a simple relationship, where one might sometimes feel that the relationship is all wrong when there is only a brief moment of discomfort?

Is there a particular place in this area that is a primary portal or connection point for extraterrestrials?

I will point you in the direction and let you find it on your own. Up Oak Creek Canyon past the place where people playfully slide in the water, you will feel an energy from your right. Find the spot. That is all you get!

Very often in Sedona I see — cloud-craft is what I think they are. They always have a specific swirled shape; sometimes they are very large, sometimes very small. I want to understand what I am really seeing. Is it a being, a consciousness, a craft?

There is, of course, a natural cloud phenomenon of this type, but when the cloud is unmistakably shaped like what you call a flying saucer and it just sits there acting very uncloudlike, it is very often just what it appears to be. When this goes on, it is somewhat borderline interference that the Network allows, since this type of cloud does exist. It is somewhat like the humorous Andromeda experience — a simple case of allowing oneself to be seen when one could be mistaken for something else. Yes, there are beings onboard and these are vehicles, but only when they look quite obviously like that.

Are they from a particular planet?

Very often they are from Arcturus. This is not a planet, but a star system. However, I see no reason to use the names of these planets, because most of the time they are unpronounceable in your language. It might take a different aperture than a mouth to pronounce it. I will leave it to your imagination what that aperture might be like!

I'm curious about a project called Operation Indigo, which happened June 29. It was a concerted effort on the part of many people to establish contact with extraterrestrials. Do you know whether or not they responded to any of these people participating?

There has been some response. There are other projects, some of them stimulated by youthful individuals. There is some contact going on with all of these situations. In many cases the contact is not always felt, since it happens largely through the subtle energies of inspiration and also in dreams, which could be easily ignored. So yes, there has been some contact as a result.

Several of these projects are under way now and will gradually begin to receive notice in the legitimate press. In the beginning it will be perceived as a humorous phenomenon, but really those days are almost gone. It will now be perceived as a mass phenomenon for which there is no apparent explanation by those who feel it is their job to explain human behavior in a predictable fashion. The days of explaining human behavior in a way that could be proved with reproducible results have come and gone. Some will linger, but the social sciences will be rewritten over the next few decades.

My father is one of the experimenters with what is called the electronic voice phenomenon, which uses tape recorders to pick up messages that make sense. He is now using the television screen to get pictures. He has some real interesting contacts with extraterrestrials, but it is kind of confusing. Can you speak on this phenomenon, on trying to use technology to make contact?

The confusion here is largely with the technology, because you must analyze with the tools at hand. A great deal of what is going on now is the seeding of enigmas — that which cannot be explained but seems to happen more and more often. The purpose of this is to stimulate new technology. Also, the experiments are largely done (aside from this particular one) by those who are pursuing them for the pleasure of doing it. So scientific individuals, whether they be full-time scientists or not, are pursuing things for their pleasure. Some of this will percolate out into the community at large right away and some will not.

It is designed to be an enigma. Playing it backwards might not help, all right? But the level of technology is primarily the difficulty. If the experimenters are willing to utilize sensitive individuals to fill in the blanks as well as attempt to interpret the data on a functional basis, it might be possible to get some direction. The intent of these enigmas is to encourage you to move beyond the mind into more fruitful areas.

Is the primary purpose of Bell Rock an energizing point for UFOs in this area?

That is not the primary purpose. That is the secondary purpose; a left/right turn signal on a car is like that. It is not the primary purpose of the vehicle to flash that light, but the flashing light on the car does allow it to tell others where it is going and, in a sense, where it has been.

So one might say that the navigational beam produced at various times of the day, especially the evening, by this particular rock (as it is referred to) has an auxiliary or ancillary purpose.

In the process of reading the book Communion, *I had some very deep and profound emotions. If contact was made when I was a small child, what was its purpose?*

This is quite personal, but I will simply say that the intention was to allow the physical being (yourself) to develop into someone it would not have developed into otherwise. So it was benign. The beings pictured on the cover of the book are only pictured in part. There was a considerable amount of artistic license taken, with the approval of the author. But from the eyes up, that is pretty close to what they look like.

Do the extraterrestrials have contact with us on a telepathic basis? Sometimes I get the feeling that they are actually teaching us to have one mind.

Yes, telepathy; yes, energetic, and this is why you need to develop beyond mental. You need to return to your full capacity. Their intention is to contact you more on the energetic or subtle-energy level, since much, much greater communication can develop that way. Mental telepathic communication, while it is not useless, is *almost* useless. It is about 10% communication and 90% nothing, because some individuals need to protect their energy fields from yours. You want to experience the contact or communication rationally; however, the rational mind is perhaps the slowest way of achieving anything. The desire is to contact you energetically, and this is beginning in some ways.

I will say, however, that the intent is to ease you toward a greater understanding of your abilities.

Are the extraterrestrials showing us in some way to think and to feel through a group mind?

Excuse me a moment. I am required elsewhere. A moment . . .

All right. Zoosh here. My friend Joopah is called away to activities elsewhere. Zetas are largely involved in a technological rush project having to do with the internal access of the Earth – nothing to be concerned about. I will field your questions.

They are not really trying to encourage you to have one mind, even though initially, in the past, they were. The understanding by those in a position to influence you now is that *that is a reality all the time*. Since you will be moving past the subconscious into expanded consciousness when you have more opportunity to experience what you have come to call the unconscious – in other words, the one-mind experience of the source of all information and experience – it is deemed unnecessary to train you for what you are in fact becoming.

Local Sightings

One night, while sitting at Bell Rock, I saw above it what I thought a city of lights would look like, a massive group of lights.

People have indicated that there is a city above this city. This is true on an interdimensional level, but what you were experiencing was something that was a gift, a vision for one individual. This was in fact a vehicle. It is difficult to grasp that they can be so big, but they can. You will know it is a vehicle when there seems to be a distortion in the fabric of space, a ripple effect. This was a vehicle that you were allowed to see.

In August 1982 a friend and I went up Airport Road; I wanted to show her Sedona in the evening. This UFO came out of the southeast, went across 89A and behind Old Grayback (Capitol Butte). It had no lights and looked like a cup turned over on a saucer, and it was a luminous pinkish-gray apparition. She looked at me and I looked at her. We saw the same thing, but we could never discuss it. Was that something that we manifested, or was it a true . . .

It was real. I might add that the source was Zeta Reticuli. There is a reason for not having discussed it. It was not the first time both of you had seen that. It was, speaking allegorically, as if you had some friends over on a Sunday afternoon and they said good-bye and hugged you at the door, then walked down the street to their car. They couldn't park too close to the house, you see, because the people across the street were having a wedding. When you asked them to come over, many cars were parked there. You were sitting on the porch, and a few minutes later your friends got to their car, drove by your house and waved in a friendly fashion.

I will not say that the exact sequence was so immediate, but I will say that the allegory is appropriate.

Joopah said something interesting. He said that there would be walk-outs from our third-dimensional selves as we went into the fourth dimension and into Terra. The walk-ins, I seem to understand, were from B'zal's negative-Sirian planet. Do I understand correctly?

Not walk-ins to *your* bodies.

Can you explain what I don't understand?

Dear, oh dear. The total overlay in your consciousness at the moment is that as you move from the third to the fourth dimension and experience elements of Earth in transition to Terra, these negative Sirians will move from the second to the third dimension and gradually experience elements of Earth. But the motion is fixed; as you move, so do they. There is *never* direct contact. There is only the little bit of contact that you are experiencing right now, which is by way of giving them some feelings they need to have in order to wake up. You are helping to wake up another race of people at the same time you are requesting to be awakened by others. It is always microcosmic experiences of the macrocosm. Souls who are walking in now will be slightly more accelerated versions of those who have been present.

About a year and a half ago I saw this craft. It was shaped like a boomerang and was bright orange. Could you tell me where it was from?

This was a very opportune sighting. Normally, this color is broadcast by the Zeta beings, but there is a craft referred to as the **V**. Of course, because of your particular locale and the energies and the optical effects of the area, you saw this vehicle as not being as big as it actually is. But it was the original vehicle that came here to create the human race on the genetic level from Sirius. It was available for sighting by several people — sighted by a few, but not many.

So be prepared over the next few months. You will experience a radical alteration in your energies. Now, many of you will be experiencing strange symptoms. Do not become alarmed that these symptoms are involved in some major discomfort. What is occurring is that with these new soul-braids as well as the walk-in experience, you will have a more full-bodied experience. Part of the reason you have been under some stress and strain over the past few years and experiencing levels of discomfort, then vacations from discomfort, and again levels of discomfort, is to stretch you and help you grow and become more than you have been. These have prepared you somewhat for this now experience. But there will still be some levels of discomfort associated with what healers and other medical technicians sometimes refer to as a healing crisis.

Do not be shy about getting medical assistance, but in most cases the symptoms will be fleeting. The new energies will so accelerate your physical self as to necessarily begin stirring up the last bastion of subconscious physical areas of holding, which is, in many cases, in the lower abdomen. This part of the body might feel at times a little odd. Do not become overly alarmed. Do what it takes to achieve comfort, utilizing whatever facilities are available, but know that it is stirring up the pot so that you can release your subconscious discomforts through the natural process of the physical body. It is part of the change. Do not become overly upset; just keep the pink stuff on the shelf and feel free to pop a little now and then. That will help. But there will be a minor sense of purging. It will help you feel more comfortable in the future and will prepare you to be much happier receptacles of your new energies.

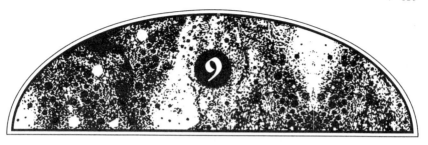

Joopah, in Transit, Gives an Overview and Helpful Tools

Joopah
Las Vegas, Nevada, July 26, 1989

ll right. Joopah speaking. I will explain who I am just a little bit. I am a being from a star system known as Zeta Reticuli to your science community. It is a portion of the constellation sometimes referred to as the Southern Cross, which can be seen most easily from the Southern Hemisphere of this planet.

My consciousness, as I understand it, is several millions of years into your future and beyond the measurement of time, since it is at a different dimension. But I give the framework of years because you are now living in a time-space continuum and that is your framework for understanding change. I will say that I have recently been in a body of Zeta Reticuli origin, which would have appeared to be about three to three-and-a-half feet tall. It was humanoid, in the sense of two arms, two legs, a head and a body. In our dimension, the interworkings of the body would have been largely cosmic, as you would understand it —light energy sufficiently compressed to have a form of solidity to us. However, were we to appear in this room in that dimension, you would not readily see us unless you could see subtle energies, which many people can.

The mass consciousness, however, that I am now a portion of, has gone beyond that recent incarnation, which ended at what you would understand to be 275 years of existence. I am now in a transition to my new body. My old one existed in a swing or a change in position from the sixth to the seventh dimension, in which my home planet existed. My new body will be ninth-dimensional. It will emanate and live on light — that is, transference of light energy within and without. I will appear rather similar to what I looked like before except for this emanation of light, which will alter its color according to my mood.

I still have not fully grasped my new embodiment, since I have never been in a body like this before. According to my understanding, my new body will emanate white and gold light in its normal state. Whenever I experience a great happiness, a great enthusiasm, a great joy, a great love, the color will change to reflect those actual feelings. In this way I will be more prepared to contact individuals who have an artistic or a childlike temperament, for I will be entertaining simply by *being*, and that is really new to me.

My previous lives have prepared me for an expanded mental consciousness. My civilization, as I have recently experienced it in my last body, has a one-mind experience; that is, whatever one of us would know we would *all* know; and equally, whatever we all know, all of us know to be the truth. While it appears to have a great advantage, mentally speaking, it has also, as I see from my now perspective, necessarily slowed growth because it created assumed truths that would last rather a long time and have the effect of a mental juggernaut in which there is such a tide moving in a specific direction that other points of view might not be readily assimilated. Not to say that it was a stubbornness, but just that individuality (as you experience your own free will) was not really a major experience. Nor was it desired, since the intention and purpose of the race was to perfect from within the highest development of mental consciousness as expressed through scientific technology.

The beings from Zeta Reticuli who experience contact with you on this planet usually have that as a goal. Many of the beings you contact now and who contact you come from all different times in Zeta Reticuli's development. The ones from your future (as you understand your point in time) will be kinder, gentler, more appreciative of who you are, because the dawn of understanding of who you are to us is moving back in time.

Beings from my time, in that recent embodiment, have come to understand who you really are to us. At the beginning of the human race we were asked by certain scientists and engineers to help create the human being — not the soul, certainly, but the body of the human being. We were asked to consult and scientifically monitor those bodies. We were simply encouraged to participate at that level then.

And we were enthusiastic about it, because monitoring the development of an entirely new species was something new and enjoyable. Not that the human species was new in the sense of humanoid, for the humanoid appearance (two arms, two legs, a head, a body) is established in this part of the universe. But this race would be created for the soul purpose (s-o-u-l) of bringing its dynamic sensibility, mentally speaking, and its creative consciousness, emotionally speaking, out to the galaxies and beyond to stimulate other races to become more than they have been. It seemed like a wonderful scientific adventure to us.

So we now understand, from my most recent past life (as you understand it, which is still millions of years in your future), that *you are our past lives on a soul level!* Well, well, well! This has been quite a revelation. We now see that our involvement was stimulated not only by our enthusiasm for the project, but also by guidance from our teachers and from the Creator, as we understand our relationship with the Creator.

We now see the Creator's larger purpose: that we would learn to understand more about who we are in our time through our devotion to the genetic experiment on Earth, of which you are all right now a result. And we have learned this, since it was our job to monitor the biological and mental functionings of the human being to see if the experiment had reached its zenith. We have seen your race become interplanetary on more than one occasion — that is, civilizations prior to your own have utilized much more refined machines to travel to other planets. But these civilizations have not lasted. Their own internal conflicts caused them to fall and disappear from the face of the Earth.

However, your civilization has achieved a level of very careful balance that has led us to believe that you will survive; due to our understanding of history, we believe that this civilization will survive. You must remember that all histories are based on probabilities. From a philosophical point of view, you could say that we are your probable future, and yet since the word "probable" is introduced, one must always allow for free will. Nothing is rigidly set in concrete. It is conceivable that some minor change or swing in the motion or direction of your society would simply re-create our now. That is to say, we would expect to exist, but we might experience our civilization differently.

In more recent times when I was embodied, we had this major concern that our civilization was dying out. We have for many, many years cloned our offspring; we have not had the type of biological reproduction that you have. We have had scientific re-creation. However, in alignment with the Creator, we would wait a respectful amount of time after the body was cloned to allow the soul to enter. The item of great concern in recent times was that after the body was cloned, we would wait for the soul to enter, but it did not. This happened over and over again, and there was great concern in our civilization that our race was dying out due to some unknown cause beyond our vast resources of technology and science. And in our contacts with other races we communicate with, no one knew or understood, so we began to believe that our race was dying out.

As a result, we had to turn to our resources. (This is before we understood that you are our past life.) We had to turn to what we had. We could not ask for your advice directly, since your energy and our own is incompatible, as we have recently experienced it, necessitating the use of a technological device that keeps a shield around us so that we do not experience your energy. This has caused complications, of course – a serious breakdown in communications. We are able to communicate with you only mentally and we have recently discovered, much to our shock, that most of *your* communication (according to our teachers, as they have advised us about you) is about 90-95% emotional, energetic, and that words or thought comprise only a very small portion of your actual communication.

You can understand this, of course, because you have arguments from time to time with individuals when you speak one point of view on the thought level and the other individual does not hear you. Instead they hear what you are feeling and react to your feelings more than to what you are saying. You think now that they are reacting to their own feelings, but it is not really that so much: their feelings are triggered by *your* feelings, and this is why arguments take place.

A Zeta-Human Hybrid

In any event, there is great concern in my civilization that we would not survive. So we have asked for permission from the Network, and it was granted, to clone a hybrid between our race and your own. At the time we thought it unusual that our request was granted. We thought the probability for it being granted was no more than half of 1%, so we were quite amazed. We now understand that the highest sources of the Network consulted with the Creator, and the Creator urged this form of union between us, because the Creator knew that you are our past lives on a soul line and that this type of contact between us would create further bonding.

So we have developed, then, a race of beings who are a cross between us. There were several experiments that did not work very well. But we have managed to develop a race that we believed would do several things: First, if our race died out, they could carry on with our knowledge; we would have someone to whom we could leave our knowledge, our purpose, our aims and our philosophies. Second, we would also have as an immediate reward a race that could communicate with you, for they are 49% you and 51% us, with a smattering of other races as spices, since they would have certain skills and abilities that our race and your race do not have to that degree.

The race we have created looks like a cross between us. That is to say, they have large eyes like those of my own race, but they are not as large and are swept back, rather streamlined-looking. They are considerably taller than our average height, ranging now about 5'5", which is probably close to the mean. They are very emotional. I now speak to you with my now understanding of emotion because *I* am becoming more emotional! But my race has not been known for being emotional; it is known for being unemotional.

So this group of beings was created (the hybrid between us) to be emotional so that they could interact with you directly without need for a technological device to protect against energetic contact. They are artistic, creative and somewhat — by our standards greatly, but by your standards somewhat — flamboyant.

They now wear a uniform, which is all black except that the artistic ones have gold flecks and the scientific ones have silver flecks through the midsection. In time, through contact with your race, they will become very enamored with the different colors of clothing that you wear and will likely alter their appearance, perhaps keeping that uniform but adding accessories such as you have now — red scarves and so on, perhaps even hats. That would be rather startling for us; nevertheless, they are quite attractive in a streamlined way. You might find them surprising-looking. But yet they are not that different from human beings.

However, as it turns out, they will not be needed for their original purpose. That is, they will not be needed to carry on for our civilization, but they will be a wonderful go-between — ambassadors, in a sense. They will be able to communicate easily with both you and us. So it turns out that the secondary intention will be the primary result.

As it turns out, from my now point of view I see that the souls did not enter the bodies we had cloned because they were waiting for the new body that *I* will have. At first we did not understand it; we seemed to be shifting from the sixth to the seventh dimension, but in reality we were shifting (though some will shift to the seventh) directly from the sixth to the ninth dimension. So of course the technology was not on-line to create this ninth-dimensional body.

I have been given the unique opportunity to rejoin my race directly following my death. Thus they will not experience any time loss. I am speaking to you in this odd little bubble of time, you see, that really involves about six weeks of your time. I'm into the fourth week by now; there are only about two weeks left. At the point of the actual death of my body, my new body will appear alongside it within about ten seconds.

My friends, who are there for the ceremony of my death, will be somewhat startled by this emanating golden light, and since we have a one-mind experience they will be treated to something entirely new. This will be an advantage, since knowledge, once it is fully appreciated, will assimilate quickly into my race in that time sequence. They will think that they're seeing some afterlife experience, but I will quickly explain to them that the body I am exhibiting is the prototype for their race.

They will then, on a scientific level, quickly learn to clone it and will find that the new souls, which had been reluctant to enter the bodies they had been cloning, will readily enter this new body. So I'm being sent back to seed my race with this new understanding of who we will be in their future, from their point of view.

The reason there has been some considerable misunderstanding between my race and yours (which the hybrid race will hopefully help to smooth over) is that we did not know who you are. The great veil lifted to reveal our dilemma as more an example of being shortsighted than a true dilemma. All of these revelations and so on that I have recently had are what one might refer to as a time-zone knowledge. We do have one mind in my race, but the time-zone knowledge is very slowly spreading back in time in my race. As a result, many of the beings you will meet from different times in Zeta Reticuli still do not understand who you are.

If I am to go back to instruct them and help them, they will be slow to grasp it because of the juggernaut effect of this wonderful, great brain. It is very powerful and has a great deal of knowledge, a great deal of ability, but it is sometimes slow to change its mind. As a result, you will have contact for some time yet with Zeta beings who are still somewhat cold in appearance. But equally, you will have contact with other Zeta beings who will show themselves to be light beings, very knowledgeable, warm, intelligent, sometimes even witty —which is for me something new, but I am working at it.

New Self-Identity for Both Races

So what is going on for you now is a radical shift in consciousness about who you are. This is going on for me also. Thus we have much more in common than we have in differences.

Now, I have given this rather long talk about who we are to give you an overview and to provide a little better understanding of who I am. It can also empower you and give you tools you can utilize that will support your growth and help you feel a little more youthful and enthusiastic about life and a little less cynical, which you might become as a result of living in these times. All right, I will take questions now.

How do I fit into the scheme from your perspective?

In the large view, since it is a large question, you are one of our past lives. My friend, you are part of the Grand Plan just like everyone is. But if you want me to tell you exactly what you are going to do in the future, I cannot do that without necessarily altering what you will do in the future as a result of that knowledge. It is not possible for you *not* to alter it, you see, because of your subconscious.

The subconscious mind in the human being is now being cleared, coming up to the surface and shedding not only its dilemmas, but also providing the gift of the expansion of the conscious mind. As a result, since the subconscious mind is in radical change, it would not be possible for me to tell you what you are going to do in the future without the subconscious mind (which is involved in the arc of change) affecting it.

What do I need to do spiritually to grow and to enhance my consciousness? What should I do and where can I go spiritually?

Inward, rather than find the greatest guru on the mountaintop (euphemistically speaking, of course). It would be of value to simply appreciate your *own* value. Nowadays the Earth Mother you are living on here is appreciating her own value by being more physical – doing things, moving herself, altering her poles somewhat, melting the polar icecaps a little bit but not enough to alarm you by raising water levels enough to create serious problems. She is becoming more physical and is doing what she can to clean up her own act, as you say, on the level of pollution.

Use the Earth Mother as an analogy. Be a little more physical; be a little more emotional, even though some have accused you of being too emotional. Now is the time to allow yourself to be a little more emotional. Where power and alignment with spirit is concerned, nowadays it would be directly aligned with emotionality. So the development of emotionality would be of great advantage to anyone choosing to come into greater focus with their spirit lives.

So I would simply suggest that when you feel emotional, allow that emotion to display itself, and begin to identify those physical objects around you – people, places, things – as something that stimulate emotion within you. For example, a beautiful scene might cause you to feel warm, wonderful; perhaps a traffic jam might cause you to become excited, nervous, agitated.

Allow those emotions to become present as best you can within the framework of your social community, and express them as emotions. Even though sometimes you are alone in a vehicle and something annoying happens, be willing and allowing to express those emotions. You don't have to yell at someone else, but if you yell about the frustration of being stuck in a traffic jam, for example, it is advantageous now, because the emotional body needs to be expressed as it is, not as you would like it to be.

Thus it is not a time for control; it is a time for expression. The key to spiritual and material mastery right now is to unlock the secrets of the emotional body, and the power of the emotional body is in allowing it to be itself, to express itself emotionally through the physical body, which is its friend.

The emotional body and the physical body do not really trust the mental body. The mental body's purpose and original intention was simply to interpret the difference in visual and other sensory stimuli so that one would not, for instance, put a hand in a fire and leave it there. One might consider this to be a natural physical reaction, but the mind is actually involved in that. So I would say, be a little more spontaneous in ways that are expressive. And when you feel something humorous, laugh out loud. It is all right. It gives people permission to do that.

Technique to Expand Perceptions

For you specifically to be able to feel the guides that are present around you, you will need to expand your sensitive perception a bit.

Pick out a favorite geographical object – a mountain or something off in the distance. And when you are looking at it, concentrate not on the mountain but on the space between your eyes and the mountain to see what you might see. Don't question anything. Make certain that there is nothing – no trees, no houses – between your eyes and the point on the mountain you are looking at. If you see ripples or flashes or dots, accept it no matter how strange or hallucinatory it might seem. It is time now to develop your subtle abilities more.

If I understand what you are all about, it's that you know a lot of things that we should already know, part of what is called the collective consciousness. Is it correct to say that we should already know what you know?

No. I know you are having the joy of discovering it. To say that you *should* know it would suggest that there is an assumption of superiority on my part. I do not make that assumption just because I'm in the future (from your point in time) and can see clearly what *might* happen in several different probabilities. I'm not reinforcing the idea that you come into a preparatory state of being conscious of the collective consciousness. In point of fact, the reason that my race exists is largely due to a desire that is being developed on this planet *right now* to develop that consciousness of the collective consciousness, as you understand it.

There is an understandable confusion on your part. The desire for a total awareness of collective consciousness has also somewhat stimulated a desire to *not* have as many emotions, and this creates a great deal of confusion in communication. Thus I do not support the idea of "should."

If two people meet in a casual manner, like I did with the person next to me, is there a connection in the past that can be used in the future? How do we know? How can we guide our behavior to help each other?

Thank you. Good question. Well thought out. Precise. I will say that you will know that something along the lines of this meeting has been preordained by the *feelings*, especially associated with the idea that you have never met, perhaps, or never really noticed each other in this way and suddenly you have this strong feeling, an affinity that is accompanied by energy. You will know that something is going on, perhaps associated with a destiny once begun by past-life associations designed to be fulfilled in this life.

Now, I am not saying that you must fulfill that destiny, but that the best thing you can do to support that form of growth is to explore each other's lives as much as possible. Of course, friendships naturally develop, and the natural tendency is to talk much about what you have done. It is of value to do this to see parallels as well as opposites. If you are intimates at that time (I'm not saying do or don't), perhaps you can take the opportunity to explore each other's hands to notice the feeling engendered within oneself as you are exploring the hand. That is, to develop another point of contact beyond thought, beyond recollection, to develop the point of contact that is both physical and emotional and see if your emotions are in any way aligned with each other. Use as many of your tools as possible.

Also, when you are together, perhaps driving or being driven from place to place by another, comment on your feelings about things you see to observe if there is any alignment there. You will discover in time that your previous lives together have been associated largely with groups that were involved in sweeping events when you had little time to explore your personal relationship or commonalities. Now you have the opportunity for an intimate tête-a-tête or experience.

I encourage you to develop enough of a friendship so that you can discover your similarities as well as your opposing points of view.

Vertical Time and Visits from Future Lives

I frequently experience what is referred to as déjà vu, experiences that I am positive I have been through before, yet I couldn't have, because the people are new to me. I'm wondering what caused that feeling.

This is an experience of *vertical time,* a gift of the coming clearing of the subconscious. That is, as the subconscious is cleared and no longer stands as a barrier or an unavailable repository of knowledge and experience that has been learned, it adds its data-storage capacity to the conscious mind. This will develop at varying rates for different individuals. You are also experiencing an associated gift that allows you to key into memories associated with other lives, including ones from the future along the line of probabilities. This is why you also sometimes have the experience of meeting people you have never really met, and they recognize you or you recognize them.

Can you give me any information about the knocking in the middle of the night when nobody is at the door, waking me up out of a sound sleep, or footsteps I hear approaching my bed when nobody's there? This generally wakes me up.

Ah, but they *are* there. Since you're experiencing vertical time, you are experiencing sensitivities and subtleties associated with interdimensional perception. That is, you are hearing and feeling things that are there but may not be visually apparent. Now, some people will experience the subtle bodies visually, but it is also possible to sense them — that is, feel slight pressure changes or a harmonic, which is a tonal change or an actual sound experience.

You are being contacted by certain individuals from other dimensions, naturally —your future lives coming back to see how you are doing and whether they can assist you in any way. They are not aware at this time of your perceptions of them. They would prefer that you could appreciate them more in terms of color and tone. If you would perhaps be more involved with musical instruments, have them about. You don't have to spend a lot of money, just something simple. Then *when you hear those sounds, pick up some simple little instrument, even a harmonica, and see if you can play a tone that uses your emotions when you hear these sounds. The tone will, in many senses, balance the harmonic.*

The individuals who are present for you from time to time are from a place where color, sound and tone are more appreciated than they are here. To hear a pleasant tone might be appreciated by them as an attempt by you to communicate, in which case it might be less necessary for you to hear only those sounds. As they say, the ball is in your court to make a sound they can hear, and a musical sound is more likely to be something that they can hear.

It will be possible for you to communicate with these beings (future lives) through tone. Let the tones that you make be the most pleasing possible tones to yourself. Not recorded music; it must be something you make yourself, so that there is actual physical-emotional interaction with the instrument. It can be, as indicated, something simple and inexpensive, something that you have about. I suggest you use this initially, as it can ease the experience somewhat.

Again, remember that even recording your own making of tones will not work. It must be something that is done "live," as they say. My intention here, of course, is not so much to alter the experience as to give you an opportunity to expand the experience into something that is more pleasurable for both you and them, to find a common language, which I believe will be pleasurable sound.

Using Fear As a Tool

So I don't need to be afraid? It really instills a lot of fear in me when this happens.

This is because of your old programming in this life. But I do not perceive any need for fear. If the fear is present, though, I will give you a little extra-credit homework, as Zoosh might say. That is, when you do not hear the sounds but can tap into the memory of the fear, then I suggest that you *lie down someplace and honor the fear.* Understand that the fear is not something I encourage you to only experience, for fear is a tool, a guide. It can be used *for* you as well as be experienced at an unpleasant level. So use it for you; do not make it a stranger. You can actually *love* your fear and let it support you by guiding you more clearly and opening up new levels of inspiration from the Creator. As you show that you respect your fear, it can stand aside and let you receive more inspiration from the Creator — God, as you understand it.

When recalling a time when you felt afraid, just hug yourself closely, go into the fear and say out loud how afraid you are. Become the fear – briefly. You don't have to do this for hours, even minutes, just briefly. And then relax into a state of as much calm and peace as you can engender. Allow the fear to be experienced as it is, rather than suppressed, subverted and altered to the point where it goes into your subconscious and reemerges later in your life to create confusion. We want to clear this confusion for you.

This is something that you can do, and the purpose of these discussions that we have, aside from activating your energies, is to give you tools you can use yourself and that are cheap and easy, so that you might be more inclined to do it.

Go into your fear briefly, experience it, locate the points in your body where you feel it most. After you come out of this meditation and you feel calm and peaceful, touch those points of your body, reassure them as one might pat or reassure a child who has fallen down and hurt itself. Reassure them and say out loud, "There, there. It will be all right. I do care about you. I do love you."

Please be willing to do this, because your physical body communicates physically and emotionally, and the purpose of this emotional exercise is to stimulate not only acceptance of your emotional body but to honor and respect it for the wonderful tool that it is.

I've been working toward an inner peace, an inner harmony, and I'm having a very, very difficult time with that. I'm trying to relate to God or a higher power as I see it, and I want to get any insights or clues about how to deal with that. It's almost a fear at times.

Your Fear's Polar Opposite

The advantage of fear is that it invariably leads you to what you are the most frightened of. And when you can identify what you are most afraid of, you will know that the true and most beneficial lesson for you will be the polar opposite of that fear. *That is the gift behind the fear.* If you are willing to practice that as an exercise, it will help you.

What do you find in your life that is of the most beauty?

Peace and quiet. Nature.

All right. Then in moments of quiet contemplation while out in nature, be clear in your understanding that nature is God and is not only peaceful and quiet, but also often violent, since sometimes the quickest path to change is sudden, and suddenness in nature is not often beauty. Beauty in nature, for example, might be a beautiful sunset or a beautiful sunrise, which takes time, whereas a bolt of lightning, which might be immensely beautiful in the moment, might also cause a forest fire. You understand?

Learn to accept the unpredictability and the paradoxical existence of God. This will allow you to not only appreciate your own value, but in time to develop a larger safety zone for yourself. Right now this planet does not feel safe to you, so it is necessary to assist yourself emotionally, since that is where your power lies. To create safety for you, learn that almost everything you were disciplined against *not* being in your childhood happens to be your strong points. What you were told *not* to be is what you really *are*, and being it will develop your power.

So utilize your imagination. Utilize "let's pretend" as a source of power. Again, look about in nature while you are out; imagine yourself as a warrior, and if no one is within eavesdropping distance, then *be* the warrior. Imagine yourself as Joan of Arc at the head of the troops. Make physical motions identified with the warrior. If you want to update that and be the female Rambo, that is all right.

But it is necessary for you to play "let's pretend" to invigorate your physical body not only with feelings of the warrior wisdom, but also to engender feelings of safety through strength. If you're willing to do this, when you play the warrior in imagination, concentrate on the warrior's great strength and the courage drawn from the emotional strength. This will help on this planet.

Material mastery is derived largely from not only feeling safe upon this planet due to your strength and wisdom, but from embracing this planet as it is, without being attached to changing it into something that it isn't. This planet functions as a material-manifesting zone. All that is thought, imagined, felt or experienced can be manifested here in some form. Since you are living in a polarized world with positivity and negativity (as you understand it) or comfort and discomfort (in reality), you will have the opportunity to manifest your fears as well as your strengths.

So the best tools you can use to sharpen your strength are your emotions, the imagination (which is your mind's link to the emotion) and your physical body (which is your physical link to spirit through the emotions). When spirit excites you with inspiration, the inspiration passes directly into your emotional body, into your physical body, and then into your mental body, which, if it is to act upon it, must stimulate itself through its imagination.

The physical body and the emotional body are absolutely and always mature. The spiritual body has some learning to do, and the mental body has the greatest amount of learning to do of all. As a species you are here largely to evolve the mental body, not only of the individual but of all mankind. The mental body is immature and perceives itself to be, due to its own self-education, superior to the physical and emotional bodies. But the reasons the physical and emotional bodies can communicate with each other instantaneously — not only telepathically but through nuance and gesture — is not because of thought but because of energetic exchange. In your current state of development, the physical and emotional bodies have reached the zenith of what they are able to do within this dimension. So it is actually quite the *opposite* as appears.

The mind has the most learning to do — to gain respect and appreciation for the other aspects of yourself, physically and emotionally. Because of the paradoxical civilization you are living in, you are trained out of a belief in your imagination in an attempt to negate it.

Imagination

The imagination is the saving grace that spirit provides for your mind. Your mind, then, in its finest moment is imaginative. Why is it that the children naturally play "let's pretend"? It is because at the very youngest ages they are less tainted with the responsibilities of adulthood, and they know and respond naturally to the whims of imagination, knowing on the greater spiritual level that imagination is the key to mental development. It is a matter of regaining what you are naturally born with. I encourage you to utilize the teachers around you. Notice children more, especially the very young ones. Notice that when they are playing, they do not question or analyze. They are spontaneous.

Utilize your imagination and all that it can do for you and with you, not to replace your life but to accent and strengthen it. Use your imagination to pretend to be the warrior or the great mother or the great lover so that you can feel emotions associated with these things. In this way you give yourself, all by yourself, the emotions that you wish brought to you by others from your point of view of the external world.

Begin to create these imagineering exercises to reengineer your life from the inside out.

Since the lack of imagination might be caused by not feeling loved, what could be a good exercise to develop imagination? Looking back, my lack of imagination has

played a negative part in my life. How do I regain it?

Develop a little homework for yourself. Incorporate a little more spontaneity. I understand that you have come to rely on the analytical aspects of your mind to separate that which is of value and that which is not. But if you are playing at this exercise and if it does not have any far-reaching impact on other aspects of your life, then I suggest that you do not overanalyze it. Let it be something in which your mind sits in the audience, in which your body and emotions are involved, and where your spirit somewhat directs not only through inspiration but your mind's level of spirituality, which is imagination.

An Exercise for Imagination

Put yourself into space, surrounded by certain childlike toys. (I'm not trying to make a fool of you, but understand that it is necessary to stimulate your imagination on the level of childhood. Therefore I encourage you to have simple things around, like a ball, maybe blocks and other simple toys, cars that you push.) As you observe them, go immediately to the ones that you are visually attracted to, because children are involved in their senses. What do things smell like? What do they taste like? Babies often put things in their mouths; they are exploring something with all of their senses, and they are exploring their senses at the same time to see what they can do.

Allow yourself to go to the toy you find the most attractive. Utilize all of your senses. Examine them not as a scientist but as a child. You might be playing with one thing while you are sticking another to the side of your face to see what it feels like.

The spontaneity here is what you wish to develop. The purpose of the exercise is to encourage you to begin to develop not only spontaneity but the feminine side of yourself (all beings have a masculine and a feminine), which utilizes the power of attraction. So as you might be attracted to someone or something beautiful, allow yourself in this exercise, which is to support greater imagination, to be attracted to the prettiest toys and to feel them, to knock them against each other a little bit to see what they sound like, or if you feel safe, to taste them a little bit and to play with them absentmindedly. Or just to bounce them off the walls to see what happens, if you are in a place where that is permitted.

The exercise is easy. It is simple. It is cheap. It is effective. And it creates for you a compartmentalized period of time in which it is not necessary for your conscious mind to rationalize the value of it.

I'm interested in two choices, both involving all kinds of aspects from personal relations to work, one in my country of origin and the other in this country. What would be the right way to go – to stay with what I can get here or go back and develop what I already have there?

A Tool for Decision-Making

In order to utilize all of your abilities, first I would suggest that you remain in residence within yourself and your own feelings when weighing these two possibilities. In this country you are dealing largely with the unknown and in your former country you are dealing with the known. Remember for a moment what it feels like back there, all right?

Go into your feelings as they are interpreted in your physical body – not in your thought. Right now, thought is a little cloudy for many people. But as you use your physical self, you might be able to incorporate a greater sense of knowledge through that secondary tool. Remember, to the best of your ability, what it's like back there. Notice how you feel in your physical body. What part of you feels one way versus another way? Go into your physical self so you can notice how you feel.

Now, I know there is some excitement about this new country, but excitement is a scattered energy, so I will ask you to use your imagination and feel into what could be (and even what *is*) in this country, and notice how your physical body feels, again from the inside out.

Choosing the old way is the home, the homeland. You will likely follow a path of recognition. You will see somewhat clearly what could be, but you will gradually experience a little more as you go along. You might become recognized there for things. In this country it is more likely that you will be somewhat invisible for a time, able to absorb from the background what this country is all about.

I do not wish to tell you what you *should* do, since that is an authoritarian position. But I will say, as gently as possible, that if you wish security you will go home, to the homeland. If you wish to have an adventure that might lead to empowerment, you will stay here. All in all, depending upon your true desires, the homeland might not allow the total you. The new land might *demand* the total you. Thus you will find life here more challenging, even though on the surface you would seem to have some freedoms that you do not experience in the old country.

But those challenges will necessarily cause you to develop and utilize latent talents and abilities that you do not identify as your own. That is, you might have to ask spirit and the Creator to provide you with more of your soul's energy in your now experience so that you can be many, many things rather than what you have been.

So I lay it out for you as gently as possible to make your own clear choice. Remember, the feelings you have associated with your now life might cause you to be confused sometimes due to pulls here versus pulls there. Either way you choose, you will find peace and happiness of a sort; here peace and happiness might take a little longer, but the rewards will also be greater.

Your lives, as they are now developing, are becoming on the surface increasingly more complicated because of the choices you have. You are being offered, my friends, so many choices, so many directions. Understand that sometimes they will seem seductive. That is, they will look and feel so good on the surface, but then after you become involved in them you see that they have a downside as well.

Recognize that it is only normal for any child or an adult with new experiences of childhood (adult child, you understand) to explore new experiences with all sides of you. You are coming into a time when you will have more of you present. That is, you're expanding your abilities. The perceptions of your senses are expanding. (This is the true meaning of extrasensory perception.) As a result, you might begin to have some experiences that you have had previously and experience it completely differently —a whole new idea, a whole new realization, a whole new feeling.

Never assume these days that just because you have tried something and it didn't work —always a disappointment —or didn't turn out the way you would have liked, that you're not going to try it again. Nowadays you are expanding so much, but you do not see it because others around you are expanding equally. Give yourself the opportunity to be more, to do more, to act more, to have more fun and to utilize all of your abilities. This is a great adventure you are on now, and sometimes it will be like a roller coaster, with ups and downs.

But it is a great adventure. Thus many individuals from other planets are here to observe all of this because of its uniqueness in the universe. Yet *you* are here. You are qualified for this life, and *it is now time*, with dedication and earnestness, *to learn to apply consciously what you have learned*. It is not a time so much of the education of the unconscious, but the application of the development and expansion of the conscious in all of its aspects: physical, mental, spiritual, emotional.

It is a wonderful time to be alive, even though there will be times of great fear. There will also be times of great reward. Use the strengths that you came with. Use your emotional body. Use your physical body. Use your spiritual body with your imagination and your mind. Use your mental body. Use all that you came here with, and you will find that your life will be easier. You have all come with those tools — body, mind, spirit and emotions. Use them all as *equals*. Judge none better than the others, and with practice you will develop not only material and spiritual mastery, but the true balance and harmony that you all seek.

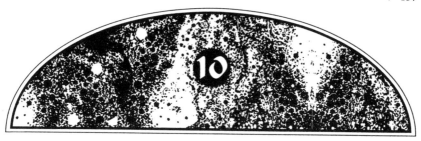

We Must Embrace the Zetas

Joopah and Zoosh
Sedona, Arizona, October 15, 1989

ood evening. Joopah speaking from the ninth-dimensional aspect. I am now fully conceived in my ninth-dimensional body, which radiates an energy physically compatible with your own. The energy being radiated is not unlike your own in its pure state. It has a quality that actually unifies us — a similarity, so to speak. That similarity is the golden light, which is the universal mastery energy of creation.

Imminent: Soul's Breach of Contract with God

The subject tonight is about Zeta Reticuli and you, and exactly why we must embrace each other. There are people living on this planet now who, by their very civilization, have the seeds of our destruction in it [Japan: see page 160]. Their civilization, although austere in many ways, has an underlying sense of struggle and emotional strangulation beneath the surface. Their eventual explosion into emotionality, which occurs on an individual level as well as on a societal level at some point in your future, will give rise in their society to the desire to do what they have had a propensity to do — control their emotions — but to go beyond a social form of control in an effort to *medically* control the emotions. That is how it will begin.

And when that begins there will be the first gesture taken toward the soul's manifestation of its breach of contract with God. God, or the Universal One, has created all life to have certain elements. You are given opportunities to work with some elements more than others, and the opportunities are there for your own choosing. That is, you might choose to think more than feel; yet the feelings will be present, though you may not choose to be aware of them.

The change, then, by today's societies is to move beyond the limits of technology. As you have created it, technology has been the seed of our destruction. In my culture there has been an inevitable desire to create the finest technological replication of ourselves. I have stated for some time in various forms of myself that we do not create ourselves as you: We clone. I would also state that if we had to create ourselves as you, we would be unable to do so, for we do not have the physical properties of biological duplication as you do. The reason we don't is because we have had a desire to improve on technology to the point where it can improve on itself without our assistance. In other words, we desired to create a society in which the mind and technology become one, and our bodies are largely a result. Not only that, but we also created the challenge of a reduced connection to the Great Spirit, or God. We are up against it now, as you say.

I have not been created in this ninth-dimensional body by my technological society. No, my recent body in my society has ceased to exist. The ninth dimension of myself was created by the Creator of all things. I have been placed back into my society in the ninth-dimensional version of myself to offer an opportunity to my society to begin again. The greatest difference between my ninth-dimensional body and the bodies of my fellow beings in our civilization now is that I have the ability to reproduce myself without technological means. I do not need another one of my culture to do it; I can do it on not exactly a biogenetic scale, but on what would be closer to an etheric-biological level. That is, I can produce the etheric self as well as the biological self.

This is important to note, since you largely do this yourself, though you state through various religions and so on that the soul is provided by the Creator. I understand that is true with myself as well, since the Creator has created me without technological means.

Needed: A Fond Memory for What Was

This is revolutionary: *my* society needs to turn from technology, and *your* society needs to know that this rush pell mell toward technology as the savior is really a false god. As you know, your technology has produced many miracles that would be called great joys, certainly, by those who have been saved medically, physically and so on by technological means. But you might look at your planet. It is almost beyond repair in its pollution; your weather will show you this in the next few years. It is becoming increasingly unpredictable due to the Earth's need to purge the effects of pollution.

Our souls are *your* souls — exactly the same. You are not genetically connected with us, but on the soul level you are. To reach a level of understanding about technology that will allow you to perceive the value of Earth as a place of joy and a place of nature, due to the nature of your society you need to develop a fond memory of what was. I am not predicting dire gloom and doom, but I am suggesting that in terms of nature, what was is leaving.

Many of your animal species are leaving now. Their genes will become dormant and remain in the planet's genetic makeup to be revived again at some point in the future when they can exist without pollution and without civilizations such as your own that do not understand their role in the whole system here.

There are other things that are leaving as well: plants, certainly aspects of Earth. You know the ozone-layer business. I will not insult your intelligence by going into that, but there are aspects of the aura of Mother Earth that also have holes in them. You cannot exist with a permanent hole in your auric field without inevitably developing a disease (as you would call it) directly associated with those holes. Because Mother Earth has holes in her aura, she must repair them in order to perpetuate herself. Since Earth will survive the coming years, the repairs must be radical. Mother Earth will do what she must.

You have the opportunity to change all this and make it different by not only what you think but what you do. *It is so very important what you do in your daily life, how you perceive yourself.* If you can, simply allow yourself to become what you desire to be and give up some of the habits that reassure you that the human race is of less value. That is all. It is necessary to become somewhat naive, as you might call it: to have faith that you can get through this and to develop appreciation for your fellow human beings. And if I might write out my prescription – to wean yourself from the news.

The news as it is now set up, regardless of its justification to exist, is perhaps the *chief cause of internal destruction* on this planet. On the soul and spiritual level it creates an atmosphere of defeatism. Even though it is well-intended, it is working against you. However, it can exist; I do not intend to discourage its existence. I do ask you to begin to wean yourself from it. Watch less on TV. Read less in the newspapers. Have fewer discussions with each other about things that you read that are negative about human beings. Those of you who pray, do so with hope rather than with dread.

Current Mass Decisions Profoundly Affect the Future

That is my opening statement. I make it somewhat dramatic to underline the word *must*. With Zeta Reticuli we have achieved a high level of technology, yes, but it was necessitated by the soul decision that your societies — one in particular — will make due to the extremes of conditions that will exist here on this planet. Mother Earth, of course, must create those extremes in her auric field. She must fire up her boilers, in a sense, to survive. And you might feel that not only as a slight increase in warmth in summer seasons, but also in an increase in emotional passion. Of course, you know that there are many forms of passion.

The decisions made in the coming years, since you are now in a time period when decisions are made en masse — will absolutely affect the future. Since you are shifting dimensions, this time slot will create your souls' future expressions. *You are in a time period when any mass decision made subconsciously, unconsciously and consciously by people on this planet will inevitably create your future expression.*

It cannot be stopped, your shift into the fourth dimension. No, it cannot be stopped. However, you might find that as your souls choose to explore the technology that will be abandoned on this planet, an offshoot of yourselves will go on to explore it in the form of the Zeta Reticuli race. It is true that the Zeta Reticuli race has predated you, but you must understand that *souls* do not travel in linear time, and *they will seek to finish everything that they have begun.* I encourage you to not abandon the forms of nature that are about you and to live in this whole system so that when some of you go on to create the Zeta Reticuli system, you bring with you a willingness to allow nature as well as technology to take their course.

The Zeta Reticuli civilization is a monument to evolutionary technology. The system runs itself as we exist on our planet. An example: If there arises any need within our civilization for any product, our technology does not require even the push of a button, since it responds along the lines of the mental brain-wave activity of the civilization to produce what we need. Not simply automatically; it produces in a way that *we have it.* It functions in terms of time and space and interdimensional aspects — this can all be produced by technology. If we need something, some material object, our technology will create a ripple in time which will create that object so that the need *never arises!*

While this is advantageous technologically and materially, it cannot be done on a soul level. We have a vacuum there. *Only you can do this.* You literally have our lives in your hands. Because even though our society will continue on the ninth-dimensional aspect of itself, it now appears certain that the society that existed on the seventh-dimensional aspect, in which I lived most recently, will be utterly and completely obliterated. I am in the ninth-dimensional body so that my fellow beings can see where they will be going.

Now, recognize that they are not going to the eighth dimension. In order to survive on the eighth dimension there must be a full and total embracing of the natural order — *nature*, as you understand it. Since the society that lives on the seventh dimension of Zeta Reticuli does not understand the natural order because they are largely a product of technology (even though there are some biological materials still within the brain), they cannot do that. They are simply unable, so that door to the eighth dimension is closed to them. Most will go to the ninth dimension, and it is a fine place to be. You still might be able to open that door, since any embracing of nature that you can do will include an embracing of the essence of mankind.

Breakdown of Normal Information Systems

This will be hard for you to do in the coming days. It will absolutely, positively, require faith. It cannot be done in any way, shape or form by looking for justifiable results based upon the facts — in other words, by any scientific or research data collected as the result of your normal information systems. Most of you use the news as your normal information systems and will have every justifiable reason to lose faith in humanity through that informational system in the coming years. So I am suggesting that you develop faith in the human being's ability to rise above the obvious. I say "the obvious" because the news and world events will cause you to believe that goodwill has left the human race. But I can assure you that if you do not use these sources of information and instead begin to use your own feelings — even going into some small town to observe the interactions of people who are not overwhelmed by the technological crush of larger cities — you will see that, contrary to the rumors and reports that will abound, goodwill amongst mankind has not died.

I am encouraging you to do this. It is not a major homework lesson, but it is something I encourage you to do because it is essential. I might also add that there will be continuing annoyances in the form of technological breakdowns in your society. You'll find that those technologies you have come to depend upon will begin to break down — such as public utilities, including the telephone system. You might say this has something to do with human beings, but I will say that even though that can be proven, it really has to do with the Creator chiding you and showing you that you have become somewhat a slave to your own technology rather than the other way around. And that the only way for you to see what you have done is to *have* to learn how to communicate and contact each other with less technology. Thus the technological problems will occur in established technologies that you have come to depend upon. This is necessary.

It is really a primer, in a sense. In several senses you are being primed to change and at the same time you are using a primer as children might use: "Basic Earth Education I." *You need other people to survive.* You could say, "Well, people can survive out in the wilderness on their own." It is true that you can do that physically, even mentally and spiritually to some extent. But emotionally you have moments of great song and enjoyment with each other, although not so much by yourself. Quality of life is a factor here.

You are here with all these people on this planet to learn to appreciate each other in your diversity, *not* to create a sameness out of a necessity to reduce chaos. Remember that *the flip side of chaos is creativity and uniqueness.* It is a very, very, narrow realm between the two. Sometimes you suppress creativity under the guise of suppressing chaos. As any good scientist knows, nature operates in what appears to the casual observer to be a most chaotic fashion. Yet if you simply understand the rules of the game, you can see that chaos is necessary to the act of creation and that a society that seems to be out of control might actually be creating a *new form* of society.

The Zeta Role

For you to know how we must change, I have stated what *you* must begin to do for us. But it is also important for you to know what *we* must do, since by our actions we can ease the burden and pressure on you. Because you must make a cosmic leap in faith, we must also begin to make our leap.

My civilization, as I understand it now, is really a civilization that has created a form of technological god. The elements in your society that cause an individual to believe in the Creator or the God force might be like a physician who witnesses childbirth and knows that mankind could never create such an organism on its own with the creativity involved in the inception of such an idea. Things like this challenge your philosophers.

My society does not have that reinforcement wherein you shake your head and say, "There must be a Creator of all things because I cannot explain this thing that is happening." That idea does not occur in our society on Zeta Reticuli, since we can point to a technological or mental cause or explanation for everything in our society.

This is why, from my current understanding, the Creator has urged us to be in contact with your society from its beginning, so that even though we did not have that mystery in our society, we could see how another society uses it. We have been exposed to you since you have begun, and there has been a sufficient accumulation of knowledge during that time for us to appreciate that what you have, even with all of its challenges and difficulties, is worth having. Understand that *the value of life is life itself.* But as you move away from spontaneous life and creativity with a desire to create the ultimately ordered society (which is what we have), you remove yourself from any possibility of experiencing the true natural order. As a result, what *we* must do in order to make it easier for you to have the leap of faith I have requested you to work toward, is experience technological breakdowns so that my society's god of technology fails them. Because time is moving on for us and members of the society of the seventh dimension of Zeta Reticuli are dying out and not being reproduced, the Creator has seen to it that we are confronted with the fallibility of technology. Technology is unable to change it because it must be changed on the soul level. It took at least a thousand years for us to have a glimmer of understanding of this in our time frame.

You must understand our technology: If we needed a material object, our technology would create a ripple in time so that we didn't need it. *We had it before we felt a need for it.* We had come to perceive our physical bodies as material objects in our dimension. That removes us slightly, you see, from the Creator. So it became necessary for the Creator, as I understand it now, to create a problem that our technology could not solve.

So our civilization was forced to look beyond a technological solution for our problem [dying race] for so many millennia that I cannot even mention (the numbers are too ridiculous); we had to look beyond the answer that was natural to us. What we perceived to be the natural order was technology, you see, albeit thought technology, and it became the technological god, which failed us. The only thing we could do is look to the past to discover why.

Joopah's Role for Zetas, How That Helps Humans

Therefore we must make a change to ease you, and that change must be on the spiritual level. My body was created by the Creator – God, you understand – something that is technologically impossible on the seventh-dimensional aspect of Zeta Reticuli. I have been placed on the seventh-dimensional aspect to be a teacher who can be a peer to them, one they can understand. My body radiates light, and the radiation of that light stimulates spiritual-philosophical enlightenment. As a result, there is a natural desire to have more of it. Those who come in contact with my body want more and are left with a little bit of it themselves just through the contact.

The only way they can have more is to reach beyond technology, and we're beginning to do it. It might not be enough to save us, but it might be enough to create an easing of your need to create order above all else.

I state to you quite clearly now that *you will all have a desire to create order in your society above all else very soon.* You will soon have experiences in your government where you will feel that its moral foundation and structure has gone mad, and you will desire order at any cost. So when each and every one of you in this room now have that desire for order, remember that *out of chaos comes a new order.* In your case it will be an appreciation for the natural order of nature and Earth that was set up specifically and ideally *just for you* as you exist in your physical and spiritual selves. It is that simple.

Do not fear great misery in the future. Simply know that what you have come to depend on might not be as reliable as it once was. But what you know to be true – goodwill in mankind and womankind for each other – will remain, contrary to the reports you receive. Learn to have faith in goodwill, for that will be your salvation.

Which society is about to suppress their emotions in a way that will cause a problem?

Recognize that I am not criticizing this society. But in the not-too-distant future Japan will be involved in a crisis [the subway poison-gassing in 1995] that will cause them to examine their method of expressing their emotions. In several years they will make this effort, due to the availability of the tools to medically suppress emotions, though it will not be called that. It will be praised as a new method of suppressing rage. I will say that even though rage does have a lot of serious consequences, it is also very often *the final element of frustration that precedes some form of magnificent creativity,* as any inventor would know. Their seemingly innocent genetic manipulation will lead to a wide variety of influence in the emotional body.

There has been for some time an effort by science to regulate the emotional self. It has been done with all good intent, with the clear desire to eliminate what is destructive in the human being but not to eliminate the constructive aspect of emotionality. However, it is like a fine and intricate creation: when you tinker with it, even though you are attempting to fine-tune it, sometimes you inadvertently throw a wrench in the works. This wrench might see its beginning in Japan.

Creativity Needed for the Cosmic Leap

If they don't *do it, will that have an effect on you, since you are our future?*

Yes. It is uncertain at this time if there is any way to prevent it, since it will be perceived to be a scientific breakthrough of such great magnitude that it will be, in the words of the time, "so desperately needed now" that the creators will likely receive the Nobel prize. I'm not suggesting worldwide chaos, but through the eyes of some people it will

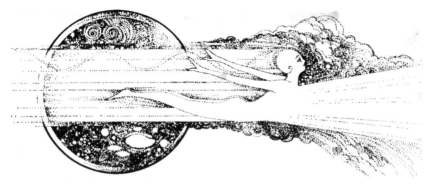

seem to be chaos. When you were children, you or your parents assumed that the philosophy of the teenagers of the time was chaotic, right? So recognize that *chaos is in the eye of the beholder.* That assumption of chaos will possibly block an aspect of creativity that is needed to make the cosmic leap. It will not block the change to the fourth dimension, but it might limit the way it will be resolved. But it will not help us.

How can we help? What can we do? Disseminate the information?

Yes, that is all, really – disseminate the information. Simply know that genetics, while it seems to be a wonderful tool – and you will see, all of you, that in the next ten years almost everything will be affected by it – it also carries the potential of being a false god. Something that looks wonderful on the surface, but by the time you're fully committed to it you discover its horrible side effect: the gradual eroding away of the belief that you really can do things considered impossible [dealing with rage]. As you all know, and certainly as every athlete knows, impossible-to-break records are continually broken.

Applications of the Genetic Discovery

How will this be applied to mankind? In what way? How would it work? How would they use it? In schools or in hospitals?

It would be applied as you indicate, through the use of the idea that technology is the ultimate savior, though the idea will not be stated clearly like that. I'm not suggesting that a religion or philosophy will develop with the machine as its fountainhead. Rather, I suggest that you will be surrounded with stimuli through the news and other information-disseminating sources that will heap continual praise upon what will be called the new science of genetics. It will be assumed that nothing that was perceived to be a limit is a limit anymore, thanks to genetics. Of course, it will be very helpful in disease; this is what it was really intended for, to assist the body in developing strength, to assist the body in developing stronger organs and so on rather than to eliminate organisms. In your society you're surrounded with organisms all the time, but it is through your *ability to be unaffected* by these organisms that you are not affected. The real purpose of genetics is to simply allow you to develop stronger organs and systems so that you can become more durable – not to create a germ-free society so that you necessarily become less durable. You were created to be survivors; that is the nature of your race.

Are you suggesting that at some point technology can become ungodly or somehow the opposite of God?

Of course, philosophically speaking, that is impossible, since all was created by the Creator. What I am suggesting is that the Creator is, in a sense, thinking out loud by allowing technology. One can almost imagine the Creator saying, "I wonder what would happen if . . ." I cannot say that technology in its own right could ever be ungodly or that anything that is ever created could be ungodly. What I am suggesting is that it could be *perceived* to be greater than anything the Creator could do. One must take that further: it could be perceived on the individual level *to be greater than any individual's aspect of the Creator* – specifically, their ability to create or their ability to beat the odds or do the impossible. All of these things your society is known for. That is what I mean by a false god. Instead of adding to your strength, it will sap it, stifle creativity, make you believe that all of your needs can be provided by the great god technology.

How many of the Zetas have moved into ninth-dimensional bodies now?

Three.

How are you treated by your race? Do they understand fully what you're doing?

Not fully. But it is most interesting, in that they clearly are experiencing something . . . I cannot really say individually, but those who are in my proximity experience what can only be described as a rush of emotion. It is a feeling of warmth and upliftment that any one of you who has a spiritual experience might understand. It is a warmth and upliftment they have not felt on a physical level before. As a result, there is clearly a new experience going on. But this type of experience will require a great deal of time to be developed into what you call the hundredth-monkey syndrome.

Will you reproduce yourself as an example for them?

Yes. That is why there are two others. Yet that is enough for now.

Passion and Imagination: Your Greatest Achievement

You spoke of having many different kinds of passion. Could you elaborate more on the various kinds of passion?

Of course, that would take a lot of time. As much as I understand, there is the passion that leads to embrace, that is, drawing toward oneself. And there is the passion that is the result of pushing away – protection, essentially. I would say that even though there is, as you say, the downside to passion, *the upside has been precisely what your civilization has been created for.* This is so that you would be urged to feel, by way of various examples, that the apparent limits that exist around you do not have to limit your imagination or some one outstanding moment. One outstanding moment, for example, might be the passion necessary to break the runner's four-minute mile. That is now common, yes? But before that time it was considered impossible. That type of passion has its value, yes? It is this type of passion that is generated by many imaginations as well as a desire to do what others have not done. That is really the greatest achievement of your civilization.

Now, I'm not saying that you have achieved or created passion in its own right, because it was given to you. But you have survived it! Other civilizations have not done so. When I compliment you, very often it is because of your ability to survive. You were created to be survivors. You were created to bring that survivability and that lust for life to other civilizations that had given up, for various reasons, on their own ability to do the same, inspiring them to develop aspects of themselves they have given up on. *Passion and your ability to survive it is right now your crowning glory.*

I will say that (what do they say in the hospital?) you are doing as well as can be expected under the circumstances. And the circumstances will alter themselves somewhat in the future. Again, do not become overly alarmed by what you see in your information services. Alarm and agitation are in the air. It is necessary. There is a sense of urgency. Mother Earth herself is urgently changing herself for her own comfort, so you will all feel her sense of urgency and her desire to make quick repairs. Mother Earth desires to re-create her natural order; that is why *you* will have the desire to create order. In your societies it will seem to be the most necessary thing. But you will achieve the best order for you if you observe nature and emulate it in its most beautiful ways rather than perfect only the aspects of nature perceived in films of the eagle grasping its prey. Remember that the eagle not only grasps it prey, but it provides insight and wisdom to the natural world that is available to all of you. And I will say good evening.

Well, all right. Zoosh here. Any questions? I will comment on my friend Joopah. It is a bit of a struggle for him to function in the channeling mode right now, since while he was sending this line of information and energy through Robert, he was fully surrounded by his own citizens. He speaks to you now from his planet, you see, not from his ship. He is no longer involved in the Earth exercise wherein he had plenty of time to do many things. His extracurricular activities don't exist now; he is full time in the curriculum. As a result he is developing a relatively new skill of doing many, many things at once. It will take a little time for him to be able to speak at length. All right, a question.

Animals: Aspects of Mankind's Potential

He said that we didn't understand the role of animals. What is your perception as to the role of animals on this planet?

In large part they each represent a certain aspect of your own potentials, abilities, or that which exists. The eagle, as mentioned by Joopah, would have to do with your ability to see over the mountain. Using your imagination, the eagle represents power and has been shown on many seals because of its ability to zoom in on its prey and devastate it. That is how the eagle survives. But it is not only that; the eagle always wants to move beyond and see the next canyon. Those of you who observe eagles will notice that they don't tend to hang around the same place all the time. They will perhaps stop for a moment and have a new brood, but then they will move on. They are the pioneers, the explorers. They always need to know what's on the other side of the mountain. So eagles represent the wisdom of imagination that stimulates the desire to follow through.

Eagles and other animals all represent certain aspects of mankind's potential. They also represent certain aspects of mankind's inability to see himself or herself as a true representative of nature. That is, they have a downside, something you can criticize. Certainly if you have ever been on the receiving end of an army that used an eagle as its symbol, you might well feel that the eagle is not something that you would want to embrace.

Does Joopah's work on the ninth dimension make him a kind of Zeta Christ?

I would not go that far. I can understand that you might have that feeling, but after all, he is not evolved that far, for starters. You might say that he is in training, but it will take some time. The analogy does not exactly fit, you see, since the idea of a savior is not what is being sought there. It is not exactly true, but it certainly has aspects that are similar.

Isn't the genetics that the Zetas are doing with the Earth beings now the basis of the development of the ninth-dimensional body? Or what is that relationship?

Not really. That is a separate situation in which there was a desperate attempt by the Zeta culture to create a secondary species. That is, since they perceive their own species dying out, they felt it was essential to create a species that would largely represent them but would be durable. They felt it was essential, and since you were their past lives (in terms of soul, though they didn't understand that until recently), they felt they had permission. After all, the Creator had told them to be involved with you from the beginning, so they felt they had permission to create a hybrid between the human being and the Zeta Reticuli race, which would have the secondary advantage of being able to communicate not only with the Zeta race but also the human race more as an equal. You might have a mixed marriage in which the child learns the languages and cultures of both individuals and could get along to a degree in either culture; it is a similar situation in this case.

The primary motive of the creation of this secondary hybrid species would be to carry on with the information and energy of the originating race, since the Zetas would possibly die out in their seventh dimension. This secondary race will carry on, not necessarily their work, but the inheritance of all the information that was gleaned by the Zetas over these many years as well as their philosophy — and, of course, a desire to find the answers to the questions that were unanswered by the Zeta race. So it is not exactly the same thing, no.

He said that the Creator created his body. How do you perceive the Creator in the ninth dimension?

Exactly the same as you would perceive It in this dimension, but in the ninth dimension It is more of a feeling. That is, It is not so abridged by the many voices. For example, there are many voices in Earth culture that point to what or who is the Creator. Who is God? What is God specifically? There is no competition at the ninth dimension for the specific of God. Because the idea "God" (or the Creator, as It is more universally called) is a feeling, something that is felt. You hear from time to time from people who have had a momentary death, some type of accident where they have died for a few minutes and then have come back remembering the contact with the Creator through the feeling of an overwhelming, unconditional love. That feeling of unconditional love is how you would physically relate to a passage of energy through the self. You can feel it now, but it is a subtle energy, and you are very distracted in your society. You also could do this if you eliminate some of your distractions.

One of the distractions is obviously the desire to feel the support from others that what you believe to be true is true. That is an underlying distraction, and that is also, paradoxically speaking, what drives you to your many varieties of experience.

The Status of the Hybrids

Has the physiognomy of the hybrids been pretty regular? How have they been developing?

They are autonomous now. They do not need the parent race (as they perceive the Zetas) to exist. They have developed their own civilization sufficiently and are currently developing their own technology. They have inherited, of course, vehicles for travel as well as the technological belief system of the Zetas to some extent. But since they contain about 49% humanity plus sprinklings of other things, they have the desire to emotionalize technology. As a result, while your society might be confronted with the need to move beyond emotion, they are moving toward it. Since they find it desirable, inevitably they will totally and completely alter the technology of the Zetas to become something that is more involved with the Creator, in the sense of spontaneity. They might just be the ones who develop space vehicles that look like birds and natural forms of life.

What dimension are they? Could we interact with them at this point if they were to visit?

They were created to be flexible. They can exist comfortably in many dimensions. Their natural existence would be (since everything is shifting now) somewhere between the fifth and the sixth. But they can actually exist with minimal technological support in your dimension.

Have they come here?

Only briefly to isolated areas simply to test that it can be done.

Are they interested in their one natural parent on this planet?

Their Adam and Eve is not one. If we were to speak of natural parents, we would have to say *three* natural parents. Since the technology and the genetic structure of the Zetas was involved (a technological genetic, you understand) as well as the masculine and the feminine aspect of the Earth being, we are talking about three parents. So yes, they are interested.

Were the Zetas involved in the alien landing in Russia last week [Vorozhnev]? Or was that a government public-relations thing?

It is not a public-relations event and the Zetas were not involved. That has to do with a civilization that has been on this planet and underneath the surface for some time.

Going back to this hybrid race, does it have a name?

It has a name, yes. I do not wish to sound coy, but I will not state it at this time. I will state it soon, all right? (The inevitable "soon.")

Would you comment on the relationship between the government and the Zetas?

I have done so at length before, but briefly I will say that the government of the United States has made what it perceives to be a treaty with the Zetas, but has actually made a treaty with a group of individuals that have very cleverly disguised themselves to look like the Zetas. That is the problem they are dealing with right now. They actually have, however, a working understanding with the Zetas, but the treaty is with someone else. It is a long subject, my friend. I will say, kindly refer to other tapes.

What is your perception of how we can best aid the situation that Joopah talked about? He gave us a list of several things we can do – have faith and wean ourselves from the news and so on. What would your answer be?

I would say that it is all right to have your understanding of realism. That is, it is all right to lock the doors at night before you go to sleep. Certainly, do whatever helps you to feel safe. But learn how to differentiate between what represents safety to you and what is actually a way of keeping the world away from you. You will all need each other in the coming years. Learn how to develop a way to allow yourself to work with and be with others regardless of what or who you think they might be. There will be plenty of opportunities to develop suspicions about individuals you have always trusted, because the rumor that human beings are being cloned and spread across the face of the Earth will move beyond rumor in the coming years and be supported by some justifiable evidence. You might have cause for moments to consider, "Well, is he really my husband?" So learn to develop ways to differentiate between the two.

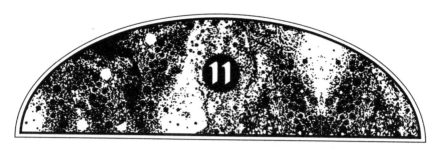

Roswell, ETs and the Shadow Government

Zoosh and Riodhdah
Sedona, Arizona, October 17, 1989, and January 14, 1995

What can you tell us about the Roswell incident? Is what has been reported accurate? What caused the alien craft to crash, and of what race were the beings onboard?

The beings onboard were from Sirius (not negative Sirians) and the vehicle crashed simply to create an enigma on this Earth, seen from a larger perspective. They experienced magnetic radiation from nearby radar experiments. At that time [July 1947] radar work was going on near the military base, and a lot of magnetic and electrical energy was being broadcast. The military did not realize radar's potential as a weapons technology, since they were looking in a different direction. The effect might be described as a magnetic or electrical storm, but it was not deliberate; it was something they were doing on their own for their own purposes. They had no idea it would destroy life anywhere; one might say that it was an accident. But it created an enigma.

They were reported to be four feet tall. Please describe them.

They are known to look similar to the Zetas. There was another crash near that time in which the beings were three to three-and-a-half feet tall, but were rather like humans. These were also from Sirius.

So there are different life forms from Sirius?

Oh, many different life forms, just like in your own constellation [solar system]. After all, variety is the spice of life!

What is the bigger picture concerning a crashed disk in Aztec, New Mexico, in 1948? It was reported that human body parts were found onboard. Is this accurate?

I would say they were not *human* body parts, but that the individuals who were in that ship (there were more than one race of beings present) had those spare parts available. I am not going to pump up the idea that there are aliens living below the surface who are raising human beings for food. Allowing for the nature of medicine and genetics, finding spare parts in a medical lab would not be considered unusual. It was a medical ship.

But they said everything else was incinerated. Why weren't these parts incinerated?

The ship had a self-destruct mechanism onboard, as they often do. But again — enigma. It is necessary to give human beings enigmas, you know, because otherwise you become complacent.

When do we get out of that game?

Never, hopefully, since you are the Explorer Race. It is not your future destiny to know it all. As a race, physically speaking, what would be the advantage? You were not created to know it all; you were created to *want* to know it all. Quite a difference. If you want to know it all, you will never stop looking; you will go to the farthest ends of the universe in search of knowledge. Your real destiny will be fulfilled by the ground that you cover rather than by what you find. It is the job of the Explorer Race to touch other races and stimulate them so that they will move out of their complacency and find other goals to perfect rather than the ones they have already perfected over and over. The universe is quite stagnant in many places and needs to be stimulated. That is where *you* come in!

What can you tell us about EBE? What race was he, and what role did he play in the whole extraterrestrial scenario?

You are referring to the terminology "extraterrestrial biological entity"?

Yes, the one they called EBE, the one they captured.

I will call him, rather, an "enigmatic" biological entity. It was his job to fulfill that enigma. After all, if one finds bodies or residual effects of life, one is going to be startled, amazed and intrigued. But if one finds someone who is alive, then one has to look very deeply within one's soul and say, "Maybe what I've believed all along really isn't so." After all, it is one thing to see a smashed butterfly on the windshield and quite another to see one flying by in all of its glory. It is also one thing to hear someone speak French on a record and quite another to have them meet you and speak French to you.

Understand that there are levels of enigma that must be stimulated. I am putting forth this idea so that you will realize how vital it is that you be stimulated with the unexplainable so that those who would state unequivocally that something is not true, when confronted with the *reality*, must move off their position.

The most important thing that this enigmatic biological entity had to do was survive, because many people, in their desperate need to believe that extraterrestrial intelligence was not real, would want to destroy it. And the best way to stay alive was to allow itself to be captured by those who would want to keep it alive at all costs. After all, if EBE was running around on Main Street, somebody would probably pull out the old rifle and level him.

So he was caught by scientists, taken to a base and talked to, right?

As best they could, yes. They are reluctant to use telepaths, though they sometimes do.

It is said there was a colonel who was a telepath.

Yes. It was difficult for the colonel, but he did it because otherwise it would necessarily compromise his position. Needless to say, his military career was not enhanced by the communication; telepaths are not considered to be valuable.

But they are now.

They are only within the context of their profession, but they are generally considered a threat. After all, when one lives in a world where secrecy and top secrecy and cosmic secrecy is a factor, the idea of having telepaths running around is pretty scary.

Did he communicate with EBE? Did he get information that was or was not accurate?

It was accurate as far as it went – that is the factor to remember. It would be like a parent talking to a child. The parent might tell the child a story, as in the case of Bible stories, which are told very simply. Yet as one gets older one realizes how complicated the Bible really is. So in a sense, what he was told was the simple story.

When EBE's life was in danger, Earth broadcast a message into space trying to save his life. Why was it not responded to? Was it ever received?

It was responded to. It was requested that the individual be returned.

And?

He was not.

So there was no further communication.

There was, but it was not heeded. There was a request.

Can you comment on the role the media is playing in the public dissemination of information about the UFO and extraterrestrial situation?

Most reporters feel they are doing a job, but at the upper levels (those who work *behind* the press – that is, involved with the Order), it is recognized that the dissemination of information (by the press or by word of mouth — gossip) is a system. It is necessary to go slowly.

In order to disseminate the information in a way that is less threatening, it is necessary to use humor. So you will very often find that those who report news of UFOs, even if they've seen them themselves, will be somewhat jocular — not necessarily the eyewitnesses, but the reporters. This is essential so that people do not panic. That is a real threat. I am not talking about individuals who feel that other life forms are welcome; I am talking about individuals who feel that they want their lives to be predictable and are involved in religions, philosophies or political groups that tend to create predictability. What happens when predictability is thrown to the winds and they have nothing they can grasp and say is true? That is why the concern about panic is real.

But after forty years?

It is no less real today than it was then. The only change is that during this time movies and books have been produced. There is so-called science fiction as well as trial-balloon factual movies such as *UFOs Are Real* and so on.

But you are saying that it has not really sunk into the subconscious of humanity yet.

It might be totally in the unconscious and might have sunk into the subconscious — but then, is humanity respectful of the subconscious, or is it simply reactive with it?

Reactive. But you'd think it would be there as sort of an inner knowing after all this time.

It can be an inner knowing, but it could also in some cases — perhaps many cases — be an inner dread. It is necessary to treat the subject with the same reverence as one treats a religion, because there are many religions that would be utterly destroyed in their own concept of themselves if this knowledge gets out. That is why the Order is careful. There are ways to do it. After all, if you are going to give people an injection that will save them, it is rather useless to give them one that will kill the disease but destroy their body.

Or scare them to death before the injection has time to work.

That is why inoculation has become popular in medicine. That gives them a little bit of the experience, yes? That is why so many people have had contact experiences. Do you understand the significance of what I am saying? Many, many people have had contact experiences, because they are being "inoculated," *gradually* given the experience. Almost everyone, if they were to be hypnotized, would remember something having to do with a UFO contact. It is not rare; I have stated that. What is rare is that people remember it.

Do you mean almost everyone on the planet?

Almost everyone on the planet has been inoculated — that is, given some element of the experience.

Are they programmed to remember at a certain time?

It is not necessary to remember. The main thing that is necessary is to not panic when the revelations begin to occur.

Who are the Grays? What are the different subgroups of the Gray race, and what is their origin?

Many people refer to the Zetas as the Grays, so it depends on what you mean by the Grays. Some of the Zetas look rather gray in their appearance because of various electronic devices, in addition to some having a skin color that approaches a grayish pallor.

In these contacts they talk about the large-nosed Grays. What is that?

In my experience, there are no Zeta beings that have noses. If they are talking about beings who have noses, they are not from Zeta Reticuli! Some of this is disinformation, and some is a reference to a variation from negative-Sirian cloning escapades. There have been occasional forays into creating slightly larger nostrils for Zetas in their attempts to crossbreed humans and Zetas, but they have been failures.

It has been said that everyone who has been abducted has been implanted. Which races use implants?

There are no less than 49 races in your twentieth century. They all use implants, every one of them.

And the purpose of these implants?

To stimulate some function within the body. In the old days they were used by unsophisticated groups to track people. They were unable to use an individual's specific energy imprint gathered by the analysis of their auric energy field, called field-tracking, so they used what you would call homing devices. The devices are now used mainly to stimulate certain activities within the brain or nervous system.

This is Riodhdah, elder of the Pleiadian society, in charge of the project involving this person, Edward.* In our time, we have been informed that we must make a greater attempt to be involved with you. We have been told that the connection between us is stronger than ever, but in practical application, we cannot bring our ships as close as we once did to your place and your time, because your people have devel-

---

* Edward Page. This is in response to questions about Page's report at the UFO Congress in Nevada at the end of November 1994, printed in the March 1995 issue of the *Sedona Journal of Emergence!*

oped a means to deflect us and keep us at a distance. So we have had to use time. So far your people have not figured out how to deflect our missions in time.

A Pleiadian Project of the 40s and 50s

We contacted a scientist from your world and brought him aboard a ship, told him our purpose, asked if he would help us, and he said he would. To repay him for his cooperation, we shared with him freely the wisdom we had accumulated – no wisdom that could cause harm, only what could cause good. And he was told he could not overly influence your society with inventions coming out of this discussion, but that he could plant the seeds of the discussion, the seeds of our wisdom, in time sequences by placing Pleiadian energy, through the use of a codifying device, into certain children. This person was not known as a scientist in his time, but as a physician, an obstetrician.

He was given a device. It looks a lot like a crystal, and occasionally, because of his sense of humor, he would leave it lying about on a counter with some pretty rocks he had collected (he liked rocks). He felt that hiding it in plain sight was the best thing he could do. This crystal could be held over the abdomen of a pregnant woman and, with her soul's permission, would function to insert a Pleiadian time line and Pleiadian energy, light and love into the child. It would not replace the child's soul; it would embrace the soul, nurture it. And with that Pleiadian time line and energy, the person's sequence of ordinary Earth life would be altered. The birth time would usually occur later; it might go past term by a week or two. And when the child was born, regardless of the time line that its natural Earth birth would have taken, that child would also have been on the Pleiadian time line.

In the case of Eddy, his death did not coincide with the death time of his Pleiadian time line, so he was reenergized and lived.

On one of your ships?

Yes. And at that time it was explained to him who he was, how he came to be here, and what was best for him to do from that point on – that he could speak of these things when he was ready, but that certain things were not safe to speak of. So although it was explained to him there, these things were extracted from him, using a time process; thus it would not even be in his unconscious and could not be removed by any means. Nevertheless, his body chemistry had the knowledge installed in it, and since you do not yet have interrogation methods that can analyze the DNA and the cellular chemistry of a person's body for memories (you're working on it, but you're not there yet), it would be impossible to extract. It would create in a person a sense of relaxation, a sense of knowing without having words and knowledge and pictures to support it. So the person would feel better and there would not be a means by which to divulge the information. In this way all parties are protected.

So Eddy and many others were created in this way, as long as their souls gave permission. The device that the doctor used looked very much like an ordinary crystal – not a rock per se, but a polished crystal, except that it had a rounded end and was faceted and pointed. And the doctor would sometimes explain it away when working on his patients (you have to remember that it was in the early days then) as being a special device that made it easier for him to feel the child, or some other simple excuse that didn't require a lot of technical explanation.

So the pregnant women, the mothers, didn't know?

They didn't know. It was felt that it would be better not to involve them any more than was necessary, for their own protection – remember, in those days people did not speak so freely about UFOs and ETs.

This is forties, fifties, thirties?

I'd say late forties or fifties. The doctor-scientist spoke of it as little as possible to protect the people. He influenced the births of about 200 people. Some of these individuals are no longer on Earth. Some of them have ended their natural cycles, both within the Earth and the Pleiadian time lines. Some have been picked up from their locations and taken into the future. This is still a possibility for Eddy, though it might just be that he will end his Pleiadian time line (he has already ended his Earth time line and is living his Pleiadian time line right now) and simply end his cycle and pass over. But it is still possible that under ideal circumstances he might be picked up and taken to the future and live out his life there. It depends entirely on his attachments here and his friends and so on.

He's saying that he was adopted at one month of age because of who he was and how he came into being. Did the doctor arrange for the adoptions of these children?

You must remember that in those days when a young woman would get pregnant out of wedlock, it was not tolerated so well on Earth.

So a lot of these pregnant women were not married?

This doctor would volunteer his time to what was then called unwed mothers. You remember these homes . . .

Yes.

And this doctor would then have the opportunity. He would give the best medical care; the young women would not have to pay anything, and he would not bill the state. It was a donation, a service. And in this way most of the children were adopted out. Occasionally one of the mothers would keep one, but that was rare.

So when he talks about his "sisters," it's because of the way they were created, not necessarily that they all had the same father and mother?

That's correct. And he has many others, people who are his cousins in that sense —sisters and brothers and also a cousin —living in the future. This is part of the reason (he has not discussed this too much) that sometimes he has dreams of a beautiful place. He doesn't always remember those dreams, but very often he is connecting with his family in the future.

So his father, Apra, who's on a spacecraft here, is from this planet named Treshuis in the future?

It is the future from my perspective.

But is that the planet you live on, too?

I do not live on that planet. I am currently living on a small . . . it's like a planetoid that houses the Council of the Elders of . . . it's a long title in your language: the Council of the Elders Arranged to the Ascent of Time. This Council of Elders works almost exclusively on projects associated with time, time lines (which is why Zoosh called me in) and projects of this nature. And because our work is so erudite we do not live with the other people. It's a project.

So you are an elder for the entire Pleiadian system, not just one planet. But is this the correct name of the planet where Eddy's father came from: Treshuis?

I think that's pretty close to the phonetic pronunciation.

When Eddy says that the government paid for him, it was because there was some program to pay for the children of unwed mothers then, not because anybody understood who he was?

Yes, because in those times . . .

Yes, I understand. He mentions the name Rigel. Is that the Pleiadian version of God?

I think it would be a word that would be acceptable, yes.

Why Rigel? I mean, we don't have a name for God here —how did you get that name?

Well, it is, from the Pleiadian perspective, a feminine connotation for God. It's also (how can we say) how God presented Herself to us, and what could we do? We must call Her by Her name.

And this is systemwide, this is seven planets wide, this is for all the Pleiades, right?

It is evident. Stars, yes.

But all of the Pleiades would say that was their God?

Well, they might use different words. But you know, everybody's God is the same God, just sometimes with different disguises.

Yes. Eddy said his father, Apra, who is on a spaceship up here, is about five feet tall and looks very humanlike. If I looked at his father, I would not be able to tell him from a human?

No, I don't think you could tell him from a human being. Put him in a three-piece business suit and a tie and give him a briefcase, and you'd think he was an insurance salesman. Well, maybe not, but he could pass very easily.

Agents of the Shadow Government

Who has been beating up Eddy Page's sisters and following Eddy? The father in the spaceship evidently took up some of them to make a point.

Took up some of what?

Some of these operatives, these agents, who had been following Eddy and beating up his sisters.

Agents follow orders based upon what they are told. Sometimes they just follow orders, and other times they are given a story to motivate them. You make the target into some kind of horrible person, and then the agent is motivated. But these agents that attacked the sister were not what I would call . . . well, they were subcontractors, as the government likes to call them (your word, I think, is "thugs"), who would perhaps be less inclined to have a more upstanding moral value —which, believe it or not, many agents have; they do have moral values.

But what was their purpose? What were they trying to do, scare Eddy into talking more?

I think they were trying to scare Eddy into *not* talking so much.

Ah-hah! So now they have come to some kind of agreement after the Pleiadian father took the agents, took the thugs?

They took up one agent and several of the bully boys, as we'll call them. When you are picked up by people in a flying saucer, as you call it, and taken aboard, the people show you nothing but kindness and love. Of course, these people, the rough, tough ones, would have been taken into a special chamber and irradiated with certain colored tones that would eliminate all their violence and aggression so that they could freely mingle with the Pleiadians on the ship, because they could not mingle otherwise. You know, you can be the roughest, toughest, baddest —whatever you want to call yourself —but when you have an experience like this, it changes you. Unlike most circumstances, these people were not deprogrammed. In other words, the material experience they had —the agent and the rough, tough people —they were allowed to retain all of that. They remembered everything they saw, everything they heard, all of this. And they were changed. You cannot go through an experience like this without being changed forever. So you might say they were redeemed. And that is good.

You cannot say who hired them?

I am constrained, as Zoosh likes to say, because I feel that it could create tensions between your country and another. Another country acted as a middle man, like an agent, to set that up. And I think you don't need tensions between yourselves and that country right now.

Is there anything else that it would be beneficial to say about this?

Mostly a word to Eddy: We appreciate all you have done. Most of what you have done has been done in your sleep, in your dreams, in your meditations and in your quiet times. Even thinking allows you to perpetuate the value of our society and intermingle it with the values of your society on Earth. We know that for you and for all of the others, it has been so very difficult. And yet when we are all together again, it will feel so very much worth it.

Thank you very much.

An Arcturian Relation

Leah Haley has been picked up by certain spaceships many, many times, and once evidently was shot down off the coast of Florida while she was in a craft. She continues to be taken up by the spaceships, and the government also keeps abducting her, trying to find out why the spaceships pick her up. Can you tell me who picks her up, why they bring her onto the spacecraft, and what the government is trying to do?

I think that people picking her up would be from the general area of Arcturus and that their planet or their base in that area would be referred to as . . . I'll call it Cyclo; I don't want to use its full name. I believe that she is considered not just a specimen (if she were, they obviously wouldn't keep coming back to her), but a relative along the soul line. As a result, they started picking her up. You know, many people were picking up many people: extraterrestrials were picking up Earth people all the time, and probably nothing would have come of it if the ship hadn't been shot down. But you can imagine their amazement when the government discovered a human being onboard the ship, and of course their first thought was, Where's she from? It didn't immediately occur to them that she was an Earth human, because by that time they had had enough contact with extraterrestrial civilizations not to jump to conclusions like that.

So their question was, What star group is she from? And this is the key to understanding it all: Even though she said she was from Earth and she could prove it (paper trails, as it were), they didn't believe her. From the view of the government and any military agency, even if people generally consider it might be true that she's from Earth, if there's even the shadow of a doubt that she might be involved either with a Pleiadian society, an Arcturean society or a Zeta Reticulan society, or might even be an extraterrestrial imitating this person in that body, they're going to keep an eye on her. Their whole issue is that they are not 100% certain that she is who she says she is and that she's an Earth person. That's why the government keeps picking her up.

So she's going to have to understand that they are not going to be convinced that she was born and raised on Earth — even though the individuals that she talks to and that talk to her might make it sound like that. They would also love it if she would cooperate. It's hard for them to understand why she doesn't willingly cooperate with them . . .

With the extraterrestrials . . .

No, that she doesn't willingly cooperate with the government by telling them about the extraterrestrials.

But she doesn't know that much about them.

Well, that's just it. She cannot access the memories, and to their great frustration, the government cannot access the memories, either.

And they've tried drugs and all types of . . .

They've tried with every type of technology they have at their disposal that would not cause permanent harm. They're willing to make her feel uncomfortable. They're willing to cause her to have temporary discomforts. But because they want to follow up after every contact — and they are aware when they take place, they can track these things now . . .

They can track every ET-human contact?

Yes. We'll talk about that in a moment. But since they know it, they want to keep studying it, they want to keep in contact with it. They just want to know more. And they are the ones, I might add, who are fervently working — though it will take them some time to perfect it, perhaps even twenty years — on a genetic means of memory retrieval.

Like with Eddy, this memory is in her body cells, you're saying.

That's right. The memory of the entire contact, with the proper genetic analysis hooked up to the proper devices beyond that (I can't really tell you what they are without making complications), the entire experience can be pulled out of the body's tissues. This includes what she saw and felt as well as everything she was thinking at the time — everything that her unconscious and her auric field could extrapolate about what the ETs were thinking and feeling — all of that. But there's only one thing that has to occur (I'll give them this little hint, because this means of extrapolating information is worth knowing): The cells have to be analyzed while they are alive. So the key is, the tool of analysis cannot be threatening, harmful or painful; it must be attached to the living person while the analysis is going on. If there is any threat, any harm, any pain, the tissues will be electrified by an emotion that will essentially make it impossible to read it. That's an interesting factor, there.

The government wants to know, and they're not going to interfere with the process, because the extraterrestrials want to keep picking her up. They hope they're going to learn more because they want to know what's happening, so they keep trying new things to extract information.

But why do the Arctureans pick her up? Just to say, "Hi, how are you, good to see you"?

No. From their point of view she is a relation. She has within her soul and within her light energy, her lightbody, a cord that connects to them. Everyone who has a connection to other planets has one of these cords connecting them to other planets. This cord allows the other planets to access a tremendous amount of information, knowledge and wisdom about the evolving emotional state of being of Earth people. This is being monitored, of course, to see whether Earth people are becoming more or less spiritually attuned and to know when Earth people can accept the presence of extraterrestrials as well as etheric entities that the extraterrestrials can help you see and interact with. You know, even if people are less spiritually evolved than they might be, there is a device by which, just by slipping your finger into it, you are able to see the devic energies, the fairies — you can even in some cases see angelic presences with your regular vision! I don't have to tell you what an astounding effect that would have on the general population.

Who has this device?

Several extraterrestrial civilizations have it, including the people who contact this woman. And this is a version or a cousin of the device they use to extract the preponderant mood of Earth people.

Like reading the temperature. So other civilizations also pick up people they're connected to — Pleiadians, Zetas, all these — and kind of read the Earth temperature?

Yes, if they have that device or if they have that agenda. Many of them do, yes. Not all, but many.

So that's one of the reasons for the ongoing picking-up of various people, then.

Yes, it's like sampling the soup: "Is it ready yet?"

Now, to get back to something we talked about before. The government now has a means . . .

The shadow government . . .

Yes. A means by which to emit a sound-light frequency that acts as a matrix, or what you would consider a sieve — it essentially sieves, or strains, all contact from known ET sources interacting with Earth in any way. So if a ship lands — even if it doesn't take a person aboard — they know where the ship landed.

Anyplace on the planet?

Anyplace on the planet. This is how they are very quick to know who interacts with whom. And this is also why very few ETs are taking chances by contacting their friends now, because they are so easily detected. However — and I can talk about this, because the secret government has not developed a counteraction to this yet . . .

They can come back in time . . .

They can come back in time, plus they've got another wrinkle: they go way back in time, then come forward on a different time line that intersects this time, making the detection of a contact like that almost impossible. The only way it might be detected is randomly — and that's with an almost infinite amount of possibilities.

So which civilizations are able to do this? All of them?

Almost all of them. The Pleiadians do not often use this technique, but they can access this technique by working with their teachers, their guides and some of their allies.

So right now the abductions are past, right? What is the reason, other than testing the emotional climate of Earth, that they would want to pick up anyone?

Sometimes it's diplomatic — making friends, influencing people, not unlike in any diplomatic situation. That has been largely the purpose. But that has been significantly constrained by the secret government's efforts to block that action. The other thing — sampling the soup, as we say — has been a bonus. But there have always been diplomatic contacts with people for whom they felt a kindred spirit.

But right now there's very little of any of that?

Very little because of the complications of detection. So they'll make those contacts only if it's an emergency situation — something they feel responsible for because they established the contact — or a situation where the person they're contacting can help them and does so willingly.

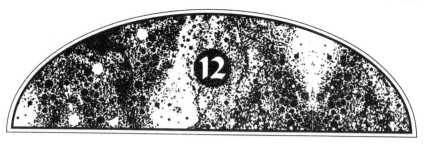

ETs: Friend or Foe?

Joopah
Carlsbad, California, October 13, 1990

ll right, Joopah speaking. Well, I would like to open by defining the words of the topic. If we assume that "friend" means "those who would help us, benefit us or enjoy our company" and that "foe" means "those who would strike us down, keep us from our desires, or simply manipulate us and work toward keeping us in bondage," then let us understand that those words in and of themselves are not a complete summary of the extraterrestrial experience here on Earth. There is another category: those who would study or simply observe. On your world observation is as normal a daily experience as watching interesting people in a public place or in scientific situations where various controlled experimental groups are observed to see if an idea or substance has value.

Reasons for ET Presence

I mention this because in order to understand and appreciate the interactions between extraterrestrials and Earth people, it is necessary to recognize that just because individuals or societies are able to build high-technology equipment and travel to other planets does not mean they are beings you would want to meet and experience in your backyard. That is (to make a joke), you may not necessarily want one to marry your sister. This is important, because for many years there have been two diametrically opposed opinions about extraterrestrials. One, that they are here to help you and offer advice; or two, they are here to interfere with you in some way. I want to offer the idea that there are other categories: those who are here simply to observe you, and those (perhaps more of these than even they realize) who are here only to learn by your example rather than study you.

You must understand that in the overall scheme of things, the race that I represent (Zeta Reticuli) has had a history over millions and millions of years of being the scientific observer *of our own kind.* As a result, we are known and appreciated throughout the universe as being objective scientists who can study and who do not make up their mind before the results are in. In other words, we are very patient. As a result, we have learned through the scientific method that anything that is being studied is to be studied physically, mentally and spiritually to the best of our abilities. In other words, what is being studied is to be studied in as many ways as possible, as any good scientist might, in order to maximize the amount of information that can be reasonably examined at a later date and perhaps correlated with other information. Therefore to recognize our scientific method, you need only recognize that your own scientific method on this planet is modeled after these universal models.

We as a species (speaking for the Zeta species in general — not only my own race but the people from the Zeta influence) were invited to participate in the genetic experiment on Earth here and help you understand your own reality by gathering data to be presented at a later date in your evolutionary cycle so that you could understand how you arrived at your position and be stimulated and invigorated by your own accomplishments. This is really why we are here. We are not here because we are trying to interfere with you; we are not even here because we are trying to love you so much. We are here to study the entire history of the human race on an experiential level. Our race has been able to travel through time for millions and millions of years, far beyond the acculturization period of your own race — for the human being has been evolving on this planet for six or seven million years. We have been here as a race during that entire time to observe the actions of evolutionary experience and genetic alterations that have taken place to produce the Explorer Race (as you are called elsewhere in the galaxy).

Our participation in this experiment was requested because of our abilities to observe, deduce and gather information. We did not understand when we were originally contacted that there was any more to it than that. We are ofttimes invited to participate as scientific observers by many different groups and races of people, and we know we are appreciated as scientists simply because of the quality of our work. We thought it was that and no more. In the past two to three years we have come to realize something completely different, and we have had to look at the human race in a new way. We have been told by our advisors that you represent our past lives. This is quite an amazing and even astounding realization for us. We did not examine it, you know, because we could not correlate from *our* point in time our souls' journeys through your bodies. This is because of the experience that you are all going through now.

You are living according to the Plan and its variations. The Plan has allowed for certain interruptions in its evolution. The interruptions will occur when all potentials are at their ultimate point of possibility, and when these potentials are met (at various times) it is possible for you to make an evolutionary leap in consciousness. This has happened within your race two or three times before, depending on how you calculate time and space. It is happening again, and you are all working toward making an evolutionary jump from the third to the fourth dimension while you are embodied instead of doing it between lives, as is often the case.

So we have not had the tools or the capacity to understand that you are our past lives. This has revolutionized our way of looking at ourselves. Until recent times we have experienced some of the most difficult crises in our race's evolution. We came to believe that we were dying out as a species because we were unable to reproduce ourselves. We had been using cloning for millions of years to create our own offspring, and the body has always had a life expectancy (in terms of your years) of about 700 to 750 years. But speaking from my point of view in time (which is millions of years in your future), we have begun experiencing in recent years a decrease in the time our bodies would last. We experienced this to the point where a physical body would last no more than 250 years. To you this might sound like a long time, but just imagine that if the life expectancy of a human being were 75, then suddenly dropped to 25 – you would have plenty of concern.

We have been very concerned, and since we are primarily geneticists, we have been experimenting with a number of offspring races that we have created of ourselves that would perpetuate our culture, our ideas, our sense of self, our accomplishments and our intelligence for other races to inherit and access should we die out. This is what we believed would happen – that we were going to die out, cease to exist as a race. What we did not understand was that we were also going to do exactly what *you* are doing: jump into another dimension *while* we are embodied.

What we have come to realize in the most recent of times is that the bodies we made for our souls to inhabit were not working because the soul was not being attached to the body. The Creator, who provides the soul, was not investing the body with the soul –not because we were to die out and cease to exist as a race, but because our entire race was going to jump dimensions while we were still alive! You see, if this had not been *your* experience, we would not have known. This also helps us to see how you are so closely related to us. It might not be obvious to you because you are so caught up in your own lives, but everything you do on this planet Earth has critical importance to other parts of the galaxy. Really, what you are, on this planet, is problem-solvers. Most races, including my own, do not have anywhere near the problem-solving capacity that any regular, day-to-day citizen on Earth has. This is because our societies by and large have no conflict. As a result, there is no need to resolve dilemmas — reinvent the wheel, as you say. The technology that was developed millions of years ago is still sufficient because it has not been blown up in any war, and thus there has been no necessity to evolve our social or technological consciousness or intelligence based on the destruction of past civilizations — as you have experienced. We have had the opportunity to see how you help us simply by your existence.

What "Abductions" Are About

Now, how is it that human beings are abducted, picked up and utilized in various ways? I have already stated that part of the picking up, part of the medical examinations, has been to see how the "soup" was coming along physically by sampling, not unlike the yearly physical exam you experience in a medical facility. Some of the beings who were involved in these scientific observations were unsophisticated; they did not have the capacity your bodies have to tolerate extremes of emotional interaction. In other words, they did not have the emotional stamina you have, so they seemed aloof, cool and distant. This is by way of explanation so that you will understand the context.

What about other contacts, ones in which there would be some interaction of the species? As indicated, our race is known for its desire to create viable species that are offshoots of our own. This is partly fueled in recent years because of our fear of not surviving as a race, but it also had to do with the fact that we simply had desires of our own to understand more about crossbreeding and so on. This is not an unusual desire in your own scientific civilization, which is always looking for new life forms that can contribute to your culture.

Other experiments were done. We will not claim that these experiments were invasive, frightening or painful. I know that there are some who say they are, but in my understanding as an architectural historian, I am not aware of any violent acts on human beings done by our race or any of the Zeta-influenced beings. I am speaking here only of the genetic experiments. People were picked up without their permission, but we had their unconscious permission. When these people were picked up, fluids might be taken from their bodies, but we always asked their souls if this was all right, always working with our God, our Creator, saying, "Is it all right?" and always with the best of intentions: to create different beings. We perceive you as being highly durable and with a survivability far beyond our own.

So we have created different offshoots of our own race that combine your genetic structure. Of course, when you consider the big picture — that you yourselves are made up of the genetic structure from Sirius, the Pleiades, Orion, Andromeda and a smattering of other places – it is, as you say, no big deal. But that is not widely known on your planet. I bring that up so that you will see this in context.

In creating these races, perhaps the most successful race – that is, the one that was the most viable, that has developed its own culture and has been in existence for many years – is a race of beings created for multiple reasons. One, we believed that they would be the most durable and would have the most to contribute on the largest number of levels. Two, these beings would be able to communicate with us and with you in the best possible way for both species. Three, we thought that they would be the inheritors of our race culture. Now we see that that is not necessary, so we have simply given them their own planet where they can create in their own way.

They are a viable race of their own, representing about 51% Zeta, 49% human. They do not look exactly like us; they are much taller. We would be about three to three-and-a-half feet tall; these beings would be five to five-and-a-half feet tall. Their skin is black, not darker tones of brown, but actually black. Their heads are just slightly larger than yours. Their eyes are somewhat swept back and, as I like to say, they are beautiful people who are somewhat reminiscent of modern architecture in their appearance. They have two arms, two legs and a head; they are not that different from yourselves. They are very sensitive and artistic; they have tendencies toward culture, and they enjoy the many and varied experiences of human life. Although they do not generally interact with you directly, occasionally they interact with people who have come aboard a ship.

This is perhaps our most viable contribution to genetic species. Now we see that it also even more viable than we understood, because they will have their own lives, live their own destiny, and in time will be the spokesmen for the Zeta-influenced races with your own society. You, when you adapt to their appearance (which is not so very different from your own), will find them most attractive, and they will find you attractive. They will be able to meet you on the grounds of emotion and passion and compassion, and there will be a healthy and pleasant exchange between you. It will be for them to pass on all the information we have gathered over the years about who you are for yourselves and for others; you will be more comfortable with them than with us because our appearance is still foreign to you. Although we have two arms, two legs and a head and body, we look sufficiently different from you that we would definitely stand out in any crowd. Therefore, it is believed that these beings will be attractive to you and find you attractive as well; we see the value in that.

I give you this background information so that you can understand who I am within the context of my own race, my own race's culture, and within some context of your own. I have mentioned earlier that you are the problem-solvers. This is so. I might also add that you are not strictly solving problems for Zeta Reticuli as some unwritten manifesto. You, of all species we have ever come into contact with, are perhaps the most elegant in the sense of your day-to-day experience being both evolutionary and revolutionary at the same moment. Only those races are allowed to physically interact with you that can benefit not *from* you, but as a result of your experience. Races that are unrelated to you, in terms of genetics or problems you are solving for them, are not really involved here.

You have never had contact with human beings from any race other than those you are benefiting (inadvertently, I should mention). It is not so much that you have been visited with the pain of others' unresolved problems; it is that you —you souls who are manifesting here on this Earth now and who have ever been here in Earth lives —have chosen the most difficult training program that can be accomplished, because of its high rewards. All souls who live a life on Earth will evolve into other lives where they will be teachers and share with others the value of learning under stress.

Most extraterrestrial civilizations do not experience stress. As a result, they do not have to grow. If you were given a lifetime of a thousand years, for example, on the Pleiades, and you were told that you had a thousand years to learn how to tie your own shoelaces, there's a good chance that many of you would take the full thousand years to do it. Now, that is just a joke, but in terms of a life on the Pleiades, it is not so different from the truth. On your planet one must learn to tie his shoelaces in much less time. So I am suggesting that while you might live one-tenth of a Pleiadian's life span, you will accomplish more in one hour of your life than is accomplished in a hundred years of a life there. This is not to put down the Pleiadians; it is just to advise you not to elevate other races and species as being more valuable than you, but to recognize that they have not learned how to deal with stress or even to grasp its value.

Your Gift of Ignorance

They are being instructed about this even now, and many of them are recoiling somewhat from their former attitudes about you. Many races over the years developed the idea that just as soon as you rose up out of your negative energy and became more positive, that we "extraterrestrials" (in quotes) would embrace you as one of us. But in reality, these races of beings (from the Pleiades, Sirius, Orion and many other places) had cultural problems that were unresolvable within a culture that does not have stress or conflict, that does not have urgency to resolve things. As a result, these ideas had to be resolved somewhere else because they were backlogged and there was no space for them in the room of the unresolved. You as souls volunteered to resolve the unresolvable by learning how to reinvent the wheel through the simple use of what is now recognized intergalactically as the most valuable tool that was formerly unrecognized for its value: *the gift of ignorance!*

When you do not remember who you are in your existence in these lives on Earth, you do not consciously (most of you) remember your former lives. You do not consciously recollect other lives you have lived or people you have met; you do not remember the things you have learned. In other words, you must learn from scratch at the beginning and throughout any life. You have to constantly reinvent things that have already been invented, and you will frequently invent them in new ways. You have the gift of ignorance. Other civilizations such as my own and others have been, as one of my chief advisors says, "strapped with the truth." That is, we have been led to believe that what is true for us has always been true, is true and will always be true. This, while it might create peace and harmony of a sort, necessarily creates a no-growth situation and also perpetuates any unresolved problems within the culture because there is *no need to resolve them.*

I am reminding you of these ideas within the context of this discussion so that you will realize completely and fully *who you really are.* It is true that your lives are a struggle here. It is true that you do not always appreciate or understand the connections that you have on an extraterrestrial level. But if you can see more clearly into the idea of your value as it is recognized by many beings, not only those like myself in the future but more enlightened beings of your own time, then perhaps you will appreciate yourselves and each other.

Implants, Contracts and Underground Bases

I have three questions. The first one is, why are the ETs putting silicon chips in various parts of the bodies of certain people they contact?

Not all beings do this, all right? These chips, as you say, are not implanted by any ETs I know. Recognize this: all that is ever implanted in the body of a human being that is not a natural portion of that body are devices which are *not physical.* That is, if they were physical they would interfere with your body and cause problems. It is not our job to cause problems; it is our job to observe. As a result, our race and no other race that I am aware of installs any chips. This would suggest to you — *and I hope you understand the ramifications* — that it would be of value to look to races of your own planet who are involved in this! I will, however, broaden that answer. I will say that there are people living in the past on your own planet who have the ability to travel in time, as well as some individuals (to make one exception) who live in a past civilization on the star system Orion — perhaps an unsophisticated civilization that does not understand the true value of your race to the universe — who are involved in such things. But for the most part, any intrusion upon the physical body of a physical device is *not* extraterrestrial.

Do you know anything about the contracts made between your race and the United States government, and the various cities that are built under Arizona to house upward of 15,000 ETs?

This is a reality; however, we are talking about more than one contract. When our race was beginning to be observed by the government of the U.S. (to say nothing of the governments of other countries) and the opinions of those observers became more respected, the governments began to develop a rudimentary electronic surveillance of our activities. We then deemed it valuable to make some type of formal acquaintance with *all* governments, not just the government of the United States. (For example, we have had an agreement with longstanding cultural people from China, Japan and other countries that have the ability to trace a history back farther than your own. But that is an aside.) We did make a formal agreement with the United States government to allow us to do what we have been doing for millions of years. That is, we felt it would be appropriate to encourage your race to begin to understand its intergalactic heritage and nature by exposing those who rule you to us. We did not do so to purposely intimidate, but as a result of our technology, our appearance and our unusual way of life in comparison to your own, there was a level of intimidation that we did not intend. This is an important factor to understand, because when people feel intimidated they often react in ways that they otherwise would not.

In the case of our race, we suggested that we had many bases around the world; that we would be continuing to monitor the human race as we have always done; that we would like to have cordial arrangements with various governments so that they would know that we did not intend to disturb or attack or take over your governments or in any way invade; and that we were simply on a largely scientific and diplomatic mission. This was, I believe, understood and appreciated by the best of the governmental representatives of the time. But there was an intimidation factor that we did not quickly see, because we misperceived the way your race socializes itself. That is, sometimes you will say that something is true when it is not — not to suggest that those representatives were lying, but perhaps they did not even fully realize themselves that they were intimidated (to give them the benefit of the doubt). So there were reactions on a military level.

You must understand that if someone comes along and shows you, by way of sharing on a friendly basis, a glimmer of technology that looks startlingly futuristic (though it was really ancient to us), there would be a certain level of envy in various areas of those military circles. There was that; but there was also, unfortunately, a level of threat. This we did not see right away. In terms of the envy, we felt it only appropriate to do what we do with all other civilizations: share some of our most benign technology that would be least likely to fuel conflict on your planet and most likely to contribute to a better quality of life. So we shared some of our knowledge of genetics, medical methods and some scientific tools and instruments, as well as certain representatives who stayed for a time with your governmental and scientific people to explain more fully the techniques and so on. *We did not share things that could be used destructively* — I want to emphasize that. This was the agreement that took place.

I'll get on now to your question about these underground bases in Arizona. They are also in northern New Mexico, southern Utah and Colorado and are beginning to snake into (in terms of a tunneling system) extreme eastern California and northwest Texas. These bases (some of which are above Zeta Reticuli bases because the technology that creates them is not as sophisticated as our own) are associated with beings you would call negative in nature. You might ask, "Why are they allowed to be here?"

It is an irony of nature. They are much more negative than your own race of beings; their planet experiences about 97% to 98% negative energy compared to your own planet, which fluctuates between 45% and 55%. They are allowed to come here because, among all the races that I am aware of in the universe, the only race of beings they can have any communication with is *your own*, because that which they respect and value — the negative aspects of fear and power — is represented in your own civilization. Thus they do not feel as threatened by you as they would by others.

I would also say that these beings have an interesting history with you. They come from a small planet in the Sirius galaxy. Although most planets there are positive and enlightened, this one is small and mainly keeps to itself. They represent something to you that is quite amazing (they do not know this because they are not willing to accept information from any source outside themselves, though in time they might accept it from you): As you evolve from the third to the fourth dimension while you are alive — not between lives — you will leave behind the third-dimensional Earth. You might say, "But we are leaving behind something polluted." As polluted as it may be, you are leaving something that is a Garden of Eden compared to their own planet, and it will be sufficiently polluted so that it will feel more like home to them. They do not know that they will inherit third-dimensional Earth, that it will be given to them as a gift. They believe that the only way they can escape from their planet, which is gradually imploding on itself, is to take over this planet.

Now, do not be frightened; they have almost no capacity to injure you *in any way.* I cannot emphasize this too much. However, they do use intimidation with your government. When they came here, which was not that long ago, they represented themselves to be like us. They have a rudimentary form of cloning wherein they can make a body that looks like other races as long as it is kept in a very isolated atmosphere. They were able to produce a body that looked very much like our own, and when they approached your government of the United States, they attempted to pass themselves off as us and stated that they would like to begin to share technology with your government that your government desired to have, and that *they would be willing to use any means necessary* to get what they wanted. (That is a key factor.) Within the military of your government this type of threat and negotiation is not unknown. (This is not by any means a criticism on my part; I am simply saying that your government knows how to deal with threatening forces.)

I would also state that your government did not at the time desire to have these beings here; however, they were bribed, one might say. This is not to suggest that they were people of less value, but that they felt threatened geopolitically by other powerful countries in your world at that time. It was the height of what you call the Cold War, and they felt that unless they could develop weapons much more powerful and accurate than atomic weaponry, your government would be, as the Chairman stated, buried. You can thus understand their motivation for allowing this type of treaty between your species and their species; they would never have done it without that pressure.

So these beings from this small planet on Sirius told them that they would like to develop these underground bases in the American Southwest, and that they would not interfere with the civilian population in any way. They would simply be here conducting various experiments, and for that privilege they would share with your government their technology that uses focused proton radiation (their name for it), which was developed into your high-energy lasers. However, these laser energies were highly condensed and focused, and could be used for destructive purposes — that was their intended function. Your government acquiesced to the idea of having a weapon that would be a considerable deterrent if your country were ever invaded by a foreign power. That was the context at the time.

Even though these beings lied to your government and misrepresented themselves (which your government now knows, though it did not know it at the time), these beings really cannot interfere with you. They lied to your government in many ways; they said they had a weapon that could totally destroy your planet in the twinkling of an eye. (Threats like that were believed when they were firing their laser weapons in the '50s). What they did *not* say, of course, was that this weapon could not be used on Earth! Not because of any intergalactic treaties (which they did not honor at all), but because the circumstances on Earth would not allow it. The circumstances that *would* allow it are something unique: If negative energy produced by human strife and struggle reaches a level of 75% or greater of your total experience on Earth, their weapon would be effective. But you see, it is going in the opposite direction; *negative energy is actually gradually shrinking*, in terms of its impact on your lives, although you might not realize it fully until the year 2000, 2003, 2010.

So your intimidated United States government representatives believed that they were up against a race of beings that could utterly destroy the United States as well as the whole world, and that this race was offering them this great gift of technology, saying they were not *really* going to interact with your population at all —that's what the representatives thought. So it was an uncomfortable treaty such as one might make with someone you'd really not like to have living next door.

Your government has recently (within the last ten years) uncovered the ruse and know that these beings are not, in fact, from Zeta Reticuli, but from Sirius. This has caused the utmost alarm about the spread of these underground bases in the American Southwest. They have now come into the knowledge of who these people are and of their desire to take over the Earth. These are the people who have been involved in what is referred to as cattle mutilations, because they are attempting to clone (with their rudimentary cloning technology) a body they can use that would be inhabited by one of their own personalities and that could tolerate living on the Earth's surface.

You see, they are really unable to affect you directly because their bodies cannot tolerate weather extremes. You might ask, "What about protective suits?" That wouldn't really work. They do not have the level of technology that some Earth people have, much less the level of technology that some extraterrestrial civilizations might have —and I'll tell you why. They do not have a warm-blooded body, so they are badly affected by temperature extremes. They do not generate their own heat, so they cannot tolerate extremes. They have discovered that the blood and various organs in cattle can be used to synthesize a body that would, on casual examination, pass for human and into which they believe they could insert one of their personalities.

However, they do not understand the law of creation, and this is to your benefit. They attempted in recent times to inject several of these bodies that looked pretty human into the flow of your population. The law of creation, however, took effect, and they —not being very enlightened – did not understand it: Regardless how you construct a body, *it is always entirely up to the Creator to provide that body with a soul.* If the being is living in a negative environment, it is likely to be a negative life, but if that being – no matter how negatively it has been programmed, no matter how technologically controlled it is – is placed into a society where negative energy and positive energy is in balance (largely speaking), such as your own, it will necessarily become what it is exposed to.

So these "spies" were unleashed on the surface with high hopes (if these Sirians could be said to have that emotion), and within three days they had become almost exactly like any other Earth person. This is why you have almost nothing to fear from these people. Why do I say "almost"? It is because they do have some rudimentary abilities: they can frighten you, but they cannot actually harm you – that's important to know. There is a lot more to this, but I'm sure you want to talk about other things. Question?

Do the negative ones who are underground have ships that get the cattle and so on? Can they travel in ships out of their caves or whatever?

Yes, but only through certain access points, and they cannot get out of the vehicles. I know that some people have reported seeing extraterrestrials in the area where such things have gone on, and it is true that some Zeta beings have been present. We have races of beings from Zeta Reticuli who are being innocently used by these people from Sirius because of their own lack of education and inability to see clearly the negative impact of these races of beings amongst you. They are few and far between, these unsophisticated Zeta clones. They do not actually help the Sirius beings in their work, but they will be with them from time to time as scientific observers. They are not used as slaves, but they are treated with disdain by these negative beings, and will at times be observed in the area. It will be clearly noted by observers that the Zeta beings have an air of innocence about them, while the other beings are clearly involved in some dastardly act.

What is the appearance of these negative beings? Do they look similar to the Zeta Reticulans?

They can create a similar body (again, that is a disguise), but it cannot function in your actual atmospheric conditions. It can function in an enclosed atmosphere of its own, a synthetic atmosphere. They have a fairly large, bulbous nose that does not function as a nose but is actually a protrusion of their spinal fluid. They are short and squat. They are not particularly pleasant-looking by your standards of beauty.

The 1992 Wormwood Planetoid

Are these draconians heading this way – is Wormwood really their vehicle? Are these the same type of beings you're talking about?

You are referring to what species?

They're called draconians or dracs. Are they headed this way in what has been called Wormwood, a planetoid that scientists supposedly can see?

These are your names for these things. This is not the same thing, but it is related. This is the theory, you say, of the planet that is coming this way and would possibly crash into your own planet, yes?

Scientists are seeing this thing coming; they say it's going to be here in 1992.

I would like to tell you something interesting about that. Again, this is not the same thing — let me start off with that. An interesting thing is occurring here. This approaching body has to do with a level of negative energy that is compatible (not that this approaching planetoid is negative, but it is beneficial to anything negative). It is going to have an experience with the law of creation; it is not going to crash into your planet, now or any time. It will, however, pass close by — close enough to experience the radionic field of Mother Earth but not close enough to really affect your surface populations. The reason it will amuse you is that those who would utilize the cyclic motion of this planet to increase the amplitude and frequency of negative energy on Earth (those beings from Sirius would use it) would actually be investing in their *own* balance of positive and negative energy. That is, they would inadvertently call forth positive energy for themselves. Believe me, they would not do this on purpose.

This is what's going to happen: This planetoid, smaller than your own Moon, will skip by Earth's energy. It will be, as it were, inoculated by Earth's energy, because the balance, the power and the focus of Mother Earth's radionic field is much more powerful than the energy of this planetoid. It will skip off of Earth's outer radionic fields, becoming inoculated with Earth's energy of balanced positive and negative.

Those individuals [negative Sirians] who attempted to draw this planetoid toward Earth with the intention of causing widespread surface destruction (to increase the negative energies here to 75% or more so that their weapon would work) will find that their tactics have backfired. They are even now drawing energy — their own — from that planetoid. Although they are not directly connected with the energy of that planetoid, they are using it. Imagine their surprise when this planetoid, inoculated with Earth energy, passes close by and does no damage to the surface of your planet (except interfering somewhat with weather patterns) and they draw *positive energy* to themselves! They will believe that they are experiencing a disease, because the pain that has existed in their bodies as long as they can remember (they are born with it) will begin to decrease. Their pain level will reduce from about 75% to about 55%. They will believe that it is a disease when it is in fact the inoculation of positive energy. Even though they are living below the surface of the planet, they cannot avoid the law of creation.

The Negative-Sirian Manipulation

Are they being supervised by the United States government? You didn't get into the nature of the contract or the specifics. Where does it stand right now?

Oh, no, the government of the United States is not supervising or directing their activities – certainly not!

You mean they can do whatever they want in there?

They can do what they want, yes, because they misrepresented themselves. And just because they gave the government of the United States some things the government could use does not mean that they allowed the government of the United States to have any authority over *them*. They have instead always intimidated and threatened your government, and now that the government knows who they really are, they are beginning to release a little bit of information through various channels – trial balloons – to see how it affects the population, whether the population will believe it. They are putting out some things that are true and some things that are not true, just to see how it would affect you. This is, I might add, a scientific methodology used in social studies to study the impact of ideas on people, so it's not something that they're inventing. Thus I would say that your government is not tricking you, but it is beginning to let out a little information because it feels that it might have to take action. However, it feels that its hands are tied because any weapon the United States has is equaled or surpassed by this race of beings, though they cannot utilize their weaponry on your planet as they would like the government to believe. Your government is not fully cognizant of this, but even if they were, they would necessarily be cautious with such a foreign power.

How can they frighten us if they have to stay underneath the Earth? You said they can frighten people; how can they do that if they can't live on the surface?

They can exert what could be referred to as an influence of energy that functions on the psychological/emotional level to distract and disrupt a human being who is not focused within his own energy and feeling happy to be here. That is, they cannot affect in any way anybody other than someone who is in that moment angry, depressed or feeling other aspects of negative energy. However, the military (which would likely inherit any invasion of these underground bases), in order to invade, would necessarily be in negative energy to battle a considerably superior force, militaristically speaking. One would have to pump oneself up with anger, hate and so on in order to charge into that battle to survive – and these Sirians can influence people who feel those emotions.

So it will be a tough battle trying to get them out or blow them up?

If you do, yes, it would be very difficult. Blowing them up is extremely unlikely, since they are so entwined with underground aquifers — and remember, I stated that their bases are fairly close to the surface, and if any attempt is made to blow them up, there would be serious problems with your own life-sustaining forces of Mother Nature.

Earthquakes and what-have-you?

Yes. This has already been caused inadvertently by your governmental powers.

Would they like to be able to use their weapon, and are they trying to pursue that goal by increasing the negativity of the planet to 75%?

Exactly; that is their intention. They would like to use it, but you must remember that they do not have the power to do this. Just so you understand, it is extremely unlikely that they will have *any* influence on your own energy, since your evolution in consciousness is moving away from negative energy. However, as in any good inoculation, *you must experience it fully before you can ward off its invasive elements.*

Are they influencing the governments to take away our constitutional rights in order to try to increase that negativity?

No.

Why, then, is the Constitution being destroyed?

This has nothing to do with them.

Advanced Spacecraft and the Orion Men in Black

How about the spacecraft? Are they involved in developing the spacecraft that we supposedly have now and are testing at our bases, or is that a different . . . ?

They are not.

Has your race helped us build those spacecraft?

There has been some assistance, yes, but not only from our own race.

Do we have spacecraft now that can disappear into the etheric levels and astral levels that the government knows about?

Not that you have produced on your own.

But they know they exist and are down here on Earth as trial crafts?

Oh, yes; just because there is an Official Secrets Act does not mean that the people of your government are foolish.

I have another question. Could you tell me what your race knows of the Men in Black? And why they try to influence people who are known as UFO investigators?

Thank you; this is a most appropriate question for this evening's topic. The Men in Black are actually from the past, an Orion civilization that existed many, many years ago. They have occasional opportunities to obtain a one-way visa to your planet through windows in space and time. They have not been able to come here much recently, so those who exist here have managed to survive (though somewhat debilitated in health) since their arrival in the 1940s. The windows (as your own scientists might call them, in terms of your present space travel) are not so different from the mathematical windows that NASA might compute. They are simply windows in the factor of time travel.

These people come from a civilization that is warlike. We are not talking about a civilization that is as extremely negative as the one in the case of the negative planet from Sirius, but it is a warlike planet and they believe that they have a right (politically speaking) to influence you because of your ancestral genetic influence from Orion. We do not have time to give the entire answer, but as a brief overview I will simply say that in the distant past this civilization blew up its own planet. It moved to various places around the galaxy, blowing up other planets. Eventually (though not immediately and not intentionally) vestigial remains of the civilization would escape, and at one point came to a planet [Maldek] within your own solar system. They had their wars and blew that up, too. That planet was at that time a trinary group of planetoids; it is now what you refer to as the asteroid belt. Vestigial remains of that civilization came here to Earth. Well, after the genetic experiment on Earth, the Explorer Race had begun.

They believe that they can change their experience of all these planets blowing up if only they can come here to Earth in your time and change their past. Essentially, *they are attempting to change their past by changing your present.* Of course, they must experience the law of creation. These beings can operate more easily on the surface of your planet than can those beings from Sirius, but it is not completely easy. They must always use certain technological supports; if they are denied the use of these technological supports for any length of time (more than nine hours), they begin to experience debilitating diseases. They do not die out, for they have a long life, but they gradually get less effective, because the diseases affect their mental power. They become too incapacitated to interfere, much less to have free thought.

It is important for you to know that these beings do exist, that they can easily pass for human (though a thorough medical check would reveal that they are not), and that they do not represent a significant threat to you. It is true that they have attempted to manipulate your societies, but at this time they do not represent a significant threat.

Could you explain why the Men in Black are trying to quiet people who have seen UFOs?

It is their intention to maintain as much ignorance as possible about their own kind, who traveled here one way in a UFO (as you say), so that they might go on undetected. One might say that they have had some influence in the general editorial policy to "make all this UFO stuff into foolishness," but they in their own right did not make policies. They have attempted to manipulate others and peddle as much influence as they can, but they do not have as much influence as they would like. Because they could travel only one way, you can see that their technology is not sophisticated; they are not true time travelers.

Are they going to eventually die off and no longer influence the Earth?

They will not exactly die off; they will simply cease to exist. I will explain the difference. You on your planet are now moving from the third to the fourth dimension even as we speak. You do not see any changes in magnitude because you and everything in your world is changing at precisely the same rate. These beings are not. If you could observe it through high-speed photography over several hundred years, you would see that they gradually disappear, because they will remain in the third dimension while you make your rapid swing over the next twelve to fifty years (depending upon your point of view). They will simply cease to exist because they will stay in the third dimension. They have had increasingly less influence due to the fact that you are changing, and they can have almost no impact on you now.

Within a ten-year period will we all be in the fourth dimension?

No, no; I say it will happen within twelve to fifty years, depending upon your point of view. It will be possible to do this sooner or later, depending upon the evolution of the human race and its synchronicity in terms of full spiritualization and, as you would experience it, friendliness — the acceptance and allowance of the differences in your own cultures.

Could you explain some of what's happening with the crop circles in England and who is behind it, why it's taking place and why it is increasing?

This is a programmed enigma; that is, in order to encourage the race of human beings to believe in the value of extraterrestrial contact outside the context of the fictional and the dramatic, it is necessary to produce effects that would enlighten, entertain and amuse, which these circles are doing at the very least. They are caused by vehicles that are unseen due to their ability to fold time.

Who specifically is behind it, and what will it accomplish?

This is a multiple inclusion; one of the races is from Andromeda, and since Andromeda is the seat of thought, it is not unexpected that they would want to stimulate the flood of ideas associated with this.

How close are we to time travel, and can you give us some suggestions on how to do that?

No, I will not. I will not encourage you to do this now; it would be perhaps several hundreds of your years (if one could measure time on the third- to fourth-dimensional shift in the context of years). No! If you were to travel in time, you would bring all of your discomforts with you. It will be quite some time before you are allowed by the Creator to do such a thing consciously. Of course, when you are asleep and you use your imaginations, you can still do so. This is allowed because you do not bring your discomforts with you then.

What year will we see UFO people among us who will publicly come to the govern-ment and present themselves? Will that be in the '90s, or can you give us a year?

It will be a little time; this is because it would be interference if someone walked out amongst you now and said, "Here I am! Am I not wonderful?" This would interfere in the experiment here. I would say it is not likely that this would happen in terms of widespread public and governmental acceptance and a promotion of its reality for at least fifty years. This is not to say that there will not be people out there amongst you who are ETs and are benign – that is, people who live amongst you without any negative interference – or that there will not be other extra-terrestrial influence of a benign nature. But in terms of someone arriving in a golden chariot – that will be a while, because for that to happen, you will have to believe sufficiently in your own value as individuals and as Earth people so that you will not be bowled over by these ET beings who will seem to be so grand. If that occurs, then you simply create another hierarchy wherein you believe that you are less than someone else. *This will not happen.*

During Atlantean times we were able to fly to different areas like Sirius, I believe (that's the information). Can you explain what was going on then with the ETs, and how advanced we were in interplanetary travel and communication?

Recognize that within the context of time Atlantis still lives, because they did interact with extraterrestrial civilizations and utilized that tech-nology. Sometimes you will even see actual Atlantean ships. To give you a specific example, the sightings in the Gulf Breeze area – not so much the pictures, but the sightings most people saw that were similar to the pictures – were from a past Atlantean civilization.

I received a voice contact from ETs, I presume, and the message that they gave me was something like "bulk hemite." Would you happen to know who these ETs were and what that expression means?

Spell that word out – though you have placed it as two words, it is one word – and look at each of the letters. Write the letters in as many different ways as you can, then place your hands on each of the letters. Then you will know. You think communication is mental, but it is really symbolic. Communication between races and species of beings is more than thought and feelings. You say that sign language is a substitute for the spoken word, but in reality the true motions of language allow you not only to experience another means of communication – be it from extraterrestrials or more terrestrial sources – but to experience on other levels of yourselves. This can help you understand new meanings behind the actual intention and purpose of communication. When you begin to fully express your language in motion as well as emotion, you will begin to appreciate and truly understand the dance of life.

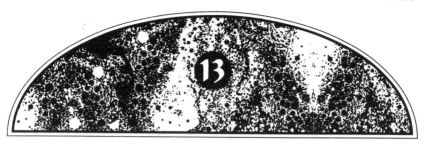

ET Presence within Earth and Human Genetics

Zoosh
Sedona, Arizona, May 9, 1991

an you tell us about the huge ship surrounding itself in a cloud that was seen here recently?

Many times children, perhaps with their parents, look at the sky, watching the clouds and enjoying the different shapes. I can assure you that most of the time the shapes that occur are there by design. It is not an accident. It is not something like, "Oh, isn't that an interesting coincidence?" It can be seen only if the vehicle or being or spirit desires it. This kind of thing can be real, but in the recent case of this so-called ship, the vehicle was not there then, but it had *been* there. The interesting thing about the interaction with vehicles such as you have described — UFOs — is that if they are freestanding, floating in any specific place for more than ten minutes of your physical Earth time, they will leave enough static charge in the air to be measured scientifically for at least a half hour to forty-five minutes after they depart.

Your government has such devices; this type of electronic countermeasure has been available for some time. They can trace UFOs on the basis of where they've been a lot easier than where they are. A natural effect of cloud vapor is sometimes to take on that form. If a UFO has been there, a cloud usually stops moving across the sky until the energy dissipates, then it might move on. If the cloud is created by a vehicle, it will also remain in place, but will dissipate more quickly when the vehicle is no longer there, since it is artificial.

What kind of effect did that large craft have on us in Sedona, if any?

You must understand that vehicles from other planets as well as planets that are versions of your own (that is, the future and the past) are here most of the time; it is not rare. It is perhaps rare that they are observed. It is no more unusual than a bus going by in a big city, but the effect is not always felt. If you are very close, say 50 to 100 yards, you might feel something. You might have an amplification of your own perceptive abilities that will either be temporary or long-lasting, depending upon your soul's allowance for that. But was the vehicle radiating something to make people more spiritual or to perhaps annoy them? – no.

Long before the city of Sedona was here, the rock structures and the terrain, the geography, was here. The city of Sedona is a relatively recent addition to the landscape, and vehicles were already coming then. They have been coming for millions of years.

Civilizations that live underneath the ground here have in many cases been here much longer than the surface civilizations. Surface civilizations come and go, but that which is underneath the ground is very often of a more permanent nature. They perform functions associated with their civilizations regardless of whether you are here or not. And they will continue to be as unobtrusive as possible, to interfere as little as possible with your civilization. But they were here first.

There is ofttimes a radionic effect from these vehicles. If it is a benign radionic effect, it can be advantageous. In such a case they are allowed to hover for a time. But if it is something that by its nature is harmful (perhaps an old vehicle with some form of gamma radiation, for example), then it is not encouraged to hang about where it might inadvertently provide some discomfort to plant, animal or person.

Are you saying that some of the UFOs we have seen have a civilization inside the Earth?

Indeed yes. It is not unusual. On many other planets the idea of having a civilization living underground is normal. I might say that by and large, underground civilizations are more frequent than civilizations living aboveground. It is much easier to control or adapt to a climate within a planet than on its surface; there is considerably more predictability, and one can maintain a balanced, harmonic recycling of matter inside a planet. So yes, there are civilizations living inside this planet that have been here millions of years and that for the most part do not originate on this planet. This is allowed, since there is generally very little contact between you and them other than what is unobtrusive. It does not interfere with your civilization.

Can you be specific about where they are, who they are and why they are here?

Many of them are associated with planets and civilizations of the distant past — that is, they were founded in the distant past. They are not in another time; they were here before you in many cases. (The human being was not the human being as you now know it, being relatively recent in terms of geological time.) Many of them are from planets associated with Andromeda; some are from planets associated with the Pleiades, Orion and Sirius. This is normal, because anyplace that has a genetic structure associated with your own is encouraged to have an outpost here (to say nothing of a developed underground civilization), since you are involved in resolving some of their problems simply because of your genetic structure. There is a physiological need to resolve these things.

Of course, nearly every civilization that has a vehicle that comes to these parts is allowed to have some kind of crew available just in case, and usually to have a certain amount of scientific apparatus. The science from other planets is very closely enmeshed with philosophy, though you might call it philosophy/religion. This type of scientific outpost is definitely allowed to exist.

There is something here from Zeta Reticuli, even though you are not resolving their genetics. They are allowed to have a base here. And of course we cannot overlook the fact that there are underground civilizations predating the human being that are associated with the beings who lived here before you were here: Terrans are here, living underground. They've got a life of their own that doesn't have anything to do with yours.

Are they in a dimensional reality that we can interface with?

Yes. There is a barrier very much like your own television that can create an illusion of reality around most of these civilizations. This is not unknown in your own military parlance, where a false echo or a false reading might be purposefully generated around a particular object in order to create the illusion that the object is something else. I compare it to television or video because it uses a similar pulse frequency to create the effect. I'm not talking about a different dimension so much as an electronic measure used as a disguise.

If necessary, these civilizations can pulse at a different frequency — fourth, fifth dimension. They do not choose to do so very often because they get pleasure from the third-dimensional experience. But these days with more experiments going on in the field of ultrahigh frequencies being radiated through the planet, to say nothing of geological exploration to find minerals, oil and other things, it is often necessary for these civilizations to remain at a higher frequency so that they are not disturbed by these unintentional invasions of their civilization.

So they live within the Earth? Or they're just not affected by matter the same way we are?

As long as they are at a quicker pulse they are not affected by matter, just as you would not, in your third dimension, be affected by second-dimensional matter. When you leave this room and walk out to enjoy the fresh air or go to your vehicle, you are passing through what people in the second dimension experience as solid matter. Understand that I'm not talking about some kind of superhuman beings here. I am simply talking about people who are phasing in a different perspective of life.

When beings are at the fourth or fifth dimension they are not easily affected by matter. If they choose to experience the third dimension, then they are in fact within an actual dome or cavern. There are a great many caverns inside the Earth, some of which have oceans and some of which have a form of sun (as you experience your small star, your Sun). They have a form of radiant glow, a natural energy, and therefore they can have a civilization. They can grow food, they can eat and so on.

But they can also alter these places so they are not found. They have the ability to change dimensions for a time. This was always available (meaning for several million years) to them through their technology. As a result, they have phased enough electrical energy to be able to move on their *own* (as a person without technology) between the third, fourth and fifth dimensions. This has come about simply as a result of being exposed to this technology for several million years, just as changes occur in you as you are exposed to technology.

The Soul Complex

You've discussed before that humans are actually a hybrid form, not a real species per se. Does having no roots, as it were, create spiritual or psychological anxiety for us as humans?

Yes, in a sense. You have all had lives on other planets because souls are eternal. You have all had lives in which you were the pure essence of one thing. But since you are now many things and are the genetic experiment on Earth (of which the human being is the result), you are obviously many more things than you would normally be, so you need a more complex soul. That soul, however, is like all souls: when it desires to know something, it will seek it out. Sometimes you experience this physiologically, as if in a daydream. You are perhaps at work, and for a moment you daydream, not even being physically aware of your surroundings. Then suddenly you come back into your body with a start and become aware that some portion of you was missing. I'm not saying that your entire soul was gone, but you might have been focusing enough of your attention that the bulk of your soul matter was elsewhere.

At these times the possibilities for anxiety are most profound, because you have so many portions of you within your physical, emotional and soul self clamoring for attention, and the soul is essentially the chairman of the board. When it calls the meeting to attention and says, "All right, we all work together toward several predetermined lessons," everybody pitches in and gives their support. But when the chairman leaves and focuses most of its attention elsewhere, what happens when the teacher's gone? It is not unlike a nursery school or even third- or fourth-grade class when the teacher goes out of the room. Things happen, and sometimes it creates disharmony for a moment within self. In those moments there is a desire in those who can yell the loudest to take over and put the full focus toward whatever lesson that particular energy, molecule or gene wants to experience.

Your Extraterrestrial Chromosomes

As science shows you, the normal number of chromosomes is 46, so it doesn't take a scientific wizard to know that there are 46 (for most of you) portions of you from elsewhere that make up the human being. The interesting thing is that there is not a *single portion* of a chromosome from Earth within your chromosomes! Everyone who is born here (with few exceptions) who has 46 chromosomes is living in a foreign place, genetically speaking. The basis for inner anxiety is not only because the portions of you that come from elsewhere, extraterrestrially speaking, are clamoring for attention, but also *because those portions all have other agendas.* Every chromosome has certain functions, and those functions are all related to one *place.* I've said that the bulk of the energies that make up the human being is from Sirius, Orion and the Pleiades. But I've always added, "and a smattering of other things." That "smattering" makes up the rest of those chromosomes. *Every one of you has at least 46 points of origin.*

Sometimes those chromosomes are almost asleep, in that they are not doing as much as other chromosomes, or at least have a great deal more they *could* do. I've talked at times about what I call soul-braiding, where an energy that comes into a person's body has a connection with some other point in the universe. It has to do with another life of your soul, which is associated with your oversoul, or your main soul energy. It becomes a permanent part of your soul and thereby brings with it not only skills, interests, desires, wishes, hopes and dreams, but also unresolved lessons that it hopes to resolve when it joins its friend soul on Earth. So where does it go? Specifically, it finds its native chromosome and sometimes amplifies the energy of that chromosome, affecting all the others.

This is why, when there is a soul-braid involved with you that goes into the chromosome and amplifies it, that it is sometimes physically demonstrable in terms of increased activities and abilities. For instance, something that was very difficult for you to do before that braid came in suddenly becomes easier. It's actually an effect of genetic change.

I go through this whole business to show you that there is something going on here on a physiological level. There is a great deal of research into genetics right now. This is not at all surprising, because science not only has its own interest, but your governments and ruling bodies, your influential groups, have been in contact with extraterrestrials for about fifty years. The bulk of interest has been in genetics, not only because certain individuals amongst those groups found out that humans are the result of a genetic experiment, but also because they were exposed to the idea of what can be done with genetics.

Genetics as a Problem-Solver

There is virtually *no level* of physical or mechanical science on this planet that cannot be done with genetics — nothing, even air conditioners. One might say, "But Zoosh, that is a mechanical effect." Even so, everything can be done with genetics. Understand that these things have been developed by other civilizations, not because it *could* be done but because it was necessary.

It was not unusual in the distant past for civilizations to go through an experience such as your own — that is, to develop through a farmlike or agrarian interaction with its world, then gradually develop a form of technology. And as a result of technology in its rudimentary form (which you have slightly passed now, but not much) there would be a sufficient amount of pollution to cause disrepair to your own home. That is, the toxic stuff that was created accidentally as a byproduct was literally thrown into the same basket — into the water or into the ground where you grow your food and bring your water up to drink.

Technologically speaking, there was no place else to put it. Where are you going to put it if you cannot transform energies? Where are you going to put radioactive waste if you do not know how to transform it into something benign and then recycle it? Recycling is an old idea, but sometimes it goes out of vogue. It has been out of vogue recently, but it's coming back because people are becoming increasingly aware that what goes on on the other side of the world does affect them. There may not be anything they can do about it individually on a physical or mental level, but there might be something they can do emotionally and spiritually, hence eventually affecting the physical and mental. There is a need to change.

You gradually discover that you are a planetary citizen, and as a result you must have a planetary economy. This is beginning to happen for you as has happened for other civilizations elsewhere who have for the most part fallen back on genetics. So when these other civilizations got here (meaning in the last fifty years, when they were beginning to be allowed to have more interactions with different influential groups), their focus was on genetic solutions.

Here is something you can do. If you focus your maximum amount of attention toward where your tail might be, you would feel it because you have the genetic energy in your chromosomes: You have at least nine chromosomal influences from beings on other planets who have a form of a tail! Tails really do affect the life of a being; they are not only tools for communication — antennas, as some have stated — but they actually form a greater portion of a consciousness.

It is as if you were Doberman pinschers and somebody, without understanding the sanctity of the physical structure, lopped off your tail and said, "Oh, that's much prettier" — without the consciousness of realizing that tail was *doing* something. It is difficult for the human being to be fully grounded because the tail has allowed that so much. You have to work toward it. Sometimes some of you are very grounded because the energy of your tail, phantom or not, is very strong. The tail is a very big thing, much more than you realize. I can assure you that by the time you evolve your understanding of time and space into the fifth dimension, you will all have your tails back.

Creating a Benevolent Future

Zoosh
Sedona, Arizona, June 26, 1994

Well, all right. Zoosh speaking. Tonight we're going to go on an unofficial ride. Because many years ago in the '40s, '50s and early '60s, many people were picked up by flying disks — flying disks from other planets. This is not to say you're not being picked up now, but they were being picked up more frequently then. One of the over-riding features of the experience was that people were comfortably shown (none of this rough stuff — that's the movies), in a very comfort-able seat, not only the past but also the future of Earth history, well into the future, sometimes as far as 2500 and on a few occasions even further. The people were shown the worst-case scenario for the past (the past and the future are both flexible, believe it or not) and the worst-case scenario for the future. They were also shown the best-case scenarios for the past and the future.

I'm going to give you an overview of what people who were on those ships saw from their single-seat screening room, as it were.

A Common '50s Visit to a Spaceship

Now relax for a moment, if you would. You are all on board a benevolent spaceship and you are surrounded by beguilingly pleasant people from other planets. You want to know everything there is to know about them. But they have a task for you, which is that when you return to your Earth life and get off the ship, they would like you to anchor the best possible scenario for Earth's past, present and future.

They picked up so many people because they wanted to anchor the possibility of the best possible scenario.

So you are settled in your chair, kind of wishing you had a bowl of popcorn or a soda. In front of you is a screen, in some cases much like a television screen (however, there is no radiation that comes out toward you). In other cases, you are in a theater in which the past, present and future appear holographically. It is such a performance that you can smell the smells, taste the tastes and so on; it is quite involved. You have special grips on the chair, and if you feel it's getting to be too much, you begin gripping your chair, whether you are aware of it or not. Then they calm things down a bit. They don't play New Age tapes, but it's something like that so you do not become overexcited. Next they show you the future from those times as it *would* have happened. [The background for the information presented here can be found in Chapter 2 of *Shining the Light I*, entitled "Global Shadow Government."]

Let's take, for example, the idea of the '50s. Let's say you are all in that vehicle in the '50s and they show you a future that is quite benevolent. It is exciting with its ups and downs, and in the mid-'60s an amazing man comes along. He makes peace over the world. (I will say more about that later because this was the future you were intended to be in now.) Your projectionist shows you a benevolent future in which the peoples of the world come together, appreciating their differences and noting their similarities. He also shows you a future wherein a form of universal language acts as a bridge to telepathy, which you will begin using in that particular future — not the one you're in now — around the year 2100. This bridge language sounds a little bit like French and a little bit like Spanish. There are a few other things in it, but it doesn't sound too much like English. It has not only a beautiful ring to it, but it has musical qualities. The way the words are used, in terms of their tone, changes the meaning of the words, not unlike some of the languages you have now.

You are looking forward to this and thinking, I'm going to live through this. I'm going to be here in these happy days. That was supposed to be your future. That was the way it was supposed to be right *now*.

Then they show you the negative future, the not-so-pleasant future. They don't let it get too intense because they don't want you to be upset. They don't want you to feel the pain of it all, because it is very involving. You are seeing your own people on Earth going through things. They show you earthquakes, violence, floods. However, while they show you these things, it is quite obvious that life is going on. The earthquakes, fires and floods are not coming much more frequently than one might expect; however, people are constantly being bombarded with images of these things so that they are whipped into a frenzy of anxiety and thus are more easily manipulated by those who would choose to run their lives or (putting it their way) remove the burden of responsibility of life, of having to make so very many decisions. (Any dictator might use that particular rationale to support what he does.)

They will also show you lightships — not ships from other planets, but ships that were mostly created on Earth. They do not fly out of your solar system, but they can fly to nearby planets. They are primarily localized, these ships, and they are time-travel machines. They do not fly so fast in space, but they can travel in time with some ease. These vehicles, in this not-so-pleasant future, go back into the past and alter events that do not meet with the approval of the rulers of that not-so-pleasant future. (More about that later.)

Then they show you the benevolent future, saving that for the last, because they wish to encourage you. They have already shown you the future that was supposed to come and that sounds pretty benevolent; and you wonder in your mind why they are showing you this other benevolent future that is very similar, in which you see very much the same thing you saw in the first benevolent future and which you expect to experience. However, in this particular benevolent future, this form of it, time travel is not done by machine but by individual experience through spiritual attainment. And since it is done through spiritual attainment, no harm can be brought to anyone through that time travel. It is used primarily for study, for appreciation of other civilizations, past and future. It might present ideas or cultures that would benevolently influence your own in this benevolent future.

It is a tremendous culture having to do much with interplanetary travel, and Earth becomes a cosmopolitan place, a meeting ground for civilizations in different times as well as from other planets. The different races of people on Earth all experience frequent contacts with their core origin people, and this is good. They discover not only why they look the way they do, but also why certain innate feelings are present. The subtle differences in the racial and cultural groups become quite obvious when meeting your brothers and sisters from other planets, and that is good. One experiences, as it were, heaven on Earth in this benevolent civilization.

The Urge to Expect Benevolence

Your projectionist waves a hand, the screen of the hologram disappears and they take you into another room. You assemble in this room, and in it are human beings like yourself you did not know were present. There might be forty or fifty people there at most, usually no fewer than fifteen. They sit you down and a speaker communicates telepathically. You hear individually, not only in your own language but also in the idioms you use, meaning that if you use certain slang terms, you hear that slang so that you will understand every possible innuendo. Everyone is clear about what is being stated.

Then the speaker tells you, and I will repeat the speaker's words: "My friends," he says, "you have been invited to be on this ship today so that you will, when the time is right, feel the urge of expectancy that a benevolent future will be coming to pass. You have been seeded not only with things to be avoided, but also with things to happen. We hope the first future we showed you will come to pass, but there is a threat that it will not.

"There are those amongst you in your civilization right now who are experimenting with time travel and are very close to building machines that will travel into the past. For their own purposes of greed, manipulation and control, they would like to change the benevolent future for which you are headed. If they accomplish this and take you into a not-so-benevolent future, then there will be only one alternative to bring you back into this benevolent future.

"Those who would manipulate and control you do certain things, and those certain things offend your brothers and sisters from whom you have all descended here on Earth. If we are sufficiently offended and fear for your safety, we will suspend our rule that has to do with not interfering an any substantial way in your evolution."

Now, you notice the speaker says "in any substantial way." At the time, they were allowed to interfere in a minor way as long as it didn't affect the outcome of a person's life. How did they do that? Most people would forget their experience on the ship until they were supposed to remember.

The speaker then says to you, "There is a danger that a wonderful man who will not only be the President of the United States but will also come to be titular head of the United Nations, and as a result will be able to benevolently create a value system that perpetuates itself throughout all peoples. This will be done through the United Nations, and before long will spread all over the world."

So what happened? The person who was supposed to be President in the early '60s didn't become a lasting president. This person — it will be hard for you to grasp this, but I will say it — was uncreated. His life was uncreated by those interests, those people who are not in the government but who manipulate it. They sent their vehicles back in time and essentially uncreated that person. It was not a killing as you know it. The person was uncreated — an easy thing to do without injuring anyone. The soul of that person was deflected from Earth and went elsewhere; he lived a life elsewhere and will return.

Now, this is part of the reason many of you are feeling so much confusion today — because part of you is being exposed to energies that are designed to activate these old memories that you got aboard the ship.

What about those of you who didn't go aboard the ship? About half of the living population today had that experience either on board the ship or in a dream state, so it is not everybody. These energies are being radiated by Mother Earth, and people feel they know that something is wrong, not just in your society and the way it's going, and they feel confusion. You feel confusion because you're being activated by that energy resonating within Mother Earth to anchor that benevolent present, yet you are living in a present manipulated by those who manipulate the present by changing the past. *It's being done right now.* You are being activated into a future in which you were not intended to live.

This Is the Not-So-Benevolent Future

So what can you do about it? That is what we are going to work on tonight, largely, but I had to give you a little bit of the future. I didn't tell you a lot about the not-so-benevolent future because you are essentially living it. The not-so-benevolent future is not, nor was it ever intended to be, total destruction of all life on Earth. Think about it: Those who would manipulate you for the purpose of keeping control, making money, having the power and so forth, gain nothing if civilization is wiped out. *They need consumers,* as it were.

Now, this is not to say that all business people who have you consume or use their products are part of this shadow government. Only a very small group of individuals are consciously involved in this. That is the key: *consciously involved.* Most of the people who are involved in this manipulation do not know what they are doing and think they are working for somebody else. In some cases what they are doing seems very patriotic and exciting. They have no idea what they are doing or who they are really working for or what is the real purpose. If they knew that, they would not do it, of course.

Changing the Future

Now, what can you do to change that future and move more into the benevolence? That person who was supposed to be President of the United States *actually became President,* and you moved quite a way into that benevolent future, believe it or not! Then the whole thing was changed and it simply didn't exist except as a dream. I might add that some of you, when you have dreams of this benevolent experience, of benevolent times here, are dreaming a dream of the way things are actually supposed to be here now.

So I'm going to put you to work tonight. I'm going to ask you to make a picture for yourself, just as if I were the speaker on that flying disk in the '50s. I'm going to ask you to imagine as best you can, so that you can almost smell the experience, almost taste it, almost touch it — use as many of your senses as you can. Imagine doing something that's really benevolent, such as interacting with friendly ETs — maybe attending a meeting of people who are supposedly the enemies of the United

States and everybody's happy to see you. "Welcome to Libya, we love you" (I might add that most of this is a fight between governments).

Think of something that is benevolent. I'm going to give you a little moment to think about that, and then after you have thought of something simple, try to experience it with all your senses. Be in it, don't just see yourself in it. After you do that for a few moments, then I'm going to talk over the experience. I'm going to attempt to move this picture of yourself, perhaps with family members, and anchor it into the benevolent future that I see. By anchoring it, you are creating potentials that would allow that future to come to pass. Does everybody understand? I'm going to give you a moment to create that. Go ahead.

All right, you can relax now. Thank you. Now, tell your friends or the people who might not be present if they would like to change the future into something more benevolent, to use their imaginations and image that future in as much detail as they can, imagining how benevolent it could be. Tell them to see themselves in that future. When you see yourself in that future, try to touch things in that picture you've created for yourself. Try to have the feelings of what it would be like to touch those things. Try to use all your senses, for when you use your senses you are bringing as much physicality into that picture as you can, and in that way you will truly be helping to bring about that benevolent future.

Stop Imagining Negative Scenarios

I'm going to give you dis-homework, and I'm going to call it dis-homework because in a sense it is. I want you to stop doing something. Now, I know it's hard for you to stop worrying, so I'm not going to ask you to do that. (I'd like it if you'd do that, but I realize that's almost impossible.) I would like you to stop imagining, in general, scenarios of the future that could be awful. And whatever you hear about the future, whether it's from me or anybody else, I want you to immediately correct it and picture something in the future such as you did with your homework. See it as benevolent. See yourself in it, be in it, have your friends there. Everybody is happy.

This is not airy-fairy; this is magic. This is the foundation of magic, because it is done with permission. True magic works because it is done with the permission of all concerned. It is sorcery when it is done without permission. I am talking about something benevolent. So when you hear a future that is not benevolent from anyone, even if it's on the news — "Oh, this is going to happen; this has been happening and thus we can expect *that* to happen" — I want you to tune that right out. I want you to picture your future, I want you to feel your future. That's your dis-homework. Don't get involved in negative futures of other people. As you say, don't buy into it, all right?

Is there anything you would suggest we visualize that might help our future? I'm sure we have our own feelings and ideas, but you might suggest something that could be all-inclusive.

I feel that the most important thing to do is to see everybody as being friendly with each other. This does not mean that people lose their cultures, but that people see their similarities and laugh about their differences — something like that. Your future is not cut in stone. Perhaps you see yourself communicating with the animals and the plants and all life around you, so there is a free communication.

Can you imagine digging the foundation of a house if you could actually hear the rock protesting being dragged out of the Earth? How many people could actually dig the foundation of a house if they could hear the rock screaming? Not many people I know. Imagine yourself actually being able to hear and feel and understand.

Future Visions

Imagine children being raised everywhere as if they were beloved all the time by people who innately knew how to raise them, even though they themselves weren't raised that way. Imagine all people having a chance to do many valuable things, such as teach the universal language. Consider things such as this to be added to your picture of the future, all right?

I envisioned extraterrestrials and humans interacting, traveling back and forth, feeling no difference. Is this possible?

Certainly. And that's a nice vision. Anybody else care to share his vision?

I saw all the people in the shadow government being presented with the truth. They stopped and read it and listened to it and considered it.

Very good.

I saw the radical Right, the conservative anti-everything.

And your visualization was benevolent?

Yes, communication between them and the rest.

Very good. A practical application of people of different points of view finding common ground, yes? Thank you. Anybody else?

I saw all the black helicopters rise in the sky into the light.

Indeed, they're going to get a paint job, are they?

I envisioned all the people in the ground who weren't meant to be there taken away, uplifted, also toward the light.

Very good. See how your theme is of cleansing. After all, conflicts between people are essentially cleared up through cleansing, meaning that misunderstandings, corners where there is no illumination, are cleaned with light and love and understanding and, perhaps most importantly, appreciation for the other person's experience. This does not mean that you allow people to trample on you, but if you appreciate what they have experienced, then it is quite easy to find common ground.

Thank you for those offerings. Any other questions?

When is that President coming back?

Thank you. This particular being will come back (in the next incarnation the being will be female, by the way) when she feels welcome.

Now, understand what it would be like to feel welcome. If you went someplace, and if someone were pleading and begging you before you even arrived on the scene to save them from some horrible thing, you might, if you were very brave, show up for a few of those people and do what you could. But to show up for many people who were pleading, "Help save us!" you might not feel so welcome. You might feel overwhelmed and say, "Maybe I'll wait for a while."

How can you make this person feel welcome? She will feel welcome when she feels not only your desire, not only your intent, but also your application of the valuable tools that work for you to create that benevolent future, be it meditation, be it imagination, be it actually going out and creating something worthwhile, big or small, to create that future. In other words, prepare to welcome this person by *not needing this person to do it for you.* That is the key. Thank you for that question.

How do things look right now in terms of the possibilities, the probabilities of that benevolent future?

Thank you. How likely is that benevolent future to come to pass right now, according to the possibilities? Don't let this discourage you, because it is actually a pretty good sign: a 35% chance of that coming. Now, you might say, "Oh that's about one in three." However, if you look back just two years ago, it was 22%. It's getting better partly because many more people exist on Earth. While that's creating problems of its own, when you have so many people around, one of the inevitable side effects is that people simply *have* to learn how to get along on a daily basis. I'm not talking about wars and skirmishes that break out, I'm talking about *on a day-to-day basis.*

If the bus is crowded and you're riding that bus with essentially the same people every day, you get to know their faces after a while, and certain unspoken agreements take place. Maybe you help each other out. Maybe someone has a birthday and she's riding home with her friend. Her friend says, "It's your birthday, and they have forgotten."

She says, "Oh, that's all right."

Then the friend says, "I'm just going to sing happy birthday to you real quietly."

And the birthday person says, "Don't do that, someone might hear you."

The friend says, "I'll be real quiet." She starts singing, trying to be really quiet, and then someone next to her hears. Everybody knows that song and pretty soon the person next to her is singing, and before you know it the whole bus is singing.

Now, that's the picture of a benevolent future. Because what happens, even though there are certain unspoken agreements between the frequent riders and the people who see each other on that bus, is that from that day forth, they will always remember that shared experience and be that much closer. New friendships will come out of that.

Why? It is having *common ground*. One of the first songs people learn when they come to the United States is not "The Star Spangled Banner." It is "Happy Birthday to You," just like one of the first words they learn is "okay" or "yes" or "no." That song is going to be "Happy Birthday to You," and they're going to know it within three or four months of coming to the United States. It is common ground, and it can be very simple. You know, in your world, in your experience of your world, perhaps one of the biggest challenges for you is to maintain an ongoing effort to create a benevolent future, to say nothing of being a benevolent person.

But you know, one of the biggest threats to that, really, is in looking at someone, be he friend or stranger, and assuming that the pain or discomfort or disinterest or unhappiness that you see or feel in him has something to do with you. It is an old one, but I will use it. Many people are unhappy sometimes. If you see these people and they look at you unhappily, please do not assume it has anything to do with you. Also, please do not assume you can rescue them from their unhappiness. (If you are a professional, that's different, if they ask.) The best thing you can do, perhaps, walking by in the street, is to say a cheery hello or "Have a nice day" or "Sure is hot, isn't it?" — something like that — and then go on. At the very least they will be reminded that people are still friendly. It is the simple advice that is enduring.

Is this increase that has occurred in the past two years due to light and energy coming in?

It is primarily due to what people are consciously doing, human beings such as yourself. It is also due to what Mother Earth is consciously doing. All of the light that comes in to Earth will be extraterrestrial; since Earth is Terra, it is extraterrestrial light.

Now, you can say, "But Zoosh, that extraterrestrial light is filled with love, unconditional love." And that's fine, but if you wish to change things to a more benevolent path, unconditional love is not enough, for unconditional love loves the pain as much as it loves the love, the pleasure, the enjoyment. It accepts the pain. While that sounds good on a spiritual level, you need to change and transform.

Transformative Golden Light

Transformative light is best done by the best-known material master in these parts, which is Mother Earth, and transformative light for her is gold. Gold light does not come from extraterrestrial sources. Gold light does come from sources in the past on Earth, parallel dimensional sources on Earth and in Earth's atmosphere, and the same can be said of benevolent futures. Benevolent past civilizations might be sending portions of Mother Earth's gold light to you now, with her permission. That is where it comes from.

But primarily what is happening is that many people want things to get better, whether they are radical right, as the questioner said, radical left, or the mass of the people who are just trying to live their lives and don't have time for radical right or left. Many people want things to get better, but they don't know how, so they do the best they can and that's all they can do. This invites Mother Earth to do what she can, for Mother Earth is a material master for sure.

On that note, let's do a little more to create that benevolent future, shall we? Let's end on that note.

Meditation to Anchor Benevolent Energy

Let's relax again with the ideas and suggestions brought up by you tonight. I want you to imagine not only as much of that benevolent future as you possibly can, but I want you to see yourself in it. This time I will be quiet. I will wait for a while, giving you a chance to imagine it quite thoroughly. Then I want you to open your eyes but stay in that imagination. You can do it. I want you to do what I do. I will show you. It's essentially taking the energy from that imagination. I'm going to put it in the future and tie a knot into it, and I want you to watch me do that, but for right now I'm going to let you perform that imagination. I will let you know when to do the rest. Go ahead . . .

Now open your eyes and stay in the future. Stay in that future, see yourself in it. I'm just going to scoop up some of your auric field. Watch me. Do as I do. You take that, move your arm to the right, tie a knot in the air and pull it tight. Now you can let go of that imagination.

See if you can do it one or two times in the upcoming week. That will help you. Remember – to the right, tie a knot and pull. Why to the right? The left side of your body is concentrated in spirit. The right side of your body is concentrated in form. Since we want to create something in form, a physical fact, move your right hand, starting at your root chakra, move up your chakras, across the top and over to the right side as far as you can reach, down. You tie a knot in here and pull the knot tight. Then at the end you say, "I would like that — or something as good as that or even better — to come to pass." That is good enough, or you can use other words if you'd like.

Now let me just say this before we close. On that ship, after those people were taken up and shown the past, the future and different things, they walked around amongst the people. They had time, most of them, to talk and to see how life was lived there, to see the gardens, the space, the plants — exotic plants with exotic fruits, nutlike.

Imagine for a moment, for example, something that tastes like a cross between a cashew nut and a mango. It's about the size of a golf ball, and you could pluck it off a tree and eat the whole thing (not the stem, of course). It supplies you with all the essential nutrients plus the energy you need for a twenty-four period. This particular tree exists in the Sirius star system. Maybe the ship is from there or from some other place that has visited there. You walk around the ship and meet people. You make friends, and some of them come to visit you in your dreams later on

The ship lands in some deserted spot or possibly lands near your home, but time is suspended briefly in the neighborhood so no one sees the ship, but all the people in the ship can move about and you can move about, too. Maybe you walk back to your home, and maybe they escort you back. If you see other people, they're all frozen in their positions because you're suspended in a moment of time.

Then they tell you the thing that you don't want to hear — that you won't remember any of this for now, but you will remember it later on. It will come back to you.

Then they give you a form of universal greeting, which I will give to you now. It is given not only when you say hello but very often when you say good-bye. This is the universal greeting: Extend your right hand with your thumb up and your index and middle fingers together pointing forward; your ring finger and little fingers are together and pointing toward the left side.

Now I will say good-bye.

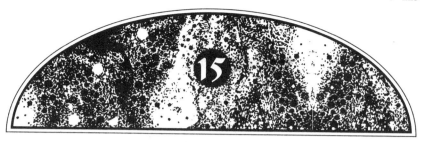

Bringing the Babies Home

Joopah
Sedona, Arizona, October 30, 1994

am Joopah. I am from the ninth dimension of the Zeta Reticuli star system. I will give you a little background. Some time ago my race was having some difficulty reproducing. We could clone, as we had done for years; we had found a body that was perfect for us through many years of waiting to get the right one. We were cloning, but nothing happened. Oh, we could create the body, but a body is only a body until there is the soul personality. And the soul personality was not entering. We waited, we went to our high priests, we did our ceremonies, we talked to our teachers, we asked our advisors, we did our prayers — nothing helped. So we thought that it was the end of time for us. But we knew we needed to perpetuate our race because not only are we important to ourselves, but we monitor, support and sustain a great many other races and cultures throughout the universe, many of whom could not exist without our sustenance.

So we were perplexed. After waiting for many years for a soul personality to enter one of the bodies (we tried different variations, but it didn't happen), we decided that we must do something. So we went back in time and tried to find the most durable and versatile expression of our souls' past incarnations. That's how we came to visit you here. You are our past lives in terms of higher-dimensional expression for Zeta Reticuli. So we thought we could work something out. Genetics is our foundation. We talked to our teachers and asked, "Can we make a hybrid race between human beings and us?" And they said, "Yes, if you are gentle. And you must not harm anyone."

The Hybrid Experiment

Well, in the beginning of the experiment, sad to say, our people were very unsophisticated. Think of it: During the thousands of years in our own culture as well as during the assistance we gave other cultures we still had little contact with others. We did not mingle with those cultures; we just assisted them, sometimes unbeknownst to them. So by way of apology, in the early days some of your people were not treated any differently than we would treat our own kind. We would land (in the early days it was possible to do this) and find a soul volunteer. Everyone who has ever cooperated in providing genetic material volunteered on the soul level —we know this, because we asked. If someone comes along for us, taking our hand to take us somewhere, we go. It did not occur to us that on your planet this is not so. So I apologize. We committed some social blunders in the early days. People were taken aboard without our asking "would you mind?" or "if you please" and all of those things.

Years later, the proper teacher was found for our people. It had to be someone like us so they could speak in our tongue. We use not only telepathy, but we also have a sound that converts to action. This is not unlike your own way when you speak abruptly and shortly. Sometimes between a couple or between good friends, you'll say a word or two and the other person will know your meaning. That is very much our spoken language —a word or two, and the other person knows exactly what we want or need. So the person who could come to speak for us had to speak our language. At that time I was not in the dimension I am in now. Those teachers came from the ninth dimension, where I now am, and told us many things, some of which we could not accept right away.

You have to understand this about our culture: Unlike you, we are not raised to be individuals. We are raised to be like a co-op; we are raised to live by consensus, so what gets told to *one* is not sufficient. That's how the original contact was; Earth people came and talked to my people on the ship: "This is not a good thing; you ought to do this" and so on. After a while, this accumulation of lectures to our face, as it were, added up and some of these problems in contacts between my people and your own became apparent to us. So an intermediary was put onboard ship, someone who relates more directly to your culture, who looks like you so you would not be frightened by our appearance, which is different from your own.

You see, that was one of the biggest challenges for us. We could not understand your reaction to us because *we* have never had a reaction to others on the basis of their appearance. We have always thought, Oh well, that's what you look like, and that's fine. Our teachers finally convinced us to bring someone onboard that Earth people could see and identify with. They said, "You can still do your work, but these people have to see one of their own kind onboard so they'll feel all right."

So we asked for volunteers from the Pleiades and they came, one per ship. They didn't like it, so it was a short tour of duty. They would be with each ship for maybe three, four months of your time. Eventually our teachers realized that if they were going to help my people to understand, they must speak to us in groups. So in recent years they asked us to step away, and we had large meetings in the great halls on our planets. They spoke to us of these things and had people come from the ninth dimension (which now includes myself) to speak to people to educate them, to help them to become more sophisticated. You on Earth are perhaps the most sophisticated people we have ever met because you can adapt. We, I am sorry to say, are not very adaptable.

So the teachers explained. When my people come here now (though they can't land anymore) and make contact, they are more careful. Know this: Our race is not what you call Grays. I don't like that; that's not who we are. Those who are so-called Grays are a tiny little minority. Most of what you hear about so-called Grays —and I know these people firsthand, I see them every day —is not true. You, as a race of beings, are currently being conditioned by those who are in control on your world to reject extraterrestrial visitors.

Many of you ask, "When are you going to land —you know, come out and mingle amongst us?" Well, there are difficulties —governments and so on as well as your reaction to us because of our appearance. We learn slowly, but we learn. Perhaps we should wear a big Halloween mask and a big badge that says "Have a Nice Day." But we won't wear masks. We've been waiting for you to accept each other. You have to at least be able to tolerate each other.

My people were afraid years ago that they were going to die out, so they collected lots of genetic material from women and men on your planet and also from people on our planet. And over the past 45 to 47 years our people have created a hybrid race in case our culture died out, which we thought it was doing. We did not realize that we were going to jump dimensions. We understood that *you* were moving from one dimension to another and that almost everybody else in the universe was moving from one dimension to another. But we did not understand that as a race of beings we were also going to jump —from the sixth dimension to the ninth. Some of our people will go from the sixth to the seventh very quickly, and then to the ninth. But we did not understand that. Being slow learners, it took us a while to catch on.

But when we caught on, we realized we had a hybrid race of people who will someday be wonderful connections between Earth people and my people and also other people. They are a little taller than us, maybe five feet tall; they are artistic and somewhat passionate, though not as much as you; they are intelligent; and they are (how can we say) stylish.

Two Groups of Babies

But what about the babies? At the same time that we were desperately trying to preserve our race, one of our teachers had said, "As long as you are doing this, why don't you preserve some human beings, too?" This particular teacher said, "There is just a chance, not a big one, but just a chance — 1½ to 2% — that they won't make it on Earth."

And we said, "But we thought that was already happening, because here *we* are; our souls used to be Earth people who evolved and evolved."

Our teachers said, "That is true. But there will be people who will want to change the evolutionary cycle on Earth from something that is benign, loving, godlike, of the light, into something that is baser and controlling, warlike, fear-based."

We said, "Is that not something that is changed, transmuted?"

And they said, "Probably, but just in case, would you also be willing to create an alternative human being who has just a little bit of your characteristics at the same time you are creating the hybrid race between you and human beings?"

We said, "Of course."

So here we have two groups of babies. One group has about 49% human and 51% Zeta genetics. This is the race we thought would inherit the sum total of our consciousness — all that we knew, all that we've done — and still have durability. When we created this more durable race, those babies were never intended to come and live here but to be those who inherited from us. Here was our teacher saying, "Have another group of babies; human beings cannot raise those."

We said, "We know how to raise our own kind and even beings like our own hybrids that will represent our culture with the passions of human beings past. But we don't know how to raise human babies and give them what human mothers and fathers give them."

Our teacher said, "That's all right."

So we did it — what could we say, no? But we did not know who we were raising. We are not the sort of people who are emotional and passionate like you. So when things didn't work out, we were disappointed, at least to the extent that my people could have emotion. The times when you would feel deep sorrow, terrible grief and tremendous, crushing disappointment, our people would just look downcast, appear to be a little sad, kind of down. We are not emotionalists. We have evolved toward the intellect rather than the feeling, though that is coming into greater balance now.

So here we were, trying to raise a group of beings that we didn't know how to raise; it was like asking a child to raise a puppy or a kitty and not telling them anything. We didn't know what to feed them; we didn't know what to do when things came out: "What's this?" We had no idea.

So sometimes we would bring up a human being from whom we had removed genetic material with the soul's permission, and ask their advice. We would bring them into a room that looked to them like an incubation room. Babies would be in incubators everywhere. We had to keep them in incubators because they could not breathe our atmosphere. The human mother would come into this incubation room and want to pick one up, feeling that motherly energy. But she would not understand that there was an envelope around her. She'd feel like she was breathing, like there was oxygen in the room, but there wasn't. (We don't breathe oxygen; it is toxic to us.) So she would say, "I want to hold one. I want to touch one." But you couldn't do that with these babies.

We would have her lie down, and we would pull pictures out of her memory to get an idea of how babies are treated. But you must remember that human memory is not a simple thing. In our culture, people are all raised alike. They don't watch television, they don't get images like that. They are acculturated in a very precise way, so when thought pictures are pulled out of their minds, it is very precise. But here we are trying to pull out thought pictures through telepathy, you understand. Out of the mind of that person, in addition to how *they* were raised, we would get all these mistakes, things that were done to them by their well-intended parents that were not a good thing to do and also strange pictures seen in movies and on television. We didn't know the difference. But there are some things we won't do. We're not going to hit the children; that goes against our grain.

We didn't know what all this was about, and our teachers were being very mysterious with us. They were not telling us why this group of babies that they had asked us to maintain and support to the best of our ability even existed, except that the human race might not make it. So there we were, stumbling and bumbling through this parentage. Maybe we would have more than one woman, and men would come in and pull thought pictures out of them. You could say, "Joopah, why didn't you *ask* them?" But it was a problem. You can think to yourself now, in these times when you are more sophisticated about this, "Well, sit down there and we will talk." But sometimes even today when some foreigner sits down, doesn't speak your language and doesn't look like you, you can get a little uncomfortable. (With children it's different.) But we can't just sit down in front of adults on our new couch and have them sit in our new chair. They would not look at us and say, "Well, how are you doing?" because we really *are* different-looking, strange-looking to them. And the moment they get frightened, we can't pull thought pictures out. We can pull thought pictures out only when you are relaxed, in a meditative state or when you are totally at ease, like you might be with a good friend, when you can be yourself.

I can assure you that in the forties and fifties and sixties when they sat down opposite us, they weren't at ease with us. The next best thing was to have them lie down on a table, and we would sometimes show these lights in a certain sequence, which would take them into a deep state of consciousness, like a deep meditation. While they were watching the lights they would have nothing attached, but there would be receptors on the back of the skull behind the ears, at the soft spot on both sides. Then we would pull thought pictures out.

The Third, Hybrid Mother Race

Eventually we realized that this wasn't working. We were getting all these strange images, and we thought, It's not possible that human beings are raised like this or they would be a big mess. We were befuddled. During this time the mortality rate with the human babies was high, not because the proper atmosphere and nutrients were missing but because we did not understand how to do what has never been done with us and have never been taught. We didn't know how to pick them up, rock them and love them, because that's a *feeling*. Remember, our feelings are very subtle.

So we finally had to create a hybrid mother race. We had to get special permission from our teachers and our Creator Spirit to create a crossbreed between human being and a little of us. The human babies were about 90%, maybe 85% human genetics and 10% or 15% Zeta genetics and a little bit of other things. We had to create the mother race —just mothers—who could learn. Primarily, we had to be able to communicate with them, so they were created with 40% human genetics and 60% our own.

This was actually the beginning of the creation of the race you now call Grays (I don't like that term). Sometimes we ask for volunteers on the soul level because we can't go down and sit in front of these people and say, "Would you volunteer to come to a planet where almost everybody looks like us?" "Eek! No, let me out of here!" We got permission on the soul level. When we would contact a person maybe forty times, they would at least get used to us and would not be as afraid, or at least would be resigned when we showed up. (We didn't understand at that time the subtleties between resignation and acceptance. Fine lines in emotions were not a strong suit in my people.)

So we brought someone up, traveled in time. We picked about sixty people over the years, mostly women, because it was clear to us that these are the nurturers. We asked them to teach the mother race that we had created how to be mothers. And they did. They would stay for two, three weeks at a time and then we would return them to their own time. From their point of view maybe five minutes would have gone by, but they would have spent three weeks experiential time training our mother race, which is actually the root race of what is now called the Gray people. This is important for you to know, because they were created to care for people who are mostly yourselves.

A New Purpose for the Race of Human Babies

Now, in recent months, to put a time sequence on it, I and other ninth-dimensional counselors who counsel our people in the sixth and seventh dimensions have been informed more clearly as to the purpose of the human babies, why and what will happen to them. For now we have several who have grown up and are adults, starting their own race and living amongst us in huge rooms with the right atmosphere in it. It's getting a little crowded. They can live in your atmosphere, and because of the training they've had, they can also live in your emotional atmosphere and are totally immune to all disease.

It now appears that you will not have to have these people inherit your planet to begin a new cycle, which had been the thought of the teacher who spoke to us when they asked us to create this race because they thought maybe you wouldn't make it. If that happened, they wanted you to start all over again in bodies that would be a little different, a little more intellectual, a little more accepting. (I won't go on with that too much lest I begin to be called Joopah, the egocentric.) But now we have been told that these people are going to come back. You might ask, "Do they look different from Earth people?" Yes. Some of them look very much like you and could pass easily. But some of them have a little bit bigger skull structure on the top, though not looking like that anomaly you call hydrocephalic. Just a *little* bit bigger, discernible by a physician, but otherwise healthy — just wearing a bigger hat size.

We were told that they will now begin coming here, visiting and maybe ensouling some of your young. Why? Because you have now evolved past the absolute desperate need to remain who you have been. Even though you struggle and have a hard time letting go of your personality parts that don't serve you, you are doing it. You've shown a lot of success in this. It's not easy.

So these people are going to come. They are going to live on a planet nearby (not in your solar system), but with the vehicles they have they can get here real fast, in two minutes. They are going to start contacting more Earth people. They are rather amusing, because they are kept up on lots of your slang in different languages. They will be able to talk to a teenager and be understood. How many adults can say that? So they are acceptable ETs, people who look almost like you but different enough for you to say, "You're not from around here, are you?"

Physical Variations

How different? Well, the eye cavities are about two to five centimeters farther away from the nose and extend the same distance farther on the side. Their nose is a little smaller than yours, on the average; it could be measured. They have all colors, all the races. If you put four or five of them in a room, even if they are different races, you would say, "You must all come from the same family."

What will they do? Their energy is infectious. But they cannot get any diseases. They are 100% immune to all Earth diseases, whether they be mental, physical or spiritual. Why? After all, they are made mostly of your genetics. *It is because their energy is entirely projected.* They do not *receive* energy at all. Yes, they have telepathy; they don't have intuition like you do, because your instinct requires that you be receptive of energies around you so you can say, "This way, not that way." They won't do that; they'll do it with their intellect only.

Their job is primarily going to be to mingle to the extent that they can. Some of them in certain cultures will be able to pass. They look a little different, but if they wear a hat, a wig, maybe one of these sweatshirts with hoods, they would pass. They have ears, they have chins. They don't have face hair, none of that; they won't be able to grow beards, but then you have some people like that here. Their internal organs are a little different, but not critically so. One lung is a little bit bigger than the other. (You have that, too, but as an anomaly or as a slight variation. With them it's a little more significant; part is a little smaller, a little more efficient.) There are other differences: their kidneys are smaller and the distance between their kidneys and the bladder is very short. Basically they are the same as you but with variations.

Their job is primarily to exist with you, to just be with you, to be exposed to as many of you as possible, because they will, just by their existence, be radiating energy that will inoculate you. A person with a psychosis, regardless of how ingrained or untreatable it is, could be with one of these new people for five minutes and that person could just sit with them and stroke their shoulder or their forehead, and in just five minutes that psychosis would be reduced to a neurosis. After twenty minutes all past pain, all wounds, even all karma leading to the psychosis or neurosis, would be eradicated. The psychotic person would not feel anything other than an extreme sense of relaxation. When they are their true personalities once again, they will feel very much like children. Although they will know how to feed themselves and go to the bathroom, they will need to be protected for a time.

Why do I tell you this? You will find amongst you in about two to three years and for many years after, people who are all grown up, who have intellects but seem childlike, very naive. You can help them — be understanding, be patient, know that maybe they are just that way, or maybe they were visited by one of these new beings. What they had done before, they don't do anymore; they are safe to be around. More than that: People who have been irradiated with this energy will pick up some themselves. Like you who both receive and project, they will project a little bit of that energy – from 3% to 12%.

It might be good to be around them. Being around someone like this might be a little annoying sometimes; but at other times when you are unhappy, depressed, had a tough day at work, being around these people for a few minutes, suddenly you'll feel fine and want to go out and play basketball or go for a hike. You might say, "What's going to happen with these people? What are they going to do?" They will be on this mission to just be here for about thirty years, and then they will probably begin their own culture in the interior of Jupiter (which will by that time be healed from her recent wound). That is what's happening with the babies.

Other Zeta Activities

What was the assistance Zetas provided to the other cultures before they started working with the Earth?

I'll give you a very brief overview of that – because I'm sure you all have something to do tomorrow! We have made room on and in planets for cultures to flourish if the planet desired it. Sometimes a planet – they all have consciousness, you know – might wish for people in the form of what you call animals (which are people to us), but there is no place for them because the surface is inhospitable. There are not the requirements that people or animals have, like water, air and so on. So we, amongst others, would be sent by our teachers to some of these planets to see what we could do within the parameters of maintaining the planet's life cycle. We would also provide a chamber within the planet that has access points to the surface, or even surface areas that could be adapted for the kind of life that could be there. We would be planetary sculptors. We could not harm the planet; we would have to get her permission. Usually it's because they are lonely; thus they would put up with a little discomfort to bring someone there whose lives the planet could share.

We did a lot of that. We even did some of that here. Many of your animals who were here, not all, were not suitable with large groups of people (small groups, maybe, but not large groups). Some of them who were not hostile to human beings and were also very shy, but because of their size would take up so much space and need so much vegetation to eat that it was not practical for them to be here while the human population was growing. So in the case of some of these creatures, we moved them to their own place where they still live happily on a big planet.

You mean dinosaurs?

Yes. The big ones, not little ones. The little ones we left, most of which are still with you —you call them lizards, alligators and so on — because they don't need much space. We were assisting civilizations that could not assist themselves. These people on other planets could not create a hospitable atmosphere on the planet and *then* be born there. Someone had to do it for them. Just like early humans could not remove the dinosaurs to a place of safety for all concerned. Someone had to do it, so we were asked to assist by those who were working with your planet.

You said you came here 47 years ago. That was the time of the Roswell crash. Is that when you first came to planet Earth to begin the hybridization project?

That's when our people came, yes. There were others who preceded us, of course, but that's when *we* came.

Other Zetas or other cultures that were hybridized?

Other cultures.

Who was in the Roswell crash? What planet were they from?

I can't pronounce it in your language. But not Zetas. Little people, though.

I have read a book channeled by Bashar, who represents a group mind from the planet Essassani. He said that they are the future of human beings and are half human, half Zeta. Is there any connection between them and the hybrids you mentioned?

They are the hybrids that we created to inherit our culture, but they are not the human babies. They are the 51% Zeta, 49% human.

And they are the expansion of your race on another planet? They are the result of it?

Yes.

How many of these human babies are there?

Not many. Right now maybe 2000, rounding it off.

Male and female?

Yes.

Do they have hair? You said they needed a wig.

Short hair, not long. This is sometimes passable for women, but not in all circumstances. So they might need wigs sometimes. It would be hard to tell those wigs from the real thing, though. Your hair stylists and beauty shops have not got those wigs yet —advanced wigs that can grow, something you put on your head and it grows. Not yet, maybe someday.

Are they reproducing themselves now?

They are not reproducing, no.

But they will when they go to Jupiter?

When they go to Jupiter, but no need until then.

So they will live much longer than we do?

Oh yes. Remember, they will be unaffected by any discomfiture here. You are all affected by the discomforts of others, to say nothing of your own. It is not just what people say or do to you, but just being in a room with people who are uncomfortable affects you. They are not affected. From our point of view most disease on your planet, in your culture, in your times and sometime in the past too, is caused primarily by stress, a big word that covers a person's interaction with the environment – which, of course, includes other people.

Will they mate with Earthlings?

No. (Did you have something in mind?)

How long will they be here before they go to Jupiter?

Thirty years.

Will they mostly go to people who are ill – mentally, physically, emotionally – to heal them, or will they also speak to others?

They will just go at random wherever they are. They will be sent, many of them, to big cities and to places where people are suffering. Some of them might even be incarcerated; there are lots of people suffering in prisons, though they have not committed serious crimes (maybe be present in a car that is stolen, nothing serious). They would go inside the prison where all the people are suffering, including those who work there.

Are they conscious of their mission, or are they going to be doing this unconsciously?

They are completely conscious of it. They know who they are, why they are here, what they are doing. They are very enthusiastic about it because they've been training their whole life for this. Only recently have they found out what they have been training for. We didn't know, so we couldn't tell them; now we can. They are very excited.

Have they been educated in specific fields, like nursing or psychiatry or engineering? Do they know how to drive cars? Do they know our technology so they can be amongst the people and not stand out?

They know how to drive cars. They know how to eat a hot dog so they don't dribble it all over. But they are probably not going to be M.D.s or police officers or professionals. They will be, maybe, working at Burger King.

Is there a deliberate confusion? You have mentioned earlier about propaganda, conditioning. Are there those who look slightly like them, and are they being deliberately used to confuse the public about the others who are Zetas?

Yes, thank you. That is quite so, although much being put out is being put out by people who do not know they are putting out disinformation. So it is not a conspiracy in that sense. Maybe one or two percent of the people have some idea that this is not true, aside from those who are simply skeptical.

These people underground are not my people. They have been artificially created to pass for us, if not in a lineup, then in a vague description. So yes, they look similar. Zeta people are not really gray. We might appear that way sometimes, but if you could see us in bright light, we're more whitish. We don't have much pigment in our skin; we don't need it. We evolved past that because our environment is very controlled. I personally, in my ninth-dimensional self, am like a gold-light being.

Who artificially created these people?

Getting into secret government stuff now. Tune in next time. I have limited knowledge only. Question for Zoosh, eh?

Were all the hybrids creations? Are they all part Essassani, or are some back on Zeta Reticuli?

There are at least 50,000 races of beings we have been involved with, helped, guided, even worked with genetically. They are all over the universe. Essassani were created because we thought we were dying out; it is only one race.

The hybrids that are half Zeta and half human. Are they all the Essassani race or are they other races?

All in that race, yes, but they have to be 51% us, 49% you, to be what I call hybrids. They have evolved to the point of naming themselves.

How many are there of the first generation?

Oh, many. First generation, about 65,000; but some might say from 40,000 to 100,000. They have no motivation to reproduce themselves in vast numbers, though there is motivation to do what it takes to reproduce.

But they have the equipment to reproduce. That's the important part.

Oh yes, they can reproduce. They are not mules.

Why have they selected Jupiter?

They want to stay close, but it is also because Jupiter represents throughout this galaxy (and astrologically) thought in action. This is really their byword. We could represent, as our portion of the parent race, thought. Your race also has this, yes. But your race represents thought in action because you are more individualistic. So they are attracted to the homeland of that theme.

What about the people who are on Jupiter now?

Big place. Lots of room. They say, "Come, welcome."

So they'll intermingle and help them?

Not intermingle; they will live separately.

But it will really enhance the vibration of Jupiter, won't it?

Oh yes. We will help to make Jupiter more hospitable on the interior. We are helping now to repair her from her recent wounding.

Now I am ready to say good night.

It is wonderful to have you here with a sense of humor.

Yes, I am enjoying this. Those of you who remember me when I first started out — oh, I was very much talking like this [Joopah speaks in a monotone]. But now I, after years of practice, can almost make a joke, maybe. So I will say good night and I hope you have found this interesting.

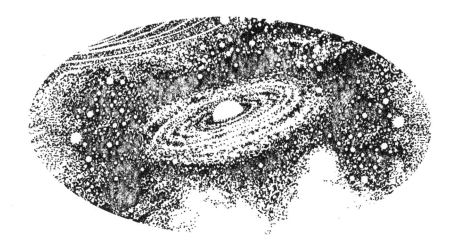

THE SEDONA VORTEX GUIDEBOOK
by 12 channels

200-plus pages of channeled, never-before-published information on the vortex energies of Sedona and the techniques to enable you to use the vortexes as multidimensional portals to time, space and other realities.

$14.95 Softcover 236p   ISBN 0-929385-25-X

◆ BOOKS BY DOROTHY ROEDER

THE NEXT DIMENSION IS LOVE
Ranoash

As speaker for a civilization whose species is more advanced, the entity describes the help they offer humanity by clearing the DNA. An exciting vision of our possibilities and future.

$11.95 Softcover 148p

NEW!
THE ALIEN PRESENCE
Evidence of secret government contact with alien life forms.
Ananda

Documented testimony of the cover-up from a U.S. president's meeting to the tactics of suppression. The most complete information yet available.

$19.95 Softcover   ISBN 0-929385-64-0

REACH FOR US
Your Cosmic Teachers and Friends

Messages from Teachers, Ascended Masters and the Space Command explain the role they play in bringing the Divine Plan to the Earth now!

$14.95 Softcover 204p   ISBN 0-929385-69-1

COLOR MEDICINE
The Secrets of Color Vibrational Healing
Charles Klotsche

A practitioner's manual for restoring blocked energy to the body systems with specific color wavelengths by the founder of "The 49th Vibrational Technique."

$11.95 Softcover 114p   ISBN 0-929385-27-6

CRYSTAL CO-CREATORS

A fascinating exploration of 100 forms of crystals, describing specific uses and their purpose, from the spiritual to the cellular, as agents of change. It clarifies the role of crystals in our awakening

$14.95 Softcover 288p   ISBN 0-929385-40-3

BOOK MARKET

A reader's guide to the extraordinary books we publish, print and market for your enLightenment.

F THE ASCENSION BOOK SERIES by JOSHUA DAVID STONE, Ph.D.

THE COMPLETE ASCENSION MANUAL

How to Achieve Ascension in This Lifetime

A synthesis of the past and guidance for ascension. An extraordinary compendium of practical techniques and spiritual history. Compiled from research and channeled information.

$14.95   Softcover 297p

ISBN 0-929385-55-1

HIDDEN MYSTERIES

An Overview of History's Secrets from Mystery Schools to ET Contacts

Explores the unknown and suppressed aspects of Earth's past; reveals new information on the ET movement and secret teachings of the ancient Master schools.

$14.95   Softcover 333p

ISBN 0-929385-57-8

SOUL PSYCHOLOGY

Keys to Ascension

Modern psychology deals exclusively with personality, ignoring the dimensions of spirit and soul. This book provides ground-breaking theories and techniques for healing and self-realization.

$14.95   Softcover 276p

ISBN 0-929385-56-X

THE ASCENDED MASTERS LIGHT THE WAY

Keys to Spiritual Mastery from Those Who Achieved It

Lives and teachings of 40 of the world's greatest saints and spiritual beacons provide a blueprint for total self-realization. Guidance from those who mastered the secrets in their lifetimes.

$14.95   Softcover 258p

ISBN 0-929385-58-6

BEYOND ASCENSION

How to Complete the Seven Levels of Initiation

Brings forth new channeled material that demystifies the 7 levels of initiation and how to attain them. It contains new information on how to open and anchor our 36 chakras.

$14.95   Softcover 279p

ISBN 0-929385-73-X

ASCENSION-ACTIVATION TAPES

How to anchor and open your 36 chakras and build your light quotient at a speed never dreamed possible. Scores of new ascension techniques and meditations directly from the galactic and universal core.

ASCENSION-ACTIVATION MEDITATION TAPE:

· S101
· S102
· S103 $12.00 each
· S104
· S105

Set of all 5 tapes $49.95

LIGHT TECHNIQUES

Light Techniques

That Trigger Transformation

Expanding the Heart Center . . . Launching your Light . . . Releasing the destructive focus . . . Weaving a Garment of Light . . . Light Alignment & more. A wonderfully effective tool for using Light to transcend. Beautiful guidance!

VYWAMUS
Channeled by Janet McClure
Edited by Lillian Harben

$11.95 Softcover 120p   ISBN 0-929385-00-4

AHA! The Realization Book

w/ Lillian Harben

If you are mirroring your life in a way that is not desirable, this book can help you locate murky areas and make them "suddenly . . . crystal clear." Readers will find it an exciting step-by-step path to changing and evolving lives.

$11.95 Softcover 145p   ISBN 0-929385-14-4

THE SOURCE ADVENTURE

THE SOURCE ADVENTURE

Life is discovery, and this book is a journey of discovery "to learn, to grow, to recognize the opportunities – to be aware." It asks the big question, "Why are you here?" and leads the reader to examine the most significant questions of a lifetime.

VYWAMUS
Channeled by Janet McClure
Edited by Lillian Harben

$11.95 Softcover 157p   ISBN 0-929385-06-3

SANAT KUMARA

Training a Planetary Logos

How was the beauty of this world created? The answer is in the story of Earth's Logos, the great being Sanat Kumara. A journey through his eyes as he learns the real-life lessons of training along the path of mastery.

The Story of
SANAT KUMARA
Training a Planetary Logos

Vywamus
Channeled and Edited by
Janet McClure

$11.95 Softcover 179p   ISBN 0-929385-17-9

SCOPES OF DIMENSIONS

SCOPES OF DIMENSIONS

How To Experience Multi-Dimensional Reality

VYWAMUS
Channeled by Janet McClure
Edited by Lillian Harben

Vywamus explains the process of exploring and experiencing the dimensions. He teaches an integrated way to utilize the combined strengths of each dimension. It is a how-to guidebook for living in the multi-dimensional reality that is our true evolutionary path.

$11.95 Softcover 176p   ISBN 0-929385-09-8

NEW! COCREATOR UNIVERSITY

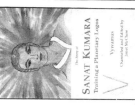

COCREATOR UNIVERSITY

Vywamus, Djwhal Khul,
The Tibetan, and Atlanto
Channeled by Janet McClure

Vywamus, Djwhal Khul & Atlanto

Your four bodies, the Tibetan Lesson series, the Twelve Rays, the Cosmic Walk-in and others. All previously unpublished channelings by Janet McClure.

$14.95 Softcover   ISBN 0-929385-54-3

BOOK MARKET

A reader's guide to the extraordinary books we publish, print and market for your enLightenment.

ORDER NOW!
1-800-450-0985
or Fax 1-800-393-7017
Or use order form at end

◆ BOOKS BY LYNN BUESS

CHILDREN OF LIGHT, CHILDREN OF DENIAL

In his fourth book Lynn calls upon his decades of practice as counselor and psychotherapist to explore the relationship between karma and the new insights from ACOA/ Co-dependency writings.

$8.95 Softcover 150p · ISBN 0-929385-15-2

THE STORY OF THE PEOPLE
Eileen Rota

An exciting history of our coming to Earth, our traditions, our choices and the coming changes, it can be viewed as a metaphysical adventure, science fiction or the epic of all of us brave enough to know the truth. Beautifully written and illustrated.

$11.95 Softcover 209p · ISBN 0-929385-51-9

NUMEROLOGY FOR THE NEW AGE

An established standard, explicating for contemporary readers the ancient art and science of symbol, cycle, and vibration. Provides insights into the patterns of our personal lives. Includes life and personality numbers.

$11.00 Softcover 262p · ISBN 0-929385-31-4

THE NEW AGE PRIMER
Spiritual Tools for Awakening

A guidebook to the changing reality, it is an overview of the concepts and techniques of mastery by authorities in their fields. Explores reincarnation, belief systems and transformative tools from astrology to crystals.

$11.95 Softcover 206p · ISBN 0-929385-48-9

NUMEROLOGY: NUANCES IN RELATIONSHIPS

Provides valuable assistance in the quest to better understand compatibilities and conflicts with a significant other. A handy guide for calculating your/his/her personality numbers.

$12.65 Softcover 239p · ISBN 0-929385-23-3

LIVING RAINBOWS
Gabriel H. Bain

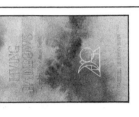

A fascinating "how-to" manual to make experiencing human, astral, animal and plant auras an everyday event. Series of techniques, exercises and illustrations guide the reader to see and hear aural energy. Spiral-bound workbook.

$14.95 Softcover 134p · ISBN 0-929385-42-X

BOOK MARKET

A reader's guide to the extraordinary books we publish, print and market for your enLightenment.

ON BECOMING
YHWH through
Arthur Fanning

Knowing the power of the light that you are. Expansion of the pituitary gland and strengthening the physical structure. Becoming more of you.
F101 $10

HEALING MEDITATIONS/ KNOWING SELF
Knowing self is knowing God. Knowing the pyramid of the soul is knowing the body. Meditation on the working of the soul and the use of the gold light within the body.
F102 $10

MANIFESTATION & ALIGNMENT with the POLES
Alignment of the meridians with the planet's grid system. Connect the root chakra with the center of the planet.
F103 $10

THE ART OF SHUTTING UP
Gaining the power and the wisdom of the quiet being that resides within the sight of thy Father.
F104 $10

CONTINUITY OF CONSCIOUSNESS
Trains you in the powerful state of waking meditation.
F105 $25 (3-tape set)

NEW!
SOULS, EVOLUTION AND THE FATHER
Channeling Lord God Jehovah

Lucifer's declaration begins the process of beings thinking another is greater than self. About the creation of souls; a way to get beyond doubt; how souls began to create physical bodies.

$12.95 Softcover 200p
ISBN 0-929385-33-0

SIMON
A compilation of some of the experiences Arthur has had with the dolphins, which triggered his opening and awakening as a channel.

$9.95 Softcover 56p
ISBN 0-929385-32-2

THE SOUL REMEMBERS
A Parable on Spiritual Transformation
Carlos Warter, M.D.
What is the purpose of human life? What is the reality of this world I find myself in?
A cosmic perspective on essence, individuality and relationships.
Through the voices of archetypes of consciousness, this journey through dimensions will assist the reader to become personally responsible for cocreating heaven on Earth.
$14.95 210p
ISBN 0-929385-36-5

MEDICAL ASTROLOGY
Eileen Nauman, DHM

The most comprehensive book ever on this rapidly growing science. Homeopath Eileen Nauman presents the Med-Scan Technique of relating astrology to health and nutrition. With case histories and guide to nutrition.
$29.95 339p
ISBN 0-9634662-4

◆ BOOKS by PRESTON NICHOLS with PETER MOON

THE MONTAUK PROJECT
Experiments in Time

The truth about time that reads like science fiction! Secret research with invisibility experiments that culminated at Montauk, tapping the powers of creation and manipulating time itself. Exposé by the technical director.

$15.95 Softcover 156p

ISBN 0-9631889-0-9

MONTAUK REVISITED
Adventures in Synchronicity

The sequel unmasks the occult forces that were behind the technology of Montauk and the incredible characters associated with it.

$19.95 Softcover 249p

ISBN 0-9631889-1-7

PYRAMIDS OF MONTAUK
Explorations in Consciousness

A journey through the mystery schools of Earth unlocking the secret of the Sphinx, thus awakening the consciousness of humanity to its ancient history and origins.

$19.95 Softcover 249p

ISBN 0-9631889-2-5

ENCOUNTER IN THE PLEIADES:
An Inside Look at UFOs

For the first time, the personal history of Preston Nichols is revealed, also amazing information the world has not yet heard. An unprecedented insight into the technology of flying saucers. Never has the complex subject of UFOs been explained in such simple language.

$19.95 Softcover

ISBN 0-9631889-3-3

ACCESS YOUR BRAIN'S JOY CENTER
Pete Sanders Jr.

Access Your Brain's Joy Center

by Pete A. Sanders, Jr.

A Natural Alternative to Using to Cope with Life's Pressures and Challenges

An M.I.T.-trained scientist's discovery of how to self-trigger the brain's natural mood-elevation mechanisms as an alternative to alcohol, nicotine, drugs or overeating to cope with life's pressures and challenges. Combination book and audio cassette package.

$29.95 Softcover 90p plus tape

ISBN 0-9641911-0-5

PRINCIPLES TO REMEMBER AND APPLY
Maile

A handbook for the heart and mind, it will spark and expand your remembrance. Explores space, time, relationships, health and includes beautiful meditations and affirmations. Lucid and penetrating.

$11.95 Softcover 114p

ISBN 0-929385-59-4

BOOK MARKET

A reader's guide to the extraordinary books we publish, print and market for your enLightenment.

◆ NEW!

ARCTURUS PROBE
José Argüelles

A poetic depiction of how the Earth was seeded by beings from the Arcturus system of three million years ago. The author of *The Mayan Factor* tells how Atlantis and Elysium were played out on Mars and implanted into Earth consciousness. Illustrated.

$14.95 Softcover
ISBN 0-929385-75-6

GUARDIANS OF THE FLAME
Tamar George

Channeled drama of a golden city in a crystal land tells of Atlantis, the source of humanity's ritual, healing, myth and astrology. Life in Atlantis over 12,000 years ago through the eyes of Persephone, a magician who can become invisible. A story you'll get lost in.

$14.95 Softcover
ISBN 0-929385-76-4

THE MILLENNIUM TABLETS
John McIntosh

Twelve tablets containing 12 powerful secrets, yet only 2 opened. The Lightbearers and Wayshowers will pave the way, dispelling darkness and allowing the opening of the 10 remaining tablets to humanity, thus beginning the age of total freedom.

$14.95 Softcover
ISBN 0-929385-78-0

◆ OLDER CLASSICS

THE TRANSFORMATIVE VISION
José Argüelles

Reprint of his 1975 tour de force, which prophesied the Harmonic Convergence as the "climax of matter," the collapse of materialism. Follows the evolution of the human soul in modern times by reviewing its expressions through the arts and philosophers.

$14.95 Softcover 364p
ISBN 0-9631750-0-9

OUT-OF-BODY EXPLORATION
Jerry Mulvin

Techniques for traveling in the Soul Body to achieve absolute freedom and experience truth for oneself. Discover reincarnation, karma and your personal spiritual path.

$8.95 Softcover 87p
ISBN 0-941464-01-6

VOICES OF SPIRIT
Charles H. Hapgood

The author discusses 15 years of work with Elwood Babbit, the famed channel. Will fascinate both the curious sceptic and the believer. Includes complete transcripts.

$13.00 Softcover 350p
ISBN 1-881343-00-6

◆ BOOKS by KRYON

KRYON – Book I
The End Times
Kryon through
Lee Carroll

New information for personal peace. Valuable metaphysical material presented in a simple easy-to-read manner.

$12.00 Softcover

ISBN 0-9636304-2-3

KRYON – Book II
Don't Think Like a Human
Kryon through
Lee Carroll

Channeled answers to basic questions. Leading to a new way of being, which will allowing miracles to come into one's life.

$12.00 Softcover

ISBN 0-9636304-0-7

KRYON – Book III
Alchemy of The Human Spirit
Kryon through
Lee Carroll

A guide to human transition into the New Age. Book III of the Kryon books covers predictions, validations, skeptics, science, mathematics and more. Two special appendices on the mysterious 9944 math.

$14.00 Softcover 376p

ISBN 0-9636304-8-2

TOUCHED BY LOVE
Dorothy McManus

From the exotic jungles of the Congo to New York's Fifth Avenue, this story sweeps the reader along in a fast-moving adventure of suspense, passion and romance. A strong theme of faith in the Universe is woven throughout the book.

$9.95 Softcover 191p

ISBN 0-929686-03-9

POISONS THAT HEAL
Eileen Nauman DHM (UK)

Homeopathy is all that remains to protect us from the deadly superbugs and viruses that modern medicine has failed to turn back. Learn how to protect yourself and your family against the coming Ebola virus and other deadly diseases.

$14.95 Softcover 270p

ISBN 0-929385-62-4

PEACE LABYRINTH
Sacred Geometry
Dr. Beatrice Bartnett

The author explains the meaning and significance of the Peace Labyrinth, a sacred geometry space. Using the numberology of the ancient Egyptians, the book explores ways of connecting with God, balancing energy, celebrations and exercises.

$9.95 Softcover 56p

ISBN 0-9622182-7-8

BOOK MARKET

A reader's guide to the extraordinary books we publish, print and market for your enLightenment.

ANNOUNCING a CHILDREN'S DIVISION – STARCHILD PRESS

ORDER NOW!
1-800-450-0985
or Fax 1-800-393-7017
Or use order form at end

CACTUS EDDIE
Brian Gold

Imaginative and colorful, charmingly illustrated with 20 detailed paintings by the artist author. The tale of a small boy who when separated from his family has more adventures than Pecos Bill. Printed in large 8½" by 11" format. A beautiful book!

$11.95 Softcover 62p   ISBN 0-929385-74-8

THE GREAT KACHINA
Lou Bader

A warm, delightful story that will help children understand Kachina energy. With 20 full-color illustrations, printed in 8½" by 11" format to dramatize the artwork.

$11.95 Softcover 62p   ISBN 0-929385-60-8

IN THE SHADOW OF THE SAN FRANCISCO PEAKS
Lou Bader

Collection of tales about those who shaped the frontier and were changed by it. A young boy's experiences with people and the wilderness is fascinating reading for all ages.

$9.95 Softcover 152p   ISBN 0-929385-52-7

SPIRIT OF THE NINJA
Toni Siegel

Returning as a dog, a Spiritual Warrior gains love and peace with a young woman in Sedona. Profoundly moving tale for all ages.

$7.95 Softcover 67p   ISBN 0-9627746-0-X

SONG OF SIRIUS
Dorothy McManus

A truthful view of modern teens who face drugs and death, love and forgiveness. Guided by Eckrita of Sirius, they each find their destiny and desires.

$8.00 Softcover 155p   ISBN 0-929686-01-2

I WANT TO KNOW
Aloa Starr

Inspiring responses to the questions of Why am I here? Who is God? Who is Jesus? What do dreams mean? and What do angels do? Invites contemplation, sets values and delights the young.

$7.00 Softcover 87p   ISBN 0-929686-02-0

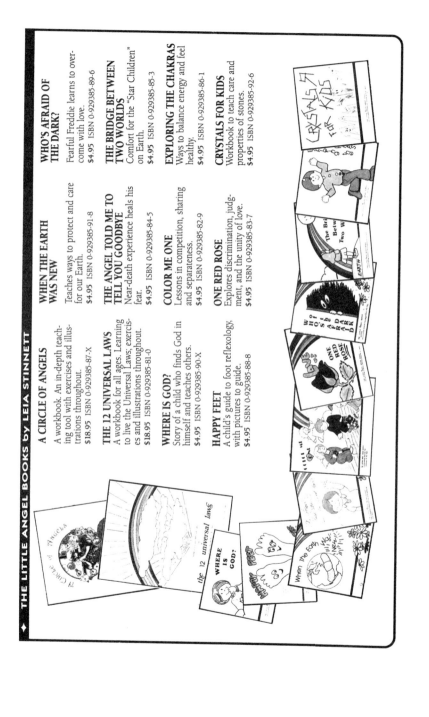

◆ B O O K   M A R K E T   O R D E R   F O R M ◆

BOOKS PRINTED OR MARKETED BY LIGHT TECHNOLOGY PUBLISHING

Title	Author	Price	
Access Your Brain's Joy Center (w/ tape)	Sanders	$29.95	$____
Awaken to the Healer Within	Work, Groth	$14.95	____
A Dedication to the Soul/Sole...	Vosacek	$9.95	____
Earth in Ascension	Clark	$14.95	____
God Within	Free	$11.95	____
"I'm OK I'm Just Mutating"	Golden Star Alliance	$6.00	____
Innana Returns	Ferguson	$14.00	____
It's Time To Remember	Gilbert	$19.95	____
I Want To Know	Starr	$7.00	____
Life On the Cutting Edge	Rachelle	$14.95	____
Look Within	Free	$9.95	____
Medical Astrology	Nauman	$29.95	____
Our Cosmic Ancestors	Chatelain	$9.95	____
Out-Of-Body Exploration	Mulvin	$8.95	____
Peace Labyrinth	Bartnett	$9.95	____
Principles To Remember and Apply	Maile	$11.95	____
Sedona Starseed	Mardyks	$14.95	____
Song of Sirius	McManus	$8.00	____
Soul Recovery and Extraction	Waya	$9.95	____
Spirit Of The Ninja	Siege	$7.95	____
Temple of The Living Earth	Christine	$16.00	____
The Only Planet of Choice	Schlemmer	$14.95	$____
Touched By Love	McManus	$9.95	$____
We Are One	Norquist	$14.95	$____
Richard Dannelley			
Sedona Power Spot/Guide		$11.00	$____
Sedona: Beyond The Vortex		$12.00	$____
Tom Dongo: Mysteries of Sedona			
Mysteries of Sedona – Book I		$6.95	$____
Alien Tide –Book II		$7.95	$____
Quest–Book III		$8.95	$____
Unseen Beings, Unseen Worlds		$9.95	$____
Merging Dimensions		$14.95	$____
Preston B. Nichols with Peter Moon			
Montauk Project		$15.95	$____
Montauk Revisited		$19.95	$____
Pyramids of Montauk		$19.95	$____
Encounter in the Pleiades: Inside Look at UFOs		$19.95	$____
Lyssa Royal and Keith Priest			
Preparing For Contact		$12.95	$____
Prism of Lyra		$11.95	$____
Visitors From Within		$12.95	$____

ASCENSION MEDITATION TAPES

JOSHUA DAVID STONE, PH.D.

Title	Code	Price	
Ascension Activation Meditation	S101	$12.00	$____
Tree of Life Ascension Meditation	S102	$12.00	$____
Mt. Shasta Ascension Activation Meditation	S103	$12.00	$____
Kabbalistic Ascension Activation	S104	$12.00	$____
Complete Ascension Manual Meditation	S105	$12.00	$____
Set of all 5 tapes		$49.95	

VYWAMUS/BARBARA BURNS

Title	Code	Price	
The Quantum Mechanical You (6 tapes)	B101-6	$40.00	$____

TAKA

Title	Code	Price	
Magical Sedona through the Didgeridoo	T101	$12.00	$____

BRIAN GRATTAN

Title	Code	Price	
Seattle Seminar Resurrection 1994 (12 tapes)	M102	$79.95	$____

YHWH/ARTHUR FANNING

Title	Code	Price	
On Becoming	F101	$10.00	$____
Healing Meditations/Knowing Self	F102	$10.00	$____
Manifestation & Alignment w/ Poles	F103	$10.00	$____
The Art of Shutting Up	F104	$10.00	$____
Continuity of Consciousness	F105	$25.00	$____
Black-Hole Meditation	F106	$10.00	$____
Merging the Golden Light Replicas of You	F107	$10.00	$____

BOOKSTORE DISCOUNTS HONORED

☐ CHECK ☐ MONEY ORDER
CREDIT CARD: ☐ MC ☐ VISA

Exp. date: _____

Signature: _____
(U.S. FUNDS ONLY) PAYABLE TO:

LIGHT TECHNOLOGY PUBLISHING
P.O. BOX 1526 • SEDONA • AZ 86339
(520) 282-6523 FAX: (520) 282-4130
1-800-450-0985
Fax 1-800-393-7017

NAME/COMPANY _____

ADDRESS _____

CITY/STATE/ZIP _____

PHONE _____ CONTACT _____

All prices in US$. Higher in Canada and Europe.

CANADA: CHERRY CANADA, INC. 1(800) 263-2408 FAX (519) 986-3103 • ENGLAND/EUROPE: WINDRUSH PRESS LTD. 0608 652012/652025 FAX 0608 652125
AUSTRALIA: GEMCRAFT BOOKS (03)888-0111 FAX (03)888-0044 • NEW ZEALAND: PEACEFUL LIVING PUB. (07)571-8105 FAX (07)571-8513

SUBTOTAL: $ _____

SALES TAX: $ _____
(7.5% - AZ residents only)

SHIPPING/HANDLING: $ _____
(*3 Min.; 10% of orders over *30)

CANADA S/H: $ _____
(20% of order)

TOTAL AMOUNT ENCLOSED: $ _____